eds Trinity

Motivating Language Learners

MODERN LANGUAGES in PRACTICE

The Modern Languages in Practice Series provides publications on the theory and practice of modern foreign language teaching. The theoretical and practical discussions in the publications arise from, and are related to, research into the subject. *Practical* is defined as having pedagogic value. *Theoretical* is defined as illuminating and/or generating issues pertinent to the practical. Theory and practice are, however, understood as a continuum. The series includes books at three distinct points along this continuum: (1) Limited discussions of language learning issues. These publications provide an outlet for coverage of actual classroom activities and exercises. (2) Aspects of both theory and practice combined in broadly equal amounts. This is the *core of the series*, and books may appear in the form of collections bringing together writers from different fields. (3) More theoretical books examining key research ideas directly relevant to the teaching of modern languages.

Series Editor
Michael Grenfell, *Centre for Language in Education, University of Southampton*

Editorial Board
Do Coyle, *School of Education, University of Nottingham*
Simon Green, *Trinity & All Saints College, Leeds*

Editorial Consultant
Christopher Brumfit, *Centre for Language in Education, University of Southampton*

Other Books in the Series
Cric Crac! Teaching and Learning French through Story-telling
   ROY DUNNING
Effective Language Learning
   SUZANNE GRAHAM
Fluency and its Teaching
   MARIE-NOËLLE GUILLOT
The Elements of Foreign Language Teaching
   WALTER GRAUBERG
The Good Language Learner
   N. NAIMAN, M. FRÖHLICH, H.H. STERN and A. TODESCO
Inspiring Innovations in Language Teaching
   JUDITH HAMILTON
Le ou La? The Gender of French Nouns
   MARIE SURRIDGE
Switched on? Video Resources in Modern Language Settings
   STEVEN FAWKES
Target Language, Collaborative Learning and Autonomy
   ERNESTO MACARO
Training Teachers in Practice
   MICHAEL GRENFELL
Validation in Language Testing
   A. CUMMING and R. BERWICK (eds)

Please contact us for the latest book information:
Multilingual Matters, Frankfurt Lodge, Clevedon Hall,
Victoria Road, Clevedon, BS21 7HH, England
http://www.multilingual-matters.com

MODERN LANGUAGES IN PRACTICE 12
Series Editor: Michael Grenfell

Motivating Language Learners

Gary N. Chambers

MULTILINGUAL MATTERS LTD
Clevedon • Buffalo • Toronto • Sydney

Library of Congress Cataloging in Publication Data

Chambers, Gary N.
Motivating Language Learners/Gary N. Chambers
Modern Languages in Practice: 12
Includes bibliographical references and index
1. Languages, Modern–Study and teaching. I. Title. II. Series
PB35.C517   1999
418'.007–dc21   99-22423

British Library Cataloguing in Publication Data

A CIP catalogue record for this book is available from the British Library.

ISBN 1-85359-449-0 (hbk)
ISBN 1-85359-448-2 (pbk)

Multilingual Matters Ltd

UK: Frankfurt Lodge, Clevedon Hall, Victoria Road, Clevedon BS21 7HH.
USA: UTP, 2250 Military Road, Tonawanda, NY 14150, USA.
Canada: UTP, 5201 Dufferin Street, North York, Ontario M3H 5T8, Canada.
Australia: P.O. Box 586, Artamon, NSW, Australia.

Typeset by Archetype-IT Ltd (http://www.archetype-it.com).
Printed and bound in Great Britain by WBC Book Manufacturers Ltd.

Contents

Foreword

The adoption of the comprehensive school as the norm in secondary education in this country resulted in the opening up of the curriculum to a wide spectrum of abilities. In modern languages, for generations the preserve of selective schools, teachers had to find ways of making their subject accessible to middle and low ability learners, validating their teaching by use of graded objectives and the end-of-course Certificate of Secondary Education. For many pupils, however, foreign languages held little appeal and were jettisoned with alacrity at the option stage. These disenchanted learners would say in later life, if they thought about it at all, that they were just 'no good at languages', or that languages were 'boring' or 'useless' or 'too difficult'.

Despite all the efforts of course writers over the ages to make the language learning experience pleasurable and rewarding, the subject has never really shaken off its 'hard' image. The classic *French Without Tears*, one of the earliest primers to promise its users a painless passage to foreign language proficiency, has been much imitated throughout most of the twentieth century. During the same period, methods, such as the direct and the oral, the audio-lingual and the audio-visual, which all claimed to be *the* way to learn a foreign language, have come and gone, each proposing to rectify the failings of its predecessor and each failing in its turn to point the way to the end of the rainbow.

With the advent of the National Curriculum, secondary school pupils can no longer opt out of foreign language learning, with the result that many Year 10 and 11 classes contain pupils who are at best reluctant to continue with their course. Teachers are therefore faced with challenges as never before to make the learning experience a positive one, to make their pupils want to learn, to turn compulsion into a virtue. For *having* to learn is one thing, *wanting* to learn is another. Take the first of these from the second and the difference is, of course, the key factor of motivation. Teachers dream of classes packed with interested, hard-working, inquisitive pupils, who by so being present no behaviour problems and allow the experts in charge of their learning to blossom and glow in their enjoyment of passing on their skills and knowledge. Reality, though, is different and not infrequently harsh. Pupils of the motivated, joy-to-teach variety *are* present, but often not in sufficient numbers to make teaching the delight it might be, and teachers are all too frequently faced with the kinds of demotivated learners described in Chapter 1 of this book.

The book goes on to examine the complex factors which combine to form the driving force which motivation is. Like teaching methods themselves, the definition of motivation has varied through time and has given rise to different and sometimes conflicting descriptions and interpretations. A range of these is examined and analysed before a model is selected as being most appropriately applicable to the field of modern language learning. At the empirical centre of the study is evidence gathered from cohorts of school pupils in England and Germany at successive stages in their progress through secondary education. We gain rare insights into the factors influencing their attitudes towards foreign language learning, including their experience in primary school, their perceptions of people from other countries and their parents' own attitudes and foreign language proficiency.

The research focuses sharply on the two factors which are central to the issue of motivation: the perceived usefulness and the perceived enjoyment of the foreign language course which learners are offered. Not surprisingly, the influence of the teacher is of prime importance and there is much to learn here from the evidence of pupils' own evaluations of the activities they are asked to engage in. What seem to be the most promising avenues to be followed through the complexities and pitfalls which lie in the path of the teacher of foreign languages? Though teaching styles are as individualistic and idiosyncratic as learning styles, it seems clear that into pupils' learning experiences can be injected certain stimuli which may reverse the negative attitudes which all too many bring to the foreign languages classroom. Although many of us are not in the position to replicate exactly the inspirational events described in Chapter 11, we are forcefully reminded of the invigorating potential offered by both everyday contacts and chance encounters for heightening learners' enjoyment and sense of purpose.

Modern foreign languages occupy a unique position in the school curriculum. The skills by which they are learnt are complex and demanding, and their inseparable association with cultures of other countries frequently challenges learners' personal and sometimes parochial views of the world. But the opportunities offered by this same uniqueness can be exploited in exciting ways, tapping into the potential of motivation which makes learners' experiences both enjoyable and memorable. Languages teachers at all levels will appreciate the combination of scholarship and practicality which characterises this book and will gain a new sense of the vital role they play in the educative process.

Dr Colin Asher
Senior Lecturer in Education
School of Education
University of Leeds

Acknowledgements

I should like to take this opportunity to thank the following people without whom this book would not have been written: Professor David Sugden and Dr Peter Tomlinson for their guidance and wise counsel; the teachers and pupils of the schools in Leeds and Kiel for their hospitality and friendly co-operation; Nick Nelson and Sandra Daniels for their patience and understanding in showing me the light at the end of the tunnel; and most of all, my parents for believing in me and always being there.

Acknowledgements

Chapter 1

Introduction

This chapter aims to contextualise the problem of motivation and foreign language learning. It touches on the status of foreign languages on the school curriculum and the influence of National Curriculum reform. An attempt is made to meet the challenge of describing the 'demotivated' or 'disaffected' pupil and to introduce the issue of distinguishing between motivation for learning in general and motivation for learning foreign languages. This provides the backdrop for an exposition of the purpose of this book and the research which informs it.

The vast majority of teachers will readily concede that the major problem is not ability but level of motivation: children have talent in plenty but many lack the interest and willingness to work hard that are needed for high achievement. (Hargreaves, 1982: 171)

The Challenge of the National Curriculum

Section 3(2)(b) of the Education Reform Act 1988 provides that a modern foreign language specified in an Order made by the Secretary of State shall be one of the foundation subjects which comprise the National Curriculum. Such a language is to be studied by pupils in the third and fourth key stages, that is to say from the beginning of the school year when the majority of pupils in the class reach the age of twelve until the majority of those pupils cease to be of compulsory school age. (DES/WO, 1991)

The National Curriculum era provides teachers in general and teachers of modern foreign languages in particular with a set of challenges likely to alter their *modus operandi* inside and outside the classroom quite substantially. The process of formally introducing a 'Languages for All' policy started in schools in August 1992. The Dearing revision to the National Curriculum (DFE/WO, 1995) required all pupils to be taking a foreign language in Key Stages 3 and 4 by August 1996, be it in the form of a full or short course. This revision claimed to reduce the number of pupils which its predecessor allowed to be 'disapplied'. For some schools 'languages for all' represented nothing new. For others the implementation of such a policy was and continues to be daunting. It is interesting to note that since the time of this study, the 'languages for all' policy has been reconsidered – perish the thought that anything in education should remain stable, if only for a short time. It now appears that modern languages is one subject area which may be sacrificed in the interest of certain categories of pupils gaining 'work-related learning opportunities'. (See 'Sick of school? Try work . . . ' *Times Educational Supplement*, 10.7.98 in which the Secretary of State's intentions are outlined.)

Modern foreign languages have a history of not enjoying a very positive or attractive image for pupils at the option stage, usually at the end of Year 9 and again at the end of Year 11:

> About 90% of pupils in the first year of secondary education are learning a foreign language, almost always French. By the fourth year the proportion learning French has dropped to about a third. (DES/WO, 1983)

> Only about 38.5% of girls and boys in an age group take a modern foreign language to public examination level at 16+. (DES/WO, 1985)

> Fewer than half of the pupils who complete the pre–16 stage will have followed a foreign language course for the entirety of secondary education. (Aplin, 1991: 3)

> Pupils' attitudes were usually positive, but the enthusiasm evident in many beginners' lessons was less often apparent at Key Stage 4. (OFSTED, 1995: 6)

O'Keeffe and Stoll (1993) as a result of a year-long survey on truancy in 150 English schools suggest that most 14–15 year old pupils who play truant do so to avoid particular lessons, not because they dislike school. The most unpopular subjects are physical education and French, followed by religious education. Complaints about lessons include lack of enjoyment, irrelevance or degree of difficulty. Pupils also remark upon the unlikeable personalities of their teachers.

Stables & Wikeley (1997) in their study into pupils' subject preferences conclude that attitudes to language learning are in 'chronic decline'. Pupils find French and German difficult and of little value, it is reported:

> Unfortunately modern languages are not rated highly for their usefulness and are seen as among the least enjoyable subjects by many pupils, particularly boys. (Stables & Wikeley, 1999)

Table 1.1 Number of pupils entering GCSE French/German/Spanish 1992–98

	1992	1993	1994	1995	1996	1997	1998
French	300,876	286,138	289,901	340,155	342,751	328,299	335,698
German	98,930	106,420	110,517	126,848	132,212	132,615	133,683
Spanish	29,245	31,949	36,415	40,591	42,592	43,826	47,269

Source: DFEE statistics branch

Table 1.2 Number of pupils entering A-level French/German/Spanish 1992–98

	1992	1993	1994	1995	1996	1997	1998
French	31,254	29,886	29,101	27,497	27,490	25,881	23,633
German	11,328	10,857	10,858	10,624	10,719	10,440	10,192
Spanish	4,717	4,850	4,755	4,822	5,232	5,606	5,653

Source: DFEE statistics branch

Teachers and their teaching appear in most reports to bear the brunt of the blame for the plight of foreign languages to the virtual exclusion of other significant factors which influence the 'popularity' and shape the image of a school subject. Is this legitimate and valid?

At the time of the study it may have been suggested that the modern languages picture was not quite so bleak as it first appeared. Foreign language examination entries at GCSE were rising. Between 1991 and 1994 GCSE entries rose by 22% for German, 40% for Spanish and 4% for French. Was this a reflection of the increased popularity of foreign languages in the aftermath of Graded Tests and a more communicative approach to teaching and assessing at GCSE, or of the *dirigiste* influence of the National Curriculum? Between 1996 and 1997, however, entries for a full GCSE course in all modern languages fell significantly and there were only 3000 entries for the new GCSE short course (see Table 1.1).

The picture for A-level reflects a steady decline in entries. This fall is in spite of the number of pupils staying on in education post-GCSE increasing (see Table 1.2).

Some pupils struggle to see the point of learning foreign languages when most other nationalities seem to have an acceptable level of competence in English. There are now at least 1.5 billion English speakers around the world, and 40% of mainland Europeans speak English (O'Leary, 1998). English is widely regarded as the language of the business world and of the pop-culture. Few pupils' role-models are witnessed interacting in languages other than English. A relatively small percentage of British politicians claim no competence in foreign languages (17.3%: Phillips, 1989: 14) but how rarely we hear them speak in French/German/Spanish (in contrast to German MPs, for example). British sports stars with foreign language competence appear to be few. Compare for example Jürgen Klinsmann's (German soccer star) competence in English (French and Italian) with Paul Gascoigne's or Paul Ince's (England soccer stars who have played for Italian teams) in Italian. Gary Lineker (former England soccer star; television and radio presenter) may represent an exception with his much lauded competence in Spanish and Japanese. In the apparent absence of initiative and ambition to alter the reputation of the British as a monolingual nation, as reflected, for example, in Mrs Thatcher's unwillingness to support the Lingua initiative promoting the teaching of at least two foreign languages to each child (see 'Languages project funds threatened' *Times Educational Supplement*, 5.5.89; 'Double entendre saves Lingua' *Times Educational Supplement*, 26.5.89), modern languages retain in the perception of some pupils their image as something difficult and not really necessary.

> Languages are difficult, and I probably won't go abroad, or else I'll go to English speaking countries. (James Merryweather, aged 13, in Gold, 1995)

National Curriculum Implications

Conferences, in-service training events and informal conversation with teachers reveal concern less with rewriting schemes of work, finding money to purchase IT resources, and the testing of integrated skills, and rather more with the challenge presented by those Year 10 pupils who pre-National Curriculum may have opted out of French/German/Spanish lessons. This is not a reference to the less able and pupils with Special Educational Needs. They bring with them their own, often distinct, challenge for the teacher. Most apprehension seems to be stimulated by those pupils who may be quite able but do not appear to want to learn a foreign language and may make sure that the teacher is aware of this. Teachers categorise such pupils as 'demotivated', 'disaffected' or 'switched off languages' (see Barber, 1994b; Dean, 1994; Keys and Fernandes, 1993; Stradling *et al.*, 1991).

Characteristics of the 'Demotivated'/'Disaffected' Pupil

At the time of writing the following four pupils are in Year 9 of a coeducational comprehensive school and have been learning German as a second foreign language for a year and a half.

Wayne is gregarious, affable and usually full of *joie de vivre.* He enjoys a good chat with his classmates. When asked to be quiet, he apologises, remains silent for all of two minutes and then sets off talking again. This pattern is repeated again and again until the teacher either explodes in frustration or simply capitulates. Wayne, with the best will in the world, seems incapable of following the instruction. He does not rate German very highly. He does not rate school very highly. His father has a fishmonger's stall in the local market and Wayne intends to join the family business as soon as he leaves school. He claims that his father left school at age 15 without any qualifications and is doing very well, thank you! 'Why do I need to learn German?' he asks. 'There aren't any Germans in our market. I don't need no [*sic*] German!'

Chris hates school. He hates German. The only thing in school which he regards as worthwhile and enjoyable is football. He has a very short fuse. He hurls books across the room in anger and frustration. Even though the teacher and 29 classmates see him do it, he claims innocence. He maintains that teachers pick on him. His mother believes he is right. She cannot see the point in his learning German. 'Why can't he do something useful instead, like more maths or English?'

Hannah has the face of an angel. She is not disruptive or rude. She does not speak out of turn. In fact, she does not really speak much at all. Her handwriting is almost illegible. Homework is rarely handed in on time and when it is, is either incomplete or of very poor quality. Her mother never comes to Parents' Evenings. She does not respond to letters. It is hard to tell whether Hannah enjoys German or not. Communication is usually limited to a shrug of the shoulders.

Norman is a 'loner'. He hates school. He hates German. He hates life. He bursts into tears for what appears to be no reason at all. The girls in the class feel sorry for him and try to protect and comfort him. The boys call him a 'big, fat poof!'.

You may recognise some of these pupils from your own experience. You may not necessarily have a Wayne, a Chris, a Hannah or a Norman in your class but you may have pupils who display some of their characteristics and indeed other behaviours. Not all of the characteristics of the category of pupil which may be labelled as 'disaffected', 'demotivated', 'disen-chanted' or 'switched off' are featured in the four descriptions. Among other things, pupils may have poor concentration, low self-esteem, make little or no effort to learn, reflect the 'what's the use?' syndrome, fail to respond to praise or when they do the response is negative, distract other pupils, shout out, fail to bring materials to lessons or claim to have lost them. (See Alison, 1993.) This list is by no means exhaustive.

'Demotivated'/'disaffected' pupils are not an invention of the 1990s but have occupied classrooms for as long as there has been formal schooling. Hargreaves paints the disheartening picture of the indifferent pupil with which we may all be too familiar:

> It's boring, sir' is their most common complaint. They display a persistent lack of enthusiasm to most of what the school offers, though a skilful teacher or carefully planned lesson may capture their imagination and attention, for a moment. Whilst exams and other incentives tend to be ineffective with them, they show little active resentment or opposition. They seem to be overwhelmed by lethargy, lacking the energy to praise or condemn. They drift through their schooldays. In consequence, whilst they avoid anything more serious than a half-hearted, game-like resistance to teachers, they are nevertheless not easy to teach. Quite often they worry their parents as much as their teachers for their lifelessness and lack of initiative. (Hargreaves, 1982: 102)

Lack of motivation can also manifest itself in a manner which is much less passive but at the same time equally challenging and arguably more disturbing for the teacher. Hargreaves describes pupils who react in a more overtly aggressive way as 'oppositionals':

> They turn in overt and sometimes powerful resistance to school and to teachers. Antagonism is overt, pronounced and prolonged. They become defined, individually and collectively, as a 'discipline problem' for teachers – and sometimes for their parents.' (Hargreaves, 1982)

Stradling *et al.* provide the following characteristics of the 'reluctant learner' which may distinguish between this category and the low attainer:

- non-completion of assignments;
- lack of persistence and expectation of failure when attempting new tasks;
- high level of dependency on sympathetic teachers (needing constant attention, direction, supervision and reassurance);
- signs of anxiety, frustration and defensive behaviour;
- disruptive or withdrawn behaviour;
- apathetic non-participation in the classroom;

- non-attendance and poor attendance;
- frequent expression of view that school is boring and irrelevant. (Stradling *et al.*, 1991: 25)

What are the factors which lead to pupils joining the category of 'reluctant learners'? The media would have us believe that it is the fault of the teachers ('Do your job, teachers!' *Daily Telegraph*, 25.1.95. 'What emerges most clearly from the reports of Inspectors of Schools is that the pupils most likely to behave badly are those who have been badly taught.' *Daily Telegraph*, 23.9.95). Stradling adds the following issues to the debate:

- low expectations by teachers;
- not being sufficiently 'stretched' in lessons;
- unrealistic demands on learners;
- too many teachers, too many subjects, too little time;
- insufficient reinforcement of learning;
- timetable and course structures too inflexible to permit learners to work at own pace and thus finish assignments;
- lack of short-term learning targets to reinforce learning;
- course content and teaching methods which are insufficiently stimulating or relevant to pupils' needs;
- insufficient attention given by some teachers to individual learning difficulties;
- lack of external motivation and incentive to learn (e.g. through broader accreditation schemes, job, further education and training prospects);
- lack of parental support and encouragement;
- peer group pressure to conform to a norm of non-achievement;
- fear of success (especially among some adolescent girls);
- social disadvantage and deprivation. (Stradling *et al.*, 1991: 27)

Although the teacher cannot be held responsible for all of the above factors, the question still must be asked: who would be a teacher? How many challenges can one person face at one time? Rather than equating their job to keeping a multitude of plates in the air, they are required to juggle with something akin to hedgehogs.

Motivation re: Foreign Language Learning versus Motivation re: Learning in General

A challenge is presented in establishing a clear distinction between problems of motivation relating to modern language learning and those relating to learning in general. The Centre for Successful Schools at Keele

University has found that disaffection is a disturbingly common feature in secondary schools:

> More than 70% of 13- and 14-year-olds say they count the minutes to the end of a lesson, and 30% think work is 'boring'. . . . Between 30% and 40% of 14- to 16-year-olds say they 'don't want to go to school'. (Barber, 1994b)

It is nonetheless true that modern foreign languages as a school subject pose a range of problems for both teacher and learner which may not apply to other subject areas. Reisener, (1992: 18ff.) summarises these aspects:

- the foreign language is taught in a mother-tongue environment; the mother-tongue is sometimes used in the foreign language classroom;
- the target language is also (it is to be hoped) the language of communication within the lesson; this can lead to the problem of discrepancy between what a pupil wishes to say and is able to say and the implications of this for the maintaining of interest;
- the nature of the foreign language course: skill-orientated, intensive practice, process-dependent; the learning group has to learn together and maintain the same pace (it should be noted that Reisener is writing within the context of the selective education system in Germany; differentiation there is a comparatively new concept which appears to be little in evidence outside the still relatively small but growing comprehensive school sector);
- cyclic or spiral rather than linear progression – implications for memory;
- intensity of practice: 75–80% of lessons consist of activities focused on practice, training, automatising, habitualising, consolidating – implications of this for stress and anxiety in the class if this is not handled sensitively; if the demands made by the teacher are too great or if the lesson content is too dense, the pupil may look for escape in the form of switching off;
- complexity: the first major problem with which the pupil is confronted is the phoneme-grapheme descrepancy;
- abstraction: pupils finds themselves in the strange position of learning a new terminology for items which they can describe perfectly well in the mother tongue: this, Reisener suggests, is possibly the essential problem in terms of motivation – the lack of a real need to articulate in the foreign code;
- the process: the learner who does not participate in the process and the activities within it, does not learn; Reisener maintains that this is

much more the case in languages than in other subjects; given the spiral nature of the process, this could well be true;

- use: a problem is caused by the fact that the rewards of language learning are generally long term – the exchange with the German twin town in Year 10 does little to motivate the learner at the beginning of Year 7.

Have you ever wished to be reincarnated as a mathematics teacher?

Purpose of this Book and the Research Which Informs It

The research project which forms the basis of this book aimed to access factors within pupils' outlooks which may influence their motivation in learning modern foreign languages. Emphasis was placed on the learning of German in the UK with some reference to the learning of English and French in Germany. The areas of focus were partly influenced by work already done in the field of motivation and attitude, principally that of Burstall *et al.* (1974), Assessment of Performance Unit (DFE/DENI/WO 1985, 1986, 1987), Gardner and Lambert (1972), and OXPROD (Phillips & Filmer-Sankey, 1993). The period of the study covers the three years between 1992 and 1994. Any development in pupils' motivation and attitudes was assessed in surveys at two given points, one in 1992 and the second in 1994. This was then evaluated in terms of the nature of the development and possible influences on it.

The study included a comparative element (see Chapter 10) in that pupils of the same age and attending similar schools in Germany were surveyed on the same areas of focus. Data were compared to access similarities and contrasts. It was felt that if conclusions were to be drawn about influences on motivation in one country, some sort of baseline or comparison from another country was needed. There also exists a popular perception that motivation to learn foreign languages is a greater problem for the British than it is for other nationalities, not least the Scandinavians, Dutch and Germans. Hooley and Newcombe (1988: 400) describe the British attitude to foreign language learning as 'cultural myopia' and contrast this with the attitude of the Germans. Prag (1994) reports on the foreign language competence deficit of young people in Britain in comparison to those on the European mainland:

> In Britain, 70% of 15–24 year olds are unable to converse in a second language. Across the Channel, the proportion is much lower – 50%. (Prag, 1994: 18)

Statistics such as these represent an irresistible bandwagon upon which the media are delighted to jump:

When it comes to foreign languages, we're the dunces of Europe. (Emma Haughton in *Education Guardian*, 31.3.98)

It is often suggested that English as the language of the pop-culture is one of the factors which serves to motivate German pupils to learn it:

German-language music was the preserve of the hopelessly unhip, lederhosen-clad folk groups and the Eurovision song contest. Young Germans grew up mouthing the words to English speaking bands, making a fortune for the American and English music industries, and making life easy for Germany's English teachers. (Brookman, 1994)

Chambers (1991) posits that German pupils may see the relevance of foreign language learning in a way that British pupils fail to (see Stables' & Wikeley's references to 'usefulness', 1997, this chapter p. 2) and as a consequence are prepared to apply the rigour and diligence necessary to acquire a reasonable level of competence. He also suggests that pupils in Germany are also more tolerant of a teaching methodology which tends to be rather 'sterile' and 'unimaginative' (see also Mreschar, 1991; Piepho, 1983). In contrast, British pupils experience in many cases a teaching approach which is varied, practical (to the point of being too transactional), makes some attempt at being 'communicative' and involves implementation of a wide range of resources including hands-on experience of information and communications technology (ICT), something rarely in evidence in English classes in German schools (Frost, 1995). If this is an accurate perception, it must be considered whether British teachers get an appropriate pay-off for their investment of time, imagination and energy, especially in the light of the apparent discrepancy in language competence outcomes. (See Milton & Meara, 1998 and this study Chapter 10, p. 156.) This forms the backdrop to an investigation into the accuracy of the above perceptions and into areas of similarity and contrast in the development and nature of the motivation and attitudes between German learners of English and (in a few cases) French and their UK peers.

This study aims to access evidence on an issue which is at the very core of the language learning/teaching experience. It sets out to provide data which may inform teachers' and parents' approaches to promoting positive attitudes and where necessary encouraging positive attitude change to learning foreign languages, German in particular. It does not stop there. It goes on to provide in-class and out-of-class strategies, which have already proven successful in enhancing pupils' motivation and providing them with that which they and their teachers perceive as a positive learning experience both in terms of level of achievement and level of enjoyment.

Research Design

Figure 1.1 (based on Phillips & Filmer-Sankey, 1993: 4) summarises the context within which the study is set and provides a preview of the broad areas of questions to be investigated.

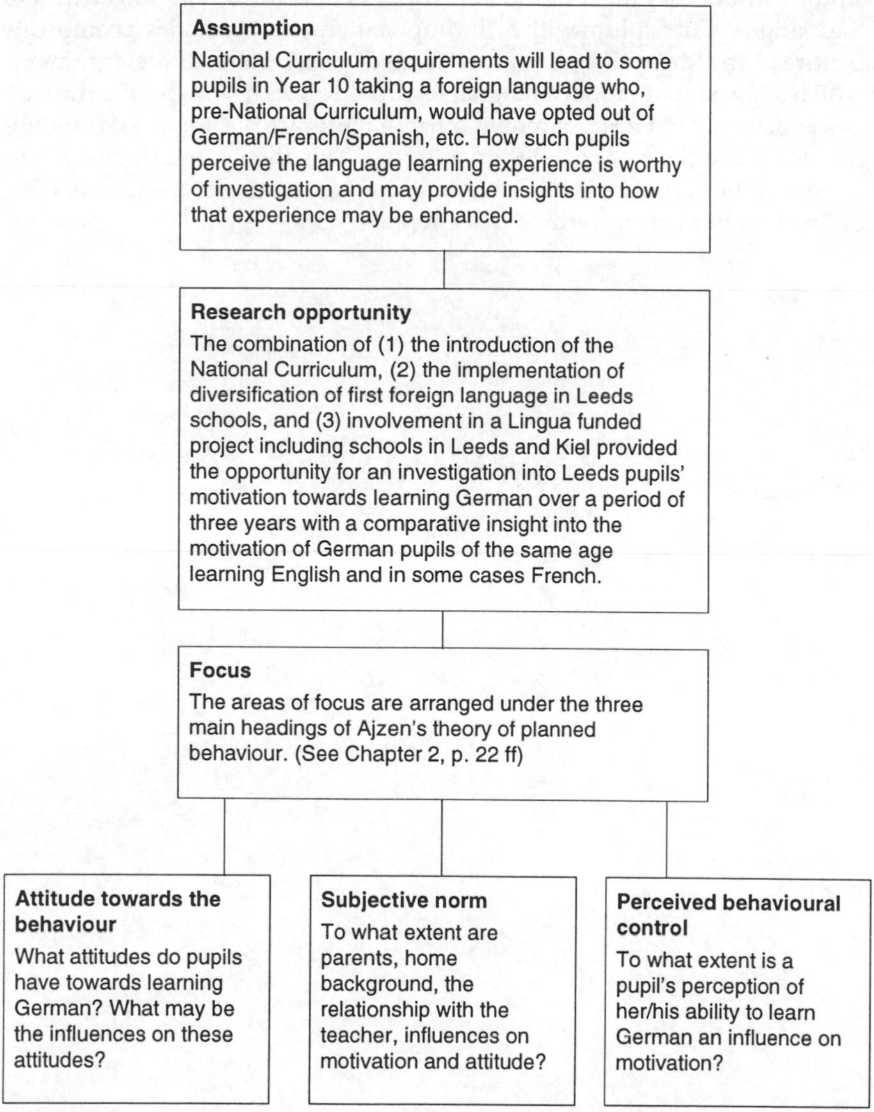

Assumption

National Curriculum requirements will lead to some pupils in Year 10 taking a foreign language who, pre-National Curriculum, would have opted out of German/French/Spanish, etc. How such pupils perceive the language learning experience is worthy of investigation and may provide insights into how that experience may be enhanced.

Research opportunity

The combination of (1) the introduction of the National Curriculum, (2) the implementation of diversification of first foreign language in Leeds schools, and (3) involvement in a Lingua funded project including schools in Leeds and Kiel provided the opportunity for an investigation into Leeds pupils' motivation towards learning German over a period of three years with a comparative insight into the motivation of German pupils of the same age learning English and in some cases French.

Focus

The areas of focus are arranged under the three main headings of Ajzen's theory of planned behaviour. (See Chapter 2, p. 22 ff)

Attitude towards the behaviour

What attitudes do pupils have towards learning German? What may be the influences on these attitudes?

Subjective norm

To what extent are parents, home background, the relationship with the teacher, influences on motivation and attitude?

Perceived behavioural control

To what extent is a pupil's perception of her/his ability to learn German an influence on motivation?

Figure 1.1 Research design

Summary

This chapter attempts to outline the factors which stimulated interest in the topic of secondary school pupils' motivational perspectives regarding modern foreign languages, with special reference to German. It places the study within the context of the 1990s, an era of change with the advent of the National Curriculum with all its implications, and provides a composite picture of the 'demotivated' or 'disaffected' pupil. Some of the arguments which suggest that modern languages provide a range of specific difficulties which may not be apparent in other subjects are outlined. An insight is provided into the research design adopted. This then paves the way for a review of the literature in the following chapter relating to the thorny issue of the definition of the term 'motivation'.

Chapter 2

What is Motivation?

This chapter strives to find the pot of gold at the end of the rainbow. It attempts to provide a satisfactory definition of motivation within the limited context and aims of this study. It is accepted that not all aspects of motivation can be covered. Other attempts to provide a satisfactory, all-embracing definition are critically reviewed. Such attempts invariably fall short, in that motivation may mean different things to different people, at different times and in different contexts.

Given that motivation, even within the confines of this study, has multifarious strands, a structural framework is needed on which to hang these. Rather than reinvent the wheel, it seems sensible and economical to exploit the work of others, in this case Ajzen (1988) and Gardner (1985). Some insight is provided into the frameworks they provide and the justification for the final selection for this book.

Introduction

Have you ever tried to describe 'motivation'? I started off with a sheet of A3 paper. I wrote 'MOTIVATION' in the centre. I then set to work in classical 'brainstorming' style. My spidergram quickly expanded beyond the bounds of the A3 sheet. I added a second and a third sheet. It was not long before the floor of my study was covered in sheets of paper. I had learned that there was very much more to motivation than I had thought. I had learned that the establishing and articulating of a concise, clear and accurate definition of motivation was more of a challenge than I had expected (see Figure 2.1).

Because motivation is such a multifaceted term, any attempt at explaining what it is requires some sort of structural model to which can be attached the categories to which the various strands may belong. Only then can some sort of order be established. Even that is not entirely satisfactory, however, because one strand cannot be detached from another. The strands are interlinked. One may influence the other. It is rather like dealing with a teacher's poor classroom management without including consideration of her[1] lesson planning, the pace of the lesson, body-language, etc. So, that provides another challenge: finding the appropriate model.

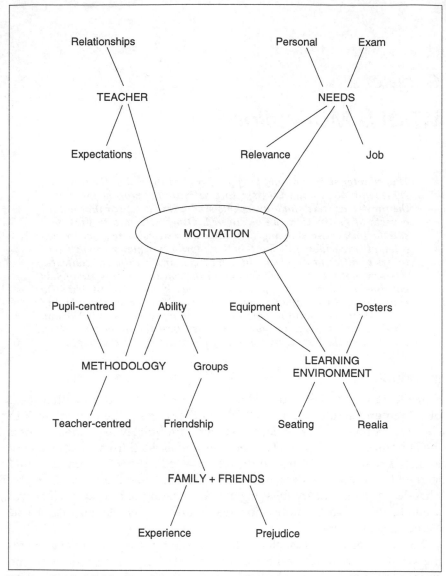

Figure 2.1 Initial brainstorming on 'motivation'

This chapter accepts the two interrelated challenges issued above. It attempts to describe what motivation is and to find the appropriate structural model to facilitate this.

General Definition of Motivation

What is it that motivates action? Is it *instinct*? This theory was developed in the nineteenth century by the psychoanalyst Sigmund Freud (1964) and the functionalist William James (1890). In Freud's view human behaviour was motivated by two instincts: (1) the life instinct (Eros), the basis for sexual motivation; and (2) the death instinct (Thanatos), which underlay aggressive motivation. Freud (in contrast to later theorists) regarded such instincts as remaining part of the individual's unconscious. James' functionalist view postulated that an individual's various instincts, such as fear, sociability, cleanliness and love, focused on the central instinct to survive.

Instinct theory was replaced in the twentieth century by 'drive theory'. A drive may motivate not just a single behaviour but various behaviours based on the same need. Hunger, for example, may motivate not only eating but also restlessness before mealtimes. Eating then reduces the drive.

Drive theory was then taken a stage further into 'neobehaviourism' (Hull, 1943) which included drive, incentive and habit as the basis of a given behaviour.

Maslow's (1954) so-called 'humanistic' interpretation went beyond the purely biological or survival oriented view and stressed man's potential for self-direction, freedom of choice, positive self-concept and ultimately self-enhancement. Maslow proposed a hierarchy of fundamental motivational bases. Once the lower needs – physiological; safety; emotional – have been satisfied, higher needs – esteem; cognitive; aesthetic; self-fulfilment – take precedence.

The 'behaviourist approach' of Skinner (1957) focuses on stimulus-response associations and cause rather than need and reason for action. Skinner's experiments on rats in his 'operant conditioning chamber' led to the development of definitions for reinforcement (any operation that increases the rate of response), punishment (any operation which decreases the rate of response), shaping (the step by step procedure in training an animal by positive reinforcement of each phase of the desired behaviour) and schedules of reinforcement (partial reinforcement involving less attention and expense because not every response is reinforced).

The weakness of the behaviourist approach, it may be argued, is that it focuses on the observable. You can see the behaviour but you cannot see what is motivating the behaviour; you can only infer what the stimulus is. The cognitive approach, by contrast, concentrates on what cannot be observed but is nonetheless accessible.

The 'cognitive approach' (see Jung, 1978: 4; Weiner, 1972) postulates that action can only be understood in relation to cognitive factors (which cannot be observed) such as thought processes, intentions, expectations and interpretation of a given situation. Weiner's (1980) 'attributions', for example, are the causal explanations given for a certain event or behaviour. Four common attributions for success are ability, effort, luck and task difficulty. Ability and effort are internal to the subject and are therefore her responsibility. Luck and task difficulty are external and the subject has no influence over these. A subject who is normally successful tends to attribute success to effort and ability. If unsuccessful, she blames effort with the implication that this internal trait can be modified. She only needs to try harder and she will enjoy success. A subject who is normally unsuccessful and experiences success tends to attribute this success to external factors such as task difficulty or luck ('It was easy, Miss'; 'I was lucky, Sir'), whereas any failure on her part is attributed to lack of ability.

Each of these categories makes an important contribution to the attempt to establish the nature of motivation but taken in isolation proves unsatisfactory. The weakness resides in the concentration on an intention model of action to the exclusion of any consideration of habitual or automatised behaviour. A car driver is able to engage the clutch before changing gear while conducting a conversation at the same time. She performs the action without giving it any apparent thought. The driver has attained a level of skill where the action has become automatised and therefore does not need conscious thought. Such behaviour does not fit into any intention model of action but is motivated in an unconscious way.

An eclectic approach may get closer to the ideal. It cannot be ignored that different motives may lie behind the same action: (1) for different people; or (2) for the same person on different occasions. An individual may have multiple motives for a particular action; she may not even be conscious of the reason for a given behaviour. To positively identify someone's motivation, therefore, is problematic.

Definition of Motivation for the Purposes of this Study

Given the complexity of motivation, especially on the levels of: (1) conscious/value-driven behaviour versus habitual/automatised behaviour; and (2) multiple motives *or* different motives for the same behaviour for the same person on different occasions or for different people, it is imperative to establish a clear understanding of motivation for the purposes of this book. It would not be possible or useful within the confines of the book to investigate all the threads which weave together to make up the concept motivation. Certain areas are required to be the focus of attention, to the exclusion of others.

This book focuses on pupils' perceptions of their learning experience at school with specific reference to their foreign language learning experience (German in particular). The research therefore only accesses those areas of motivation upon which the pupils can comment. The book concentrates on the value-driven/conscious aspect as opposed to the automatised/habitual/ unconscious aspect. It investigates the nature and quality of pupils' motivation to learn German (in the case of Leeds pupils) and English/French (in the case of Kiel pupils). Their motivation may be determined by perceived need, enjoyment or social pressures, for example. This by necessity excludes other important factors which influence motivation such as age, personality and aptitude. These could well be the subjects of other studies.

Structure for the Exposition of Perspectives and Research on the Definition of Motivation

Even when limiting the focus to the value-driven/conscious aspect of motivation, there is a myriad of interlocking issues to be examined. This demands a structural framework which accommodates as far as possible the various aspects of the definition of motivation relevant to this study. The purpose of the underlying framework is organisational. It is not to be tested as to its accuracy, validity or reliability. It has no predictive role. It serves merely to help describe. It provides the bones onto which the meat of motivation can be hung.

Two structural models present themselves above others. The 'socio-educational' model of Gardner (1985) and Ajzen's (1988) 'theory of planned behaviour'. What follows are the pros and cons of each in terms of their suitability to this study. Only one comes out on top. So why present the debate on the merits of both? The discussion, of Gardner's model in particular, gives access to other useful models which informed and influenced the development of those under consideration and provide the pieces which contribute to the complete jigsaw (insofar as any model can be complete).

Gardner's Socio-educational Model

Gardner's socio-educational model has a great deal to commend it. It is foreign language learning specific and so has much in common with the topic of this study. Gardner (1985: 124–45) describes how it is soundly based on seven other foreign language learning models each of which can be placed into one of two categories:

(1) those with a focus on linguistic process – i.e. which address individual differences in second language achievement and with direct attention to hypothesised processes operating on the individual when confronted with the task of learning or using a particular language form. To this category belong the following models:

(a) The *monitor model* (Krashen, 1978, 1981, 1982) postulates that there are two language systems, one conscious (attention to form rather than content), the other subconscious (focus on the message rather than grammatical accuracy); emphasises Krashen's distinction between 'language learning' (associated with conscious system and aptitude) and 'language acquisition' (associated with subconscious system and attitude).

(b) The *conscious reinforcement model* (Carroll, 1981) posits that language learning begins when the individual has the intent to communicate; dependent on intent, knowledge and the context, the individual responds; if the response achieves the desired goal, it is reinforced; this may result in:

(i)   the increased likelihood of the response being repeated in similar contexts; and

(ii) the acquisition of knowledge about the nature of the language itself.

(c) *The strategy model* (Bialystok, 1978) has three levels or stages:

(i)   input – exposure to the language, e.g. in the classroom, from reading magazines, watching television, meeting with speakers of the target language;

(ii) knowledge – input provides three categories of knowledge: any knowledge relevant to the second language; conscious knowledge about the language code; and intuitive linguistic knowledge;

(iii) output – a response; either spontaneous/immediate or deliberate/requiring time to be articulated.

To these three levels are applied four strategy types:

(a) formal practising: focus on grammar, pronunciation, linguistic patterns;

(b) functional practising: increased exposure to improve communication; e.g. communicating with speakers of the target language; watching films in the target language;

(c) monitoring: modifying language behaviour based on knowledge of the code;

(d) inferencing: applies mostly to comprehension and involves acquiring explicit knowledge about the language code; e.g. inferring the meaning of a previously unknown word based on the context in which it is located.

(2) Those with a social process focus – i.e. attention to the social, psychological variables which facilitate or impede second language acquisition. To this category belong the following models:

(a) *Social psychological model of second language acquisition* (Lambert, 1963a,b, 1967, 1974): this represents a theory of bilingual development and self-identity modification; self-identity and the development of proficiency in a second language are inextricably related; students learning a second language 'must be both able and willing to adopt various aspects of behaviour, including verbal behaviour, which characterise members of the other linguistic-cultural group'. (1967: 102) The model focuses on affective factors such as ethnocentric tendencies, attitudes towards the other community, orientation towards language learning, and motivation.

(b) *Acculturation model* (Schumann, 1978a,b): this concentrates purely on the identification of major causal variables relating to 'learning language without instruction and in the environment where it is spoken' (1978a: 27). Like Lambert, Schumann assumes the importance of identification with the target language community but identifies other factors including social, affective, personality, cognitive, biological, aptitude, personal and instructional.

(c) *Social context model* (Clément 1980): this places emphasis on the cultural milieu of the language communities involved and assumes that second language acquisition involves not only the 'learning of language skills but also the adoption of other patterns of behaviour of the second language community' (Gardner, 1985: 137). Central to the model is the quality of motivation in the learner which may emanate at the extremes from a social context where: (i) there is little contact with the target language community, learning of the target language is not encouraged at school or at home and fear of assimilation with the target language community may be strong; and (ii) where first and second languages have equal status, contact between the two communities is close, there is considerable support from school and home and there is a high degree of 'integrativeness'.

(d) *The intergroup model* (Giles & Byrne, 1982) focuses on the second language acquisition of a linguistic minority group and stresses the importance of maintenance of a positive self-concept. Social identity relates to the individual's concept of membership of groups. Where linguistic competence is a factor in group membership and where negative self-concept is resulting, various strategies may be adopted to change this assessment. Those who fear assimilation and tend not to be successful in second language acquisition are likely to avoid contact with speakers of the target language (the linguistic majority group) and concentrate on formal learning contexts, e.g. school. Those who are integratively orientated tend to be more successful in acquiring the second language and actively seek contact with the target language community in informal contexts.

These models, in which motivation plays a central role, inform the development of Gardner's socio-educational model which stresses the idea that languages, unlike other subjects, involve the development of knowledge and skills which are part of the heritage of the learner's cultural community.

> A second language . . . is a salient characteristic of another culture. As a consequence, the relative degree of success will be influenced to a certain extent by the individual's attitudes towards the other community or to other communities in general as well as by the beliefs in the community which are relevant to the language learning process. (Gardner, 1985: 146)

The model focuses on four classes of variable:

(1) Social milieu: influence of the cultural context in which the second language acquisition takes place. If the cultural belief is that to learn a foreign language is difficult, then the general level of achievement is likely to be low (self-fulfilling prophecy). The converse is also true. Where the cultural belief is that to learn a foreign language is not difficult, then the general level of achievement – all other things considered – is likely to be high.

(2) Individual differences: focus on four types of individual differences which influence achievement directly: (a) intelligence (speed of learning); (b) language aptitude (cognitive and verbal abilities); (c) motivation (effort and desire); and (d) situational anxiety (inhibitions).

(3) Language acquisition contexts: (a) formal contexts – language classroom or any situation in which the individual receives training, explanations or drills; (b) informal contexts – situations where instruction is not the primary aim, e.g. listening to the radio, watching television, conversation.

(4) Learning outcomes: (a) linguistic outcomes – proficiency in the language/grammar/vocabulary/pronunication/fluency, etc; (b) nonlinguistic outcomes – the attitudes and values which derive from the experience (see Figure 2.2).

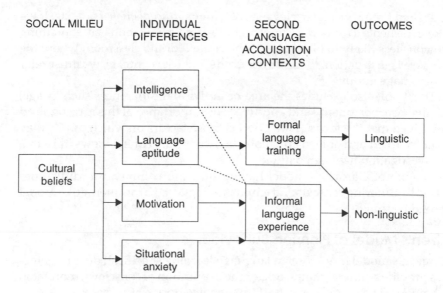

SOCIAL MILIEU   INDIVIDUAL   SECOND   OUTCOMES
                 DIFFERENCES   LANGUAGE
                               ACQUISITION
                               CONTEXTS

Figure 2.2 Gardner's socio-educational model

The attraction of this model is the central role played by motivation and the social dimension which Gardner sees as a major part of motivation. For the purposes of this book, however, with its focus on pupils' views, the model appears too all-embracing with its inclusion of informal language experience (which gets much greater emphasis in Gardner's work) and individual differences. Although Gardner claims to place under scrutiny the context 'of the student acquiring a second language in the school setting, often in environments where immediate access to the second language community is limited, if not virtually non-existent' (Gardner, 1985: 4), his research often has a context where foreign language learners have, if not immediate, then near access to the target language community, e.g. learning French in Canada. They, their families and friends may have a view of the target language community based on considerable experience of living with or close to that community. They may leave the formal learning context of the classroom and move easily and with some immediacy into an informal learning context where they hear and see the target language in authentic situations. This is unlikely to be the case for the foreign language learner in the UK, for example, for whom with few exceptions the informal learning context is not so accessible. Opinions on the target language community may be based on holidays, articles in newspapers and magazines, television programmes, hearsay. A case could be argued for the virtual irrelevance of 'language *acquisition*' contexts. If we take Krashen's (1981: 2–3) interpretation of 'acquisition' as something which is less likely to take place in the context of the classroom where the purpose is instruction, then, for the Leeds and Kiel contexts, we must refer to 'language *learning*'.

This book also excludes the area of individual differences such as age, intelligence, personality and aptitude. The importance of this is recognised but, given that the focus of attention is those factors on which pupils may feel prompted and able to articulate their consciously held views, this area of investigation has been omitted.

In spite of Gardner's model having much to commend it, difficulties posed by differing contexts and emphases suggest that an alternative model should be sought.

Ajzen's Model of Planned Behaviour

Ajzen's model is not foreign language learning specific. It does nonetheless provide a simple framework for the explication of conscious, motivated behaviour. The model consists of three main strands at its base:

(1) *Perceived behavioural control*: the perceived ease or difficulty of performing the behaviour; this is assumed to reflect past experience as well as anticipated impediments and obstacles. Perceived behavioural control is founded on the strong correlation between self-efficacy (the subjective probability that one is capable of executing a certain course of action) and behavioural achievement (see Ajzen & Timko, 1986; Bandura *et al.*, 1977; Locke *et al.*, 1984). An individual attempts to

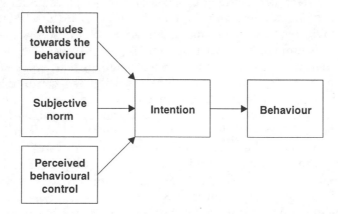

Figure 2.3 Ajzen's model of planned behaviour

perform a behaviour to the extent that they have confidence in their ability to do so.

(2) *Attitude towards the behaviour*: personal – the positive or negative evaluation of behaviour; value/pay-off – the advantages of given behaviour. An individual is likely to perform a specific behaviour if she views its performance favourably. The opposite is also the case.

(3) *Subjective norm*: social influences – an individual's perception of social pressure to perform or not. An individual's intention to perform a behaviour may be influenced not only by her positive evaluation of the behaviour but also her belief that others (or 'referents' (Ajzen, 1988: 121), usually parents, spouse, close friends) think that she should perform the behaviour.

One of these main strands or any combination of two or more of them may lead to the *intention* to act or behave. Ajzen emphasises that 'the theory of planned behavior does not deal directly with the amount of control a person actually has in a given situation; instead, it considers the possible effects of *perceived* behavioral control on achievement of behavioral goals' (Ajzen, 1988: 133). Perceived control is likely to take account of some of the constraints which may exist, as opposed to *intention* which reflects an individual's willingness to behave.

> The more favourable the *attitude* and *subjective norm* with respect to a behaviour, and the greater the *perceived behavioural control*, the stronger the individual's intention to perform the behaviour. (Ajzen, 1988: 132)

Both Gardner and Ajzen offer not only a framework which is relevant but one which is valid in that it has been shown to work fruitfully in attempted applications. Ajzen's model, however, serves the purpose of this book more readily, in terms of its organisational strength, not least for its simplicity. It includes the areas upon which pupils may feel able to articulate their views – their attitudes to languages; their view of their own ability to cope with the demands of learning German; their in-school experience; their perceptions of the influence of their parents and friends. Gardner's model provides complications and areas of focus which are not part of this book.

Ajzen's model is not perfect. It presents problems rather different to those posed by Gardner, such as that relating to the allocation of particular factors to a given strand. The difficulty of categorisation leads to potential overlap between strands. 'The teacher' serves to illustrate one area of difficulty. When Ajzen's model of planned behaviour is applied to the context of this book, the teacher plays a dominating role, arguably featuring in all three strands, i.e. 'perceived behavioural control' (e.g. the role of the teacher in influencing the pupils' perception of their ability to learn German), 'attitude towards the behaviour' (e.g. the role of teaching style on the pupils' attitude towards learning German) and 'subjective norm' (e.g. the role of the teacher as a potential 'referent'). This and similar questions may have no definitive answer and serve to illustrate that models are not clearcut or black and white but tend to lack clarity and not to fit neatly.

It is unlikely that a model could be found which would accommodate all aspects of the book neatly. For this reason, this research is informed by a range of models, including those referred to in the introduction (Chapter 1, p. 9). Accepting that Ajzen's model is given a purely organisational function, what may be regarded as weaknesses in terms of the areas of focus in this book, cannot only be tolerated but offer advantages in terms of strategic flexibility.

Summary

This chapter attempts to provide a definition of motivation for the purposes of this book. Given that motivation has many aspects, some selection has to be made to serve as a focus for the book. This is provided by the consciously held views of secondary school pupils learning foreign languages.

To facilitate the review of perspectives and research on motivation, a model providing some structural framework had to be found. Gardner's 'socio-educational model' and Ajzen's 'theory of planned behaviour' have many attributes which suggest their suitability. In the end, however, Ajzen's model was selected primarily for its simplicity and flexibility as opposed to Gardner's specificity requiring access to data beyond the perspectives of pupils.

Note

1. The feminine pronoun is adopted here and throughout the book because most foreign language teachers in the UK are women. It is also adopted when referring to pupils in order to avoid repetition of 's/he' and should be understood to refer to boys and girls.

Chapter 3

Filling the Information Gap

The previous chapter emphasised the complexity of motivation. The model associated with Ajzen's 'theory of planned behaviour' was selected with a view to providing some structure to what could be the chaos of reviewing just some of the literature on the topic and especially the work already done on motivation and foreign language learning and teaching. Figure 3.1 illustrates the three main areas of Ajzen's model which are to be exploited for this purpose.

Attitude towards the behaviour What attitudes do pupils have towards learning German? What may be the influences on these attitudes?	**Subjective norm** To what extent are parents, home background, the relationship with the teacher, influences on motivation and attitude?	**Perceived behavioural control** What may be the realistic constraints which pupils perceive as influencing their motivation to learn foreign languages?

Figure 3.1 Ajzen's categories

This chapter will take each of these three areas in turn and critically analyse work done to date on motivational perspectives of pupils learning foreign languages.

Areas of the Study Covered by 'Attitude Towards the Behaviour'

Pupils do not come to the foreign languages classroom as *tabulae rasae*. They bring with them certain attitudes born of conversations shared with family and friends, the media and personal experience of the target language community. Ajzen defines attitude as 'the individual's positive or negative evaluation of performing the particular behavior of interest' (1988: 117). If the pay-off is likely to be positive and especially if 'significant others' are disposed to approve of the intended behaviour then the intention to perform the behaviour is inclined to develop positively. The converse is also true. Within the context of this research, this translates to a pupil who regards foreign language learning as useful and/or enjoyable and who feels encouraged by, for example, parents to learn foreign languages, being more likely to feel positively motivated to participate in the learning process. The extent of the pupils' ethnocentricity, their experience of travel and of meeting other nationalities may also have an influence on their attitude to the foreign language learning experience.

General definition of attitude

If motivation is difficult to define, attitude poses no fewer problems. Attitude is linked to an individual's set of values and may be influenced by many factors. To describe a pupil as having 'an attitude' or 'an attitude problem' reflects a certain *je ne sais quoi* which makes her at best an awkward pupil. She 'has something about her' (that is, a different set of values) which makes the teacher–pupil relationship rather challenging. Research into motivation and foreign language learning reflects some difficulty with the distinction between motivation and attitude. To treat them as one and the same thing, however, is unhelpful.

Schiefele distinguishes between attitude and motive in the following terms. Attitude is individualised and not liable to much change. Motive, by contrast, is more immediate in offering the reason for the behaviour of the moment. He places attitude within the motivation model shown in Figure 3.2:

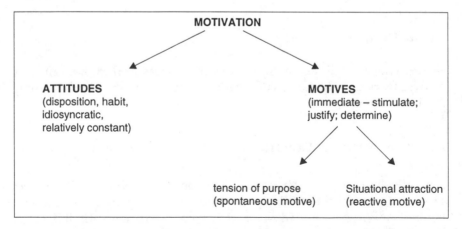

Figure 3.2 Schiefele motivation model
Source: Schiefele, 1963: 66

Gardner's work on attitude and second language learning is in keeping with the general view of attitudes as related to motivation by serving as a support to learner's overall motivation. He defines attitude as 'an evaluative reaction to some referent or attitude object, inferred on the basis of the individual's beliefs or opinions about the referent' (Gardner, 1985: 9). Attitudes are constructs, discoverable in statements of belief or opinions. Gardner endeavours to explain how attitudes relate to motivation in the foreign language learning/acquisition context in the following rather all-inclusive manner:

> Motivation refers to the combination of effort plus desire to achieve the goal of learning plus favourable attitudes towards learning the language. (Gardner, 1985: 10)

Gardner and Lambert (1972: 132) identify three categories of attitude relevant to second language learning:

- attitudes towards the target language community (group specific attitudes) (see also Brown, 1981);
- attitudes towards learning the language;
- attitudes towards languages and language learning in general.

Definition of attitude for the purposes of this study

In the light of this diversity, what is the definition of 'attitude' for the purposes of this study? 'Attitude' is taken to mean the set of values which a pupil brings to the foreign language learning experience. It is shaped by the pay-offs that she expects; the advantages that she sees in language learning. The values which a pupil has may be determined by different variables, such as experience of learning the target language, of the target language community, experience of travel, the influence of parents and friends and the attitudes which they may demonstrate and articulate.

Attitude related research and perspectives

A great deal of work has been done within the field of attitude and how it relates to foreign language learning and acquisition.

Gardner and Lambert (1972) examined attitudes as part of a motivational intensity index within the context of learners of French in Canada. They paid particular attention to three aspects:

(1) Ethnocentrism, that is suspicion of foreign people and ideas.
(2) Authoritarianism, that is authoritarian or antidemocratic ideologies, reflecting a generalised prejudice of foreign peoples.

(3) Social dissatisfaction or 'anomie', that is the feeling of finding oneself between two cultures rather than belonging to one or the other.

They conclude that the attitude of the learner towards the target language culture is the most important variable influencing foreign language acquisition. The extent to which this conclusion can be generalised from its Canadian setting is open to question. How applicable is it to the UK foreign language learning context, where, at least in the case of the languages most commonly taught in schools (French, German, Spanish), there is no immediate access to the target language community and thus apparently little or no experience of real substance upon which an attitude could be based? The findings of this study should offer further insight into this and similar attitudinal questions.

In an earlier study Lambert (1961) had found a link between ethnocentrism and poor achievement in the learning of French. He drew the conclusion that American students of English-speaking backgrounds who were in the process of studying French, generally had a negative set of stereotypes about the basic personality characteristics of French-speaking people. There was a strong correlation between this and their poor performance in learning French:

> The student who has ethnocentric or prejudiced attitudes towards foreign peoples and who makes invidious comparisons of French and American ways of life, is likely to do poorly in school French and in some aspects of comprehension, independent of any intellectual capacity or motivation to do well in French. (Lambert, 1961: 36)

Piepho comes to a similar conclusion in linking performance and level of ethnocentricity:

> All the research and experimentation with which I am familiar indicates that the most stable and highly correlated prerequisite for the variable of language performance is that of the *attitude* taken by the learner to the subject, the country and the people who speak the language . . . (Piepho, 1981: 45)

Closer to home, Burstall *et al.*'s (1974) research into primary school French, controversial though it may be in the interpretation of its findings, reveals much about the development of young learners' attitudes. She concludes that the mere process of attempting to learn a foreign language during childhood is sufficient to promote the development of positive attitudes towards speakers of that language. Pupils who like French in their *first year of learning* tend:

- to want to speak many languages;
- to want to continue with French;
- to feel that they are better at French than other subjects;
- to find French easier than other subjects;
- to feel that everyone should learn French;
- to think that French will be useful after they have left school;
- to have parents who are pleased that they are learning French;
- to want to visit France;
- to want to make French friends.

Pupils who dislike French, however, tend:

- to find it less useful than other subjects;
- to feel that only those who are good at it, should learn it;
- to feel that French is difficult;
- to feel that English is a superior language to French;
- to think that the French should learn English.

In spite of the evidence supporting the view that a healthy attitude towards the country and speakers of the target language may help lead to a healthy attitude towards learning the language, Thornton and Cajkler (1996) found in their study on 'Student attitudes to German language and life' that pupils rarely revealed the classroom and the foreign language learning experience as the source of their information about the target language community. More common was personal experience, television and radio.

Influences on attitude

In-school factors

How easy it is to misinterpret a pupil's negative attitude to foreign language learning. It may well be the case that she has a negative attitude not only to foreign languages but to school and learning in general.

Learning in general

Keys and Fernandes (1993) conducted questionnaire-based research into the experiences and attitudes of 11- and 13-year-old students in their schools in order to:

- test the hypothesis that students' levels of motivation towards schooling are lower in Year 9 than in Year 7;
- identify the factors associated with motivation towards school and learning and hypothesise causes for hostility towards school.

The main areas covered in the questionnaires were:

- personal and home background information;
- attitudes towards school and learning;
- perceptions of teachers and lessons;
- self-reported behaviour in and out of school;
- perceptions of parental interest and support.

It was found that Year 9 differed most strikingly from Year 7 in that they were:

- less likely to say that their work was interesting and more likely to say that their lessons were boring;
- less likely to say that they liked all or most of their teachers;
- less likely to agree that their teachers tried hard to make them work as well as they were able;
- less likely to agree that their teachers were making efforts to maintain discipline;
- less likely to agree that their schools had sensible rules;
- more likely to have played truant.

There was little or no difference between the Year 7 and Year 9 samples of students in:

- their perceptions of their own ability;
- their strong belief that schools should help them to do well in exams, teach them things which would be useful when they got jobs and to be independent;
- their perceptions of their parents' aspirations for their future. (Keys & Fernandes, 1993: 62)

The findings suggested that pupils who dislike school are likely to:

- find school boring;
- dislike their teachers;
- place low values on school and schoolwork;
- have negative perceptions of the ethos of their school;
- have negative views of their own ability and perseverance;
- behave badly at school;
- perceive lower levels of support from their parents. (Keys & Fernandes, 1993: 63)

Some aspects of the findings give cause for concern:

- Nine per cent of pupils indicated that they were bored in all or most lessons and a further 40–55% said that they were bored in some lessons;

- many teachers did not praise their students for good work;
- nearly 25% of students perceived their teachers to be 'fairly easily satisfied' with their students' work;
- 40% of students said that they had not discussed their work individually with their teachers during the school year;
- the majority of students perceived a high level of parental interest and support and both age groups reported talking about their career plans more frequently with their parents than with their teachers.

Many of the above issues feature in the data provided by this study. It is small comfort that they relate not to foreign languages specifically but appear to apply across all subjects.

In a study on children's attitude to work at 11 years, Blatchford (1992) reports that 17% of 175 pupils interviewed were not looking forward to secondary school. At age seven, 25% of pupils found school boring, at 11 years, 42% found school mostly interesting, 8% mostly boring, with 50% non-committal. One may have expected the enthusiasm of youth to provide a more positive response. How bleak is the prospect of teaching these same pupils in the difficult Years 9 and 10. These data are echoed in the research of Barber (1994b) who found that 'more than 70% of 13–14 year olds say they count the minutes to the end of a lesson and 30% think work is boring'.

Learning foreign languages

Aplin (1991) conducted research into why pupils opted out of foreign language courses at the earliest opportunity. At the time of the study, fewer than half the pupils who completed the pre–16 stage of education would have followed a foreign language course for the entirety of their secondary school experience. (This picture is of course altering quite significantly as the result of National Curriculum reform.) Some had opted out of foreign language courses having made instrumental judgements, for example, that other subjects, such as science, lead to better jobs. Others had developed negative attitudes towards foreign language learning. Pupils offered the following as contributory factors:

- irrelevant activities;
- unhelpful career advice;
- negative impressions about progress;
- dislike of teachers;
- lack of opportunity for contact with the country of the target language.

The Assessment of Performance Unit (APU) (DES/DENI/WO, 1985) on behalf of the Department of Education and Science, conducted a survey to assess the performance of pupils aged 13 in French, German and Spanish as a first foreign language. Further surveys (DES/DENI/WO, 1986, 1987) were carried out in 1984 and 1985 but in French only. The aims of the surveys were: (1) to establish the degree of success with which pupils could perform assessment tasks and (2) to document the knowledge and skills displayed. Listening, speaking, reading and writing tests were administered and pupils were also required to fill in an 'attitude questionnaire'. This consisted of four parts:

A: questions relating to the pupils' contact with the foreign community;
B: a list of 37 statements relating to pupils' feelings about learning foreign languages and contact with the foreign community; pupils were required to indicate the extent of their agreement on a 5 point scale (strongly agree – strongly disagree);
C: pupils' reactions to the kinds of activities which take place in the foreign languages learning classroom – indicated on a scale as in B;
D: 'any thoughts or feelings about learning French/German/Spanish which have not been expressed in Parts A, B AND C'.

The findings over the three years of the survey remained fairly constant. The following general conclusions were drawn for each of the three languages in 1983 and for French in the following two years:

- more pupils thought that the foreign language was useful, enjoyable and not difficult than the contrary;
- more pupils wanted contact with the foreign community than not;
- higher proportions of girls than boys had positive views on all these aspects;
- higher proportions of those who had visited the foreign country than those who had not, had positive attitudes. (DES/DENI/WO, 1985: 390; 1986: 219, 236; 1987: 68)

Some interesting differences in response between pupils learning the individual languages were uncovered:

- the highest proportion of both boys and girls finding the foreign language useful, was among pupils learning Spanish;
- the highest proportion of both boys and girls finding the foreign language easy and enjoyable, was among pupils learning German;
- the highest proportion of girls wanting contact with the foreign language community, was in German; the highest proportions of boys were in French and German. (DES/DENI/WO, 1985: 391)

The study revealed that about two-thirds of the pupils wanted to continue the foreign language in the following year and more than half showed interest in studying a second foreign language, if given the opportunity. It was concluded that the foreign language learning picture for pupils aged 13 was much brighter than had generally been thought.

Filmer-Sankey (1989: 5) accepts that the work of the APU gathered useful evidence, particularly in favour of German and Spanish but maintains that the generalisability of the findings may be open to question in that the sample of pupils was not entirely representative, nor were important variables taken into account such as the ability of the pupils in the sample, the course books used and varying teaching styles. This made impossible the absolute comparison between pupils' attitudes towards the three languages.

Is the positive trend suggested by the APU at age 13 being maintained at age 15? Is this reflected in GCSE examination entries which have recently shown an upward tendency? (See Chapter 1, Table 1.1, p. 3.) Or is the increase in entries merely a reflection of the implementation of the National Curriculum requirement for almost all pupils to take a foreign language up to the end of Key Stage 4? Factors identified as contributing to any enhanced view of language learning include visits to the target language country, closer connections between foreign languages and career opportunities and opportunities to start a new language (Clark & Trafford, 1996; Thornton & Cajkler, 1996). How regrettable then that the National Curriculum puts a severe squeeze on the opportunity for pupils to take a second foreign language. Given the importance of success as a motivating factor, Graded Assessment Schemes (where are they now?; see Buckby *et al.*, 1981) and a more positive approach to assessment within GCSE, may have done much to enhance the image of foreign languages.

One should not be seduced into thinking, however, that everything in the garden is rosy. Clark and Trafford provide evidence of some pupils finding languages difficult and irrelevant to their needs. Some find the classroom experience boring and repetitive ('We're not learning anything new'; 'We just think it's pointless, doing it over again'), and teaching methods unimaginative (Clark & Trafford, 1996: 43).

The research of the Oxford Project for Diversification of First Foreign Language Teaching (OXPROD) focused on difficulties pupils encountered in French, German and Spanish, organisational problems and attitudes children have to the three languages in the course of the first three years of learning. Phillips and Filmer-Sankey (1993) examined which aspects of languages pupils found most difficult, useful and enjoyable, their views of the target language people and countries. Again pupils were required to respond to statements on each area by indicating to what extent they agreed or disagreed with them. Items included the following:

(1) I'm glad I'm learning French rather than another language.
(2) French is one of my favourite lessons.
(3) I'm not interested in meeting French people.
(4) I think my parents are glad I am learning French rather than another language.
(5) I find French too hard.

Although the project was limited in terms of its scale – six 11–18 comprehensives, all in the south of England – and therefore posed problems in terms of generalisability, it nonetheless revealed some interesting findings. The following conclusions refer to pupils in their first year of foreign language learning:

- Pupils brought with them to secondary school enormous enthusiasm for foreign languages which they found enjoyable and quite easy. They were seen as useful and pupils expressed a desire to visit the target language countries.
- The teacher and her teaching methods were seen as having a major bearing on how enjoyable and easy lessons were perceived to be.
- Pupils felt positive about the target language countries and their people but reported themselves motivated more by extrinsic/instrumental factors – getting a certificate/job, etc. – than integrative factors.
- Boys and girls were equally positive about languages but girls were more enthusiastic about visiting the country.
- Pupils who had already been to the target language country (30%) were more positive about learning languages than those who had not.
- Pupils who had parents or sisters/brothers with competence in the target language were more positive than those who did not.
- Pupils enjoyed learning German more than French.
- Boys were more positive towards learning German than girls.

In Year 2 of foreign language learning the results were similar. Pupils remained positive in their attitudes but their enthusiasm was more restrained. Languages were not perceived as being any less useful or more difficult. The teacher and her teaching methods remained the most important contributing factor to attitude. The European Market, Channel Tunnel, the usefulness of German in the commercial world often featured in pupil responses. (Year 3 results were not published.)

Other factors

Pupils bring with them to school attitudes influenced by extraneous factors over which the teacher may have little or no control. *Gender*, for example, is regarded as being a significant factor in foreign language learning. Various studies (Burstall, 1975; Gagnon, 1974; Gardner & Smythe, 1975; Powell & Littlewood, 1983) have established that girls tend to have a more positive attitude to learning French, German, Spanish, etc. than do boys. (See also Barton, 1997; Callaghan 1998; Place 1997.) Clark and Trafford (1996) examined the reasons why girls tend to outperform boys at GCSE and in so doing uncovered a number of variables (attitude to modern languages; perceptions of difficulty; the in-class experience; relationship with the teacher), not all of which, predictably, were gender related. *Background* is another influential factor. Gardner (1985) suggests the influence of upbringing and context on attitude. He takes Welsh speakers as an example. Parents as speakers of a language or parents as non-speakers but with positive attitudes can lead to positive attitudes in their children. *Length of residence* in a country may also be significant, especially for those learning French/German/Spanish as a *second language* as, for example, in the case of Puerto Ricans learning English in USA or Asians in England, as opposed to a *foreign language*, the situation of the UK pupil learning French/German in a UK-based school. Age too is thought to have some bearing on learners' attitudes. Gardner and Smythe (1975) found that attitudes towards second language learning changed, becoming less positive, as learners become older. This may reflect, among other things, pupils' ability to be more objective and also the consequence of a less than positive language learning experience. McDonough (1981: 153) concludes that integrative attitudes (or does he mean motivation?) decrease in favour of instrumental attitudes after the age of 11 or 12 as maturity brings the importance of job prospects into focus rather more. Burstall (1975) maintains that attitudes are dependent to a large extent on prior *achievement* in the foreign language:

> The calculation of partial correlations indicated strongly that early achievement in French affected attitudes towards learning French and later achievement in French to a significantly greater extent than early attitudes towards learning French affected the subsequent development of either attitudes or achievement. (Burstall, 1975: 399)

This is supported by Her Majesty's Inspectorate (1985) and Oller and Perkins (1978a), especially with reference to achievement and attitude in the early stages of foreign language learning.

Teacher–pupil relationship

The teacher–pupil relationship plays an important role in determining the atmosphere of the teaching environment and this combination influences the quality of learning which takes place. Interviews forming the basis of the modern languages specific study conducted by Clark and Trafford (1995: 318, 322) reveal that both teachers and pupils regard the teacher–pupil relationship as the most significant variable affecting pupils' attitudes towards foreign language learning.

The teacher has a difficult balance to strike in establishing a relationship which allows her to be approachable but maintains the distance which the teacher–pupil relationship demands. The teacher cannot be the pupil's friend, in the purest sense. Nor must she come across as a harsh disciplinarian. Having said that, discipline which allows learning to take place must be maintained. (See Kyriacou 1992: 130–52)

How then does the teacher meet the challenge of establishing the appropriate atmosphere of learning? (See p. 49.)

> To create an effective learning experience in any classroom (whatever the school) the teacher has to be able to create a purposeful and calm atmosphere in which the 'momentum' for learning can be built. (Blum,1998: 11)

Her approach will in all likelihood vary from class to class depending on the behaviour and performance of the group and individuals within the group. Initial impressions may be significant. Tomlinson (1981: 273) warns, however, of the dangers of categorising pupils according to stereotype. A teacher's perception of a pupil may be coloured by factors such as previous achievement, conformity tendencies, physical attractiveness, seating location, neatness of writing, speech characteristics. The pupil's awareness of the teacher's perception can affect pupil motivation and performance in both the long and short term. A teacher conscious of this danger may review assumptions she may have made on a pupil and correct them accordingly, not least with regard to motivation. Tomlinson (1981: 286) stresses how knowledge of the group is as important as knowledge of individuals. If motivation is to be influenced the teacher must pay attention to group culture and group structure and within the group it is important to recognise the role of individuals.

Perry (1992) focuses on the early labelling of pupils as a significant factor in under-achievement. She refers to worrying evidence from the mid-1980s, showing that teachers quickly classify children whose achievement in the early days of the classroom appear to be lower than average, as 'low ability'. These children are often those from working-class homes or from ethnic minorities who may indeed reach school with less developed skills, and therefore lower attainment in some of the early tasks. Later research also found that there was a significant relationship between teachers' ratings of pupils' behaviour as 'naughty' or 'good' and their rating of their ability. Perry calls a 'tragedy' the fact that those 'low-ability' children were then relegated to tasks, given less academic attention and rewarded, on the basis of 'Well, what can you expect?'. As a result the pathology of the low achiever is reinforced, sending the child on an ever downward spiral of low achievement, low expectations and finally low self-esteem. (The publication of the 1998 GCSE results was accompanied by a media outcry that the gap between 'the more and less able' was widening as schools neglected those pupils not likely to feature in the league-tables for A*–C passes. 'The system meant that schools were concentrating on those pupils who were capable of higher grades to the detriment of those at the bottom of the heap', in 'League tables under fire over increase in GCSE failures', *The Independent*, 27.8.98.)

Perceived relevance

If the teacher is to motivate pupils to learn, then relevance has to be the red thread permeating activities. If pupils fail to see the relationship between the activity and the world in which they live, then the point of the activity is likely to be lost on them. Schiefele (1963) distinguishes between the difficulties faced by the secondary school teacher and those of her primary school colleagues. Pupils of primary school age, he suggests, are motivated to learn, almost regardless of the object of learning. Schiefele refers to this as 'Expansion'. (See Blatchford, 1992 and O'Connor, 1994 for an opposing view.) In the secondary sector, however, pupils tend to be more selective and to focus on what they feel is important to them: Schiefele's 'Intensivierung' (1963: 379).

This is illustrated within the German context in the findings of research carried out by Measor and Woods (1984). They found that pupils in the first year of secondary school tended to prioritise subjects in terms of their importance. Subjects such as music and art and design, for example, were given very low priority in contrast to English and mathematics which were highly valued because of their vocational relevance. More importance was attached to physical sciences by boys than girls, while foreign languages other than English were not mentioned.

Within the UK modern languages context Clark and Trafford found evidence of pupils articulating a need to make a link between their learning and the world outside the classroom. In the words of one interviewee:

> It's good to put into practice what you've learnt, you know, then you feel satisfied, I mean now we've learnt all this but we haven't put it into practice because we haven't been to France or anything. (Clark & Trafford, 1995: 320)

Lee and Dickson (1991: 11) in their work on foreign languages for lower attaining pupils, report the feeling among teachers that 'if it were to be compulsory for pupils to study the same language for five years then it should be linked to the work situation'. To this was added the need for more flexible approaches, increased support in the classroom and more non-contact time. If pupils do not see the relevance of a subject, the teacher has from the outset a major challenge.

'Teaching styles'

> Undemanding tasks and dull teaching failed to engage pupils' participation in lessons and their willing consent to learn. Teaching styles were insufficiently varied to sustain pupils' concentration throughout lesson of 50 minutes or more. (OFSTED, 1993: 25)

To what extent is teaching style a contributory factor to foreign language learners' attitude? The confines of this review allow only a scratching of the surface of this important topic. Any work on motivation and foreign language learning, however, would be incomplete without some reference to it. Teachers of modern foreign languages have striven throughout the ages to find a methodology which would meet the needs of all learners. The pendulum has swung back and forth via 'grammar grind' and the 'direct method', the audio-visual and communicative eras, total physical response and suggestopedia (see Kelly, 1976). None of these methods is bad. None provides a universal panacea to the problem of motivation. The idea that a single methodology exists which suits everyone is as erroneous as believing that the stereotypical language learner exists. Within any given group there is a range of needs, interests, background and learner-types. To target what may be perceived as the average pupil means the neglect of those not conforming to that stereotype. What follows is a brief review of two areas currently in vogue: information and communications technology (ICT), and the flexible/autonomous approach.

Information and communications technology (ICT)

The National Curriculum places great emphasis on various forms of ICT, not least exploitation of word-processing packages, overlays, self-authoring packages and e-mail. There is much evidence (Atkinson, 1992; Brown, R., 1993; Martin & Hampson, 1991; White & Wacha, 1992) to support the view that ICT has much to contribute to the enhancement of the foreign language learning experience. The computer is a medium which is flexible and promotes independent learning. Pupils enjoy working on the computer and have little difficulty in developing the necessary competence. How can ICT make a positive contribution in the language learning classroom? Writing in the target language, for example, may serve to demotivate in that performance can be inaccurate. Many drafts may have to be written before a document of which the pupil can be proud is produced. ICT facilitates correction without red pen. It can be done easily and the final product looks good.

> The use of the computer . . . provides motivation to pupils who might otherwise be reluctant to practise writing in a foreign language at all. (Lee, 1994: 93)

ICT driven grammar exercises are repeated without complaint by pupils who find them tedious when using pen and paper. E-mail facilitates writing for a real purpose and for an authentic readership. Response is likely to be almost immediate. Teachers and their pupils can 'surf the net' in their search for authentic, up-to-date materials on the topic on which they may be working.

> The World Wide Web and e-mail offer language professionals the twin virtues of topicality and authenticity. The Internet provides uniquely powerful facilities to cross borders and dive headlong into a *bain linguistique* of authentic texts and communication possibilities. (McKenna & McKenna, 1999)

Immediacy, accessibility of materials and native speakers in the target language country, use of the keyboard rather than the pen, of the screen rather than the exercise book and textbook contribute much to the learning of real life skills and to the enhancement of motivation.

Given these indisputable motivational advantages of ICT, to what extent does it impinge upon the foreign language learning reality of the pupils in this study?

Flexible/Autonomous approach

'Flexibile' or 'autonomous' or 'individualised' learning is 'in' at all levels of learning/teaching. (See Drew & Ottewill, 1998; Hurd, 1998; McDevitt, 1997; Remmert, 1997.) It represents an effort to meet the needs of learners with a range of ability and interests. Such an approach allows learners to work at their own pace through programmes and materials of their own choosing. It takes account of the age, ability and previous experience of pupils, time factors and the nature and content of the work. Each student works to an individual work plan and study guides allow for differentiation by topic and ability.

The autonomous approach is not without its problems, however. The learner who is new to the approach invariably may have difficulty in identifying those aspects of the syllabus upon which she needs to focus. She may have a global understanding of what needs to be done, but lacks insight into the detail. This is where careful liaison with the teacher can be so important, not to mention time-consuming.

Michael Evans offers reasons for the increasing popularity of a more flexible approach with pupils and teachers:

> Pupils enjoy being given responsibility for some of their work and quite naturally respond positively to work which they have helped organise. Variety of resources increases the scope for their finding a medium which they enjoy using. It also avoids the tedium which inevitably results from over-reliance on one medium (say, the textbook). There is greater opportunity for creative participation through, for instance, video or tape recording of role plays, interviews or other performances which are planned or carried out in groups independently of the teacher. The role of the teacher alters radically and the image which he or she projects is no longer one of a distant authority whose job is to apply pressure on the learner to absorb information which has been previously selected and organised. As well as becoming a facilitator of independent learning through provision and organisation of resource-based activities and the general management of a flexible learning course, the teacher is also divested of the invisible chains which tie him or her to the front of the class and is free to interact with learners in small groups or individually and thereby follow more closely the progress of each member of the class and monitor self-assessment and reflection on the learning process by the pupils themselves. (Michael Evans, 1993: 18)

Evans appreciates the complexity of causes of disaffection and does not suggest flexible learning as a panacea. He does nevertheless see the opportunity which this strategy offers for personal contact with individual pupils as a potential contributor to a more positive attitude, however shortlived, in future lessons.

To what extent are pupils in this study experiencing their teachers of foreign languages taking advantage of the opportunity which Evans identifies?

Assessment and feedback

The importance of success in motivation cannot be overstated. Olivier points out how the teacher should provide feedback to the pupil at regular intervals, measuring success not against other members of the class but against personal criteria:

> We have to learn to recognise and reward success in relation to clearly defined criteria and to enable pupils to see what they are able to do and

take pride in that. This approach also enables teachers to organise their work so as to give regular and frequent feedback to pupils. (Olivier, 1990: 50)

Olivier refers to the influence of Graded Tests (see also Buckby *et al.*, 1981) and the development of modular courses which allow pupils to take responsibility for the pace of their own learning and state when they are ready to present themselves for assessment. In this way the pupils can see where they are going, know exactly what they have to do and understand why they have to learn certain language and structures. Failure is minimised.

The importance of regular feedback, of the pupil knowing where she stands in relation to progress and teacher and pupil sharing a view of where she stands are recognised as important attitudinal issues. This is a subject which is taken up again below under the heading 'Subjective Norm'.

Summary of 'Attitude Towards the Behaviour'

There are so many factors which may contribute to a pupil's attitude. Some of these are in-school factors and the responsibility of the teacher of foreign languages: the teaching style; the atmosphere of the classroom; the teacher–pupil relationship; pupils' perception of the relevance of the target language to them; the teacher-to-pupil-feedback. Others are in-school factors but not directly the responsibility of the teacher of foreign languages but rather the school management and society in general: the general atmosphere within the school and individual classrooms; the low status which may be perceived to be attributed to a subject. Others are factors external to the school: gender; age; home background; general lack of interest in learning. While it is important for a teacher to be aware of these, she can and should only retain a limited range at the forefront of her consciousness at any given time. Consideration of attitudinal factors is only one of many plates which the teacher is required to keep in the air. And she is only human after all.

Areas of the Study Covered by 'Subjective Norm'

Ajzen defines 'subjective norm' in the following terms: 'The person's perception of social pressure to perform or not to perform the behavior' (Ajzen, 1988: 117).

Within the context of Ajzen's model, subjective norm plays an important role, especially when combined with attitude towards the behaviour. If an individual assesses the outcome of the behaviour under consideration to be positive and believes that 'significant others' support her in the behaviour, then it is likely that she will decide to carry it out.

Within the context of this study, who are the 'significant others'? To identify those who are likely to influence the foreign language learner's perception of the social pressure to perform or not is a challenging task. A 'significant other' for one pupil may have no influence of any import on another pupil.

Social learning theory

Indisputably social factors play an important role in motivating behaviour. Tomlinson (1981: 159) defines social learning theory as explaining behaviour in the form of responses not necessarily determined by primary or secondary reinforcement but by processes of imitation and more general identification. Such learning is often incidental and not influenced by the prospect of reward or punishment. Children imitating adults may be an example. Bandura (1989) suggests that people develop 'performance standards', behavioural goals and expectations by observing the actions of others and the outcomes. He provides the (rather politically incorrect) illustration of a girl whose father values achievement and praises his wife and children when he judges it appropriate. As a result the girl learns to set achievement-oriented standards for her own performance. Self-efficacy theory explicates the feeling of competence and self-control when success in meeting one's own performance targets is experienced.

Within the context of this study, how often do pupils have the opportunity of observing 'significant others' or role models 'performing' in a foreign language? How many pupils observe their parents speaking French/German/Spanish and think: 'Oh, I want to be able to do that'? How many of their pop or sports idols provide them with evidence of a foreign language competence worthy of replication? Do our politicians set them an example?

Lewin's *Field Theory*

Lewin's *Field Theory* (1952) attempts to explain possible reactions to the situation in which the individual and the goal-object are in conflict. The perceived likelihood of success of a given behaviour and its importance can be influenced by the expectations of teachers, parents, peers and the social milieu. Expectations set inappropriately low, for example, could have a retarding effect on performance. Expectations which are inappropriately high, demanding excessive effort, may lead to a person's abandoning the activity or trying to 'leave the field'. This may be temporary at first but repeated lack of success and increased negative valence leads to giving up on the activity. Success and failure influence valence, raise or lower the level of aspiration and may affect pupils' self-esteem and/or self-concept.

Nash (1976: 57) identifies pupils with high self-concept as regarding the teacher as a 'significant other'. He suggests that this is not the case with pupils with low self-concept who characterise themselves by making friends with pupils similar to them thereby forming tight circles offering compensatory security and a sense of belonging. He also stresses the influence of the support which the child receives from parents for school achievements. The greater the support and interest parents show, the more likely the child is to have a high self-esteem which in turn enhances performance.

Teachers and parents appear to have a key role to play in influencing the behaviour of pupils in the school context. If their expectations and estimations of performance are realistic, if they set the appropriate tone in terms of encouragement and support, if they provide the appropriate learning environment, it may be more likely that they will be adopted as 'significant others'. If not, there may be a likelihood that the individual's self-esteem will be damaged and she will seek refuge within the peer group.

Teacher expectations

In the absence of accurate assessment teachers used more generalised estimates of pupils' abilities which led them in some schools to *overestimate the effects of poverty and social disadvantage and to underestimate the potential ability of pupils.* (OFSTED, 1993: 16)

. . . lessons were carefully planned to meet clearly understood targets in programmes of study. Teachers communicated these objectives to pupils, *established high expectations* and set appropriate tasks. (OFSTED, 1993: 26)

The link between teacher-expectation and pupil performance is well established (see Alexander *et al.*, 1992; Brophy & Good, 1976; Burstall, 1968; Finn, 1972; Nash, 1976; Pidgeon, 1970). Appropriately high expectations are more likely to lead to appropriately high performance. If expectations are too low, sometimes as the result of misdirected kindness on the part of teachers, pupils are likely to 'live down' to those expectations (Brophy & Good, 1976; Schusser, 1972). Similarly if expectations are too high, then this leads to frustration at the realisation that the goals set are unattainable and thus to a poorer standard of performance.

The implications of teacher-expectation are emphasised when it is not applied evenly to all pupils regardless of ability. Nash (1976: 50) warns that some teachers may not even be conscious of the fact that they are transmitting high expectations to highly thought of pupils and thus enhancing their achievements, and low expectations to poorly thought of pupils and thereby potentially lowering their achievements. In this way the gap between the more able and the less able widens as the former are further advantaged and the latter further disadvantaged.

Gardner and Lambert (1972: 57, 135) point out the importance of teacher and pupil sharing a common view of the pupil's achievement and progress. Should there be a discrepancy in this perception, it can have a demotivating effect on the pupil. Research on learners of French in Canada suggests that students showing most motivation are those who reach a consensus with their teacher on what the criteria are to determine progress and achievement in language study.

As worrying as pupils not sharing their teachers' view of achievement and progress is the problem of pupils not being aware of what their teachers think. Keys *et al.* (1995a) found that about half the pupils in each age group (final year of primary school and first year of secondary school) had not had a conversation with their teachers about their work during the school year. Not knowing may or may not have a negative influence on motivation but is unlikely to do much to enhance it. How can pupils not know? Were 'Records of Achievement' not introduced to facilitate discussion of progress made, of areas for improvement and target-setting? What is happening in 'form periods'? Is the Personal and Social Education (PSE) programme so dominant and inflexible that little room is left for one-to-one pupil-to-teacher discussion of progress?

Socio-cultural issues

Stern (1983: 270) stresses the relevance of socio-cultural factors to motivation. Such factors include the general attitude to formal education, to foreign languages and the relative social status of the first and second language. Particular languages are sometimes held in either high or low esteem because of economic, political or cultural values associated with them. Students therefore come to the learning situation with positive or negative attitudes derived from the society in which they live. The instrumental value of the second language, political factors, geographical aspects, the educational framework all have a role to play. These factors will in turn be influenced by social opportunities for contact with the second language and environmental issues including the socio-economic status of the parents.

Pritchard, writing on the Northern Ireland context, identifies a link between socio-economic background, relevance of foreign language learning and motivation:

> Since it is not easy to convince children, particularly those from lower socio-economic groups, of the immediate and direct relevance of

foreign languages, there are sure to be serious problems in motivating the 'new' language learners. (Pritchard, 1991: 3)

Gardner's (1985) 'socio-educational model' of second language acquisition (see Chapter 2, p. 17 ff) reflects the influence of social milieu and in particular: (1) the cultural beliefs on issues such as whether language learning is easy or hard, (2) the development of attitudinal and motivational characteristics, and (3) the role it can play in influencing the actual level of second language proficiency attained by students in general, because of expectations imposed on them.

Parental influence

The importance of parental influence on performance in the classroom should not be underestimated (see Alexander *et al.* 1995). Feenstra (1969) in a study on parent and teacher attitudes and their effect on learners concludes that integrative motivation (i.e. reflecting a desire to become part of the target language community; see Gardner & Lambert, 1972: 157) is facilitated by the 'attitudinal atmosphere' of the home. Parents have an active role to play in the establishing of such an atmosphere by making overt efforts to help, facilitate and support the child, and a passive role in the attitude they manifest to learning and, in the case of foreign language learning, to the target language community (see also Gardner, 1968). How many UK parents have foreign language competence which allows them to help their children with homework?

Oskamp (1977) includes parental influence among the most significant determinants of attitude, along with personal experience with the attitude object, group determinants and the mass media. Children could hardly escape the images portrayed on television (*Allo! Allo!*; the Carlsberg advertisement playing on the sunbed myth(?)) and in newspapers which again paint the stereotype of the Germans monopolising the sunbeds in Spanish resorts ('Brits won't share sun with the hun', *The Sun*, 8 September 1995) and the alleged French proclivity towards violence ('The French are a violent and sexually aggressive nation', *The Sun*, 23 June 1990. A survey (Burstall, 1995) carried out by the Business Development Partnership showed *The Sun* to be the favourite national newspaper of school-age boys and girls.). The newspaper coverage of the Euro '96 football championships reflected a tabloid obsession with stimulating at best a negative picture and at worst hatred of any team against which England had to play.

Oskamp also considers age as a variable in this context. He suggests that parental influence is at its strongest in the early years. As the child matures the influence of direct experience, the mass media, direct indoctrination in school, peer group pressure and general expectations or beliefs in the cultural community play a more telling role.

Summary of 'Subjective Norm'

The teacher of foreign languages in the UK is up against it. She faces the challenge of English occupying prime position as the language of the business world and pop-culture. How much support is she likely to receive from the outside? Are family and friends in a position to offer help? Do parents have foreign language competence? How often do pupils hear a foreign language spoken outside school? What messages do pupils receive from family and friends about their foreign language learning experience? Do pupils come from an environment where foreign languages are seen as having any practical relevance or application?

What if the pupil gives the teacher the mantle of 'significant other'? The teacher already carries as part of an enormous burden the reponsibility of making expectations clear to the pupil. This is no easy task. Yet another balance has to be struck: set expectations too high and the pupil struggles to cope and eventually gives up trying; set expectations which are too low and the pupil copes without much effort, misses the buzz which meeting a challenge provides and eventually switches off.

Perceived Behavioural Control

Ajzen's 'perceived behavioural control' takes account of an individual's perception of the realistic constraints which may influence capability to perform a given behaviour. Within the context of this book, potential impediments to learning the foreign language may include the atmosphere of the learning environment and its potential to stimulate positive and/or negative emotional reactions, stress or anxiety. As with all aspects of the in-school experience, the teacher has a key role to play.

Emotion/stress/anxiety and modern languages

The link between emotion and learning, and foreign language learning in particular, has a substantial history. Findlay for example, recognises the learner's emotional resistance to abandoning the first language frame of reference and his refusal to 'grasp the foreigner's mind by entering into his mode of thought' (Findlay, 1932: 321). If successful learning is to take place, this emotional hurdle has to be overcome:

> The learner has to copy the behaviour of the native by conscious attention, practising again and again, establishing a multitude of new habits, all of them contrary to the stream of his own vernacular habits. (Findlay, 1932: 321)

In the light of this emotional dimension, which also provides a foretaste of the philosophy behind the social processing models of Clément (1980); Giles & Byrne (1982); Lambert (1963a,b, 1967, 1974); and Schumann (1978a,b), Findlay argues that rather than approaching language learning as the analysis of a foreign code, it is more appropriate to meet it as a living reality, in situations representing authentic experiences in dramatic form. Findlay clearly had a vision of Graded Objectives (Buckby *et al.*, 1981) and the so-called 'communicative era' of language learning and teaching (Page & Hewett, 1987).

Rivers (1964: 91) outlines the emotional aspects which make the language learning process difficult. Within the British context, where language learning has traditionally started at age 11, the adolescent, she suggests, is asked to return to immature behaviour in that she is required to practise strange sounds, strange words and modes of expression, to do exactly what the teacher asks and to lay aside any independent thinking. Rivers is of the view that language learning materials tended in the 1960s to be childish in terms of content, relating to family, a day at the farm, at the seaside, etc., taking learners back to their early days in the primary school. More than 20 years later Powell (1986: 65) supports this view:

> There is still some way to go, however, before the mismatch between pupils' level of sophistication in the modern world and the childishness of some of the topics and activities presented is overcome completely.

Have materials and related activities improved in the interim? Some aspects of the 'bad old days' remain but much has improved. Communicative competence, usefulness, perceived relevance may not have been universally regarded as important concepts at the juncture of the 'grammar grind' and audio-visual eras, the time at which Rivers was writing. Materials have improved considerably, going some way to meeting the needs and interests of the learner. A more autonomous approach to learning and the exploitation of ICT, problem-solving and information gap exercises, for example, which give the learner the opportunity to think for herself and a reason to act were uncommon as aspects of teaching methodology in the 1960s and were perhaps only embryonic ideas in the mid-1980s when Powell forewarned:

> One must not be seduced into thinking, however, that all is rosy in the language learning/teaching garden. It could be argued that the transaction-focused GCSE syllabus with its move away from 'childish' contexts towards more adult activities (booking hotel rooms; buying petrol, etc.), represents a shift from one extreme to the other. How many opportunities are provided to fire pupils' imagination and curiosity as

they move from the post-office to the lost property office to the tourist information office? (Powell, 1986: 65)

Rivers (1964: 91ff.) describes other problems on the emotional level which remain in spite of the passage of time. The adolescent language learner may be sensitive to her standing within the peer group and self-concept. She may hesitate to answer, to try to get her tongue around these strange sounds or show any initiative or originality, as to make a mistake might lead to the laughter of classmates and the feeling of having made a fool of herself. Rivers (1964: 92) describes the foreign language learning classroom as 'a fertile ground for frustration, anxiety, embarrassment and humiliation'. Pupils react to this in different ways. Unpleasant emotions lead some to behave in a disruptive fashion. Anxiety can lead to increased effort to avoid embarrassment or indeed passivity to meet the same end. Feelings of humiliation may lead to antagonism and negative feelings towards the teacher, the language and foreign language learning in general. The sensitive teacher is aware of this potential difficulty and, in order to meet the challenge it presents, applies trained, practised and acquired skills, the products of the experience of teaching and of life.

Anxiety, however, is not an exclusively bad thing. It can in fact have a performance enhancing influence on some pupils. Mathews draws the following conclusion from experiments conducted with language learners in America who were required to take tests while experiencing various anxiety levels or levels of 'negative affect':

> In those situations where there is reason to believe that students may have little incentive to do well, or when some students admit that they wish to do poorly, increased negative affect can cause students to function at a level of operational tension, and that at that level we can expect to obtain optimum learning and performance. (Mathews, 1996: 41)

nAch and modern foreign languages

Linked to the emotional/anxiety dimension is Atkinson and McClelland's (1953) development of the 'need to achieve' theory (nAch). They distinguish between individuals with high and low nAch. Those with a high nAch strive for success. Given the choice of a range of activities, members of this category would opt for those which would provide a reasonable guarantee of success. Extremely difficult tasks would be avoided. Those with a low nAch, who may also have Maf, motive to avoid failure, avoid moderately difficult tasks and opt for those which are either very easy, thus ensuring success, or very difficult, thus guaranteeing failure and therefore reducing anxiety by providing themselves with the excuse, 'Well, the task was far too difficult in any case'.

Burstall *et al.* (1974) and Stern (1983) emphasise the negative consequences of failure. For some learners, failure can be a stimulus to greater effort, for others, however, it provokes disappointment, disaffection and worse (Stern 1983: 340).

Motivational function of the teacher

If you have a nice teacher it encourages you to do well. But if the teacher is severe you may be scared of her, so you may not like to answer in case you get it wrong. (APU, 1985: 65)

Learning French is easy if you have the right teacher. Luckily we have.' (APU, 1985: 65)

Amidst the complexity of factors influencing behaviour, the teacher has a key role to play in shaping pupils' perception of the ease or difficulty of performing a given task, in fostering positive attitudes and stimulating pupils' desire to learn.

De Cecco and Crawford (1974) divide the motivational functions of the teacher into four categories:

(1) Arousal – if arousal leads to high levels of anxiety then performance is likely to be impaired. (Krashen, 1982: 32, refers to this as keeping the 'affective filter' low: 'The effective language teacher is someone who can provide input and help make it comprehensible in a low anxiety situation').

(2) Expectancy – underlines the importance of setting clear achievable objectives and appropriate and well-timed pay-off.

(3) Incentive – this is the stimulus which triggers off anticipations and responses; the rewards for present achievement should be provided in such a way as to stimulate future achievement. Formal qualifications are unlikely to perform this function adequately because they are long-term rewards. Short-term rewards must also be given a place. Consider for example the role of 'Graded Objectives'. (See p. 51 for the need for the judicious use of extrinsic rewards.)

(4) Disciplinary – this aims at the creation of an ordered, non-authoritarian, non-threatening, atmosphere. It is the teacher's responsibility to create a social structure in the classroom which promotes healthy interpersonal relationships and sustains all pupils' interests, needs and potential. (See p. 35 ff.)

An inextricable link exists between the appropriate learning atmosphere and the management of classroom control. The creation of an atmosphere where the rights of each individual are recognised and respected and each is given the opportunity by teacher and peers to achieve her potential, enhances quite naturally the quality of behaviour. Learning best takes place in an ordered environment where the ground rules for behaviour are clearly laid down, understood by all and adhered to. Traditionally it is the teacher's responsibility to establish and maintain that order. This function is often referred to as 'discipline'. Some colleagues would argue that in today's school the establishing of an appropriate atmosphere of learning is something which is negotiated between pupil and teacher. Others would say that such negotiation is merely a façade covering the reality of dominant teachers controlling and directing subordinate pupils. See Jahnke (1977: 93ff.) who identifies seven categories of atmosphere:

(1) 'The emotionally positive atmosphere.'
(2) 'The informative atmosphere.'
(3) 'Independence-promoting atmosphere.'
(4) 'The supportive atmosphere.'
(5) 'The rewarding atmosphere' (as opposed to 'the punishing atmosphere').
(6) 'The atmosphere of the flexible, individualised approach.'
(7) 'The stimulating, problem-solving atmosphere.'

How does the teacher get the atmosphere right? The atmosphere of the classroom may be influenced by a plethora of factors:

- the atmosphere of the school as a whole at a given time;
- the pupils' mood(s) as determined by their experience in the previous lesson:
  - have they been severely reprimanded?
  - have they just come from a rousing games or drama lesson?
  - have they just sat through a double-lesson which they found particularly dreary?
- the teacher's mood:
  - has she had a difference of opinion with a colleague/friend/partner?
  - is she feeling unwell?
  - has she just received good/bad news?
- the failure of technical equipment, e.g. the video; OHP; cassette-recorder, computer;
- the teacher's misjudging of the pupils' ability to cope with a listening task.

There are so many variables which represent the ingredients which go towards the making of the atmosphere. None of those described above will be a permanent feature of a teacher's lessons. The atmosphere may well change from lesson to lesson or even within a given lesson. No one said that teaching was easy.

Praise versus reproof/reward versus punishment

> Pupils who have no self-respect and who feel rejected, discouraged and powerless . . . have lost all faith in their ability to succeed and are not prepared to risk further loss of esteem by attempting the academic curriculum. Concentrating on self-esteem will give children the skills to communicate well, to be flexible, to get along with others and to deal with any problem or crisis they encounter. (Murray White: International Council for Self-Esteem in *The Times Educational Supplement*, 25.4.97)

> Make him feel good about himself? You must be joking! I want to knock the little shit down a peg or two. (Huddersfield teacher in response to advice on how to deal with a troublesome pupil, 1996)

Praise versus reproof/reward versus punishment are important debates in the enhancement of pupils' self-esteem and the creation of an appropriate atmosphere of learning. How the teacher approaches these issues and how her approach is perceived by the pupils play an important role in determining the quality of the classroom climate.

The application of both praise and reproof demands careful consideration. Solmecke (1983: 171) urges caution with regard to positive re-inforcement. Give too much praise and it loses its value. Pupils need to feel that their praise is warranted. How easily the trainee teacher, for example, slips into the habit of going 'over the top' with her praise of a pupil's every utterance:

Pupil: 'Je m'appelle Susan.'
Teacher: 'Super! Excellent! Génial!'

If praise is continuous, rather than to enhance motivation, it can in fact be damaging. Not only does the regularity of the praise diminish its worth, but if it is once neglected where it is deemed by the pupil to be warranted, then this can lead to disaffection and indifference. Praise must be seen to be deserved.

Atkinson *et al.* (1953) distinguish between 'extrinsic and intrinsic motivation'. 'Extrinsic' and 'intrinsic' are examples of terms which are used differently by different writers. Atkinson *et al.* postulate that, within their definition, extrinsic motivation may lead to material reward and social approval; intrinsic motivated behaviour may result in a feeling of pride and satisfaction. It is suggested that intrinsically motivated learning leads to higher quality and more sustained performance than extrinsically motivated. (See also Gardner & Lambert 1972: 147 on the merits of integratively motivated learning over instrumentally motivated learning.) They posit that the intrinsically motivated learner finds the motivation in the task itself. Extrinsically motivated learning can, in the view of Gardner and Lambert, lead to extremes of behaviour such as cheating, when the academic success and the material rewards it may bring assume greater significance than the actual learning. The teacher then is asked to strike another difficult balance between providing relatively insignificant (in material terms) extrinsic rewards such as silver stars affixed to good work, sweets (contrary to the better judgement of some parents), and in-house produced 'well done' certificates, in the hope that this might lead to behaviour which eventually becomes intrinsically motivated, but at the same time running the risk of reinforcing the pupils' possible interpretation that the point of the behaviour is the gaining of the reward. The teacher's short-term, immediate, relatively insignificant material reward becomes the end rather than a catalyst contributing to the means to the end. This represents yet another example of the teacher walking a tightrope in terms of what may be right for her pupils as a group as well as the individual pupils within the group.

Summary of 'Perceived Behavioural Control'

The teacher carries an enormous responsibility. Any constraints influencing a pupil's capability to perform a given behaviour – in the case of this study modern language learning – are likely to be linked to the teacher. If the pupil is over-anxious, it may well be the teacher's fault. If the atmosphere in the classroom is too tense, it may be the teacher's fault. If the pupils feel they have the licence to misbehave so that little or no learning can take place, it may be down to the teacher again. Does she reward too much or too little? Is the material she exploits too childish? Are the activities appropriate to the pupils level of maturity? Whether the teacher likes it or not, she carries responsibility for what pupils may perceive as constraints and this responsibility forms only a part of the total responsibility she has for the motivation of the pupils in her charge.

Summary

The purpose of this chapter was to review some of the literature on motivational perspectives. This poses a considerable challenge given the wide range of work done in this area. An attempt was made to provide insights into motivation generally and motivation as a modern languages specific issue. In order to provide some sense of structure, Ajzen's model of the 'theory of planned behaviour' was exploited. This allowed the vast array of motivational and attitudinal factors to be allocated to one of three categories. This is only satisfactory in part. Not all relevant factors can be accommodated. Not all factors fit easily into their designated category. The case of the teacher is the most obvious example. She pervades all categories. It is right that she should. The teacher has a finger in just about every motivational pie. She carries enormous responsibility.

How pertinent is the reviewed literature to the context of pupils learning foreign languages in the UK secondary school in the 1990s? Can the findings of Gardner and Lambert, based in Canada, for example, be transposed to the UK context? Have the views of pupils altered in light of the curriculum reform, changing teaching methodologies and the advent of more advanced technology? How the answers to these and other questions were accessed is the subject of the next chapter.

Chapter 4

Getting Inside the Pupils' Heads

The previous chapter reviewed some of the work done on motivation in general and motivation and modern foreign language learning in particular. It leaves certain gaps which this study aims to fill. This chapter offers an insight into the methods adopted to 'get inside the pupils' heads' to access their views on what switches them on and off in the languages and other classrooms.

What are the Gaps?

To identify with any validity the cause of pupil disaffection is an impossible task. There are so many interlinking variables that the challenge to unravel them in order to pinpoint a specific variable or group of variables with any confidence is well nigh insurmountable. Wilkins (1972: 210) articulates his awareness of the difficulty in the following terms:

> If we wish to study the effects of only one variable, it is necessary to hold all the others constant and in any real teaching situation this is difficult, if not impossible. If one attempts to take these problems into account and compares not isolated factors but groups of variables, it becomes impossible to decide which of the factors is responsible for the results one has obtained.

What do secondary-age pupils think of their in-school experience? What can we learn from their views? In the market-driven society in which we live, the perceptions of the consumers are of paramount importance, for better or for worse. In this context it must surely be for the better. This is a view supported by Ruddock (1996: 15):

> If we want to enhance pupils' achievement, why don't we take our agenda for school improvement from their accounts of learning – what helps them to work hard, what switches them off, what kinds of teaching do they value and what kind of support do they need? They are, after all, our 'expert witnesses'

Teachers may also be a valuable source of information. How reliable they may be is open to question, given that they may have a perception of the level of a pupil's motivation but may have little insight into the factors behind it:

> When teachers say that a student is motivated, they are not usually concerning themselves with the student's reason for studying, but are observing that the student does study, or at least engage in teacher-desired behavior in the classroom and possibly outside it. (Crookes & Schmidt, 1991: 480)

For these reasons, this project focuses on the views of pupils rather than their teachers.

This book, although informed by earlier projects, differs from them in terms of emphasis and detail. This project represents a product of its time. The research opportunity was provided by the implementation of the National Curriculum for Modern Foreign Languages requiring all pupils in Key Stages 3 and 4 to learn a foreign language. At the same time a policy of diversification was being energetically encouraged which meant in many schools the teaching of German or Spanish as a first or first equal foreign language on the school curriculum. With this backdrop, what new insights could be gleaned?

- What were pupils' consciously held views at a time when those who pre-National Curriculum would probably have given up foreign language learning were now obliged to continue with them to the age of 16?
- At a time of 'diversification of first foreign language', what could we learn about pupils' attitude to the learning of what had up to this point been regarded as a 'second foreign language' in the majority of schools? Earlier studies either focus exclusively on French (e.g. Buckby *et al.*, 1981 and Burstall *et al.*, 1974) or include German with French and Spanish (e.g. OXPROD: Phillips & Filmer-Sankey, 1993).
- What could pupils tell us about their motivation to work and learn in general (see Keys & Fernandes, 1993, Chapter 3, p. 39 ff) and their learning of modern languages in particular (Gardner & Lambert, 1972, Chapter 3, pp. 43–5; Burstall, 1975 Chapter 3, p. 27 ff; APU, Chapter 3, p. 31 ff); OXPROD, Chapter 3, p. 33 ff).
- How do parents influence and encourage their children in their learning of foreign languages?
- Gardner and Lambert investigate the role of the match between pupil- and teacher-perception of effort and progress. This is an area neglected, however, by UK-based studies. This book tackles this issue.
- Does class size really matter? What do the pupils think?

- What can we learn from pupils' counterparts on the European mainland? This book takes German pupils as an example. This provides a baseline for comparisons to be made and answers questions relating to the commonly held but so far unsubstantiated perception of differences in the motivations and attitudes of German pupils learning English and in a few cases French. If it is found to be true that German pupils are more motivated to learn English (and French) than their Leeds counterparts are to learn German, this may have the potential to inform teachers of foreign languages in the UK of aspects of teaching and learning which may enhance the motivation of their pupils.

Research Methodology

The accelerated longitudinal methodology adopted is shared with the OXPROD research (see Chapter 3, p. 33 ff) but differs from it in that it accesses the views of three age cohorts rather than one (multi-cohort, longitudinal method (Cohen & Manion 1991: 71)). This provides interesting insights into the development of the views of pupils and possible reasons for any development covering a large proportion of the 11–17 age range between 1992 and 1994.

The two-phase approach

The methodology for accessing individual attitudes is self-report in nature, in the form of questionnaires and interviews. It was felt to be very important that the author supervised the filling in of the questionnaires by each class and conducted the interviews, not only in the interest of validity and reliability but also to ensure that the same messages were being given to all pupils. This was an area of difficulty identified by Green and Hecht (1989) who describe one research project where the decision was made to allow the teachers of each class to supervise the filling in of questionnaires. As is the case with this study, the emphasis was on pupils' views, and so it was important that the teachers did not intervene. In one case, however, pupils asked questions relating to the survey and the teacher answered, thereby influencing and colouring the pupils' reported views:

> We had assumed that the teacher would not respond to such appeals; we were, after all, interested in the strategies pupils employed for coping with linguistic deficits. However, in one case, the teacher helped pupils with whispered prompts, and a whole set of data had to be abandoned. (Green & Hecht, 1989: 97)

In the case of this study each cohort of pupils was surveyed on two occasions, each separated by a period of two years.

Phase 1

Eleven-year-old (Year 7), 13-year-old (Year 9) and 15-year-old (Year 11) pupils from four Leeds schools filled in questionnaires covering areas related to motivation as outlined below. A number of weeks were allowed to elapse and a selected sample of 10% of the pupils were interviewed on the same topic areas. The interviews sought to confirm consistency with the answers given in the survey and to delve rather more deeply into the answers given.

Phase 2

Two years later, Phase 2 of the study, the same pupils, so far as was possible (see Figure 4.1 and p. 58), (now 13, 15 and 17 years old in Years 9, 11 and 13 respectively) in the same schools underwent the same process to offer some insight into how their motivation towards foreign language learning may have developed and the possible reasons for this. Figure 4.1 aims to explain the two-phase approach and the nomenclature relating to the age cohorts in the description of the data.

The German dimension

The project was also given a comparative dimension in that the same process was carried out in Kiel/Neumünster in northern Germany with pupils of the same age, that is, 11 year olds (Year 6 in Phase 1 only), 13 year olds (Year 8), 15 year olds (Year 10) and 17 year olds (Year 12 in Phase 2 only). This had the potential to provide some evidence to access the nature and quality of the motivation of German pupils in their learning of English and in some cases French and factors contributing to this.

Numbers participating in the survey

As is the case with any survey, the methodology adopted has its limitations. For example, the geographical compass of the research is limited to a small number of schools within one British and one German city. The survey's strength, however, resides in the number of pupils providing relevant information, that is 1481 in Leeds and 1251 in Kiel in the two phases between 1992 and 1994. The numbers of pupils (Figure 4.1) participating in both Phase 1 and Phase 2 of the survey are rather smaller, that is 322 pupils in Leeds and 402 in Kiel. The difference is more extreme in the case of Leeds schools than for those in Kiel/Neumünster. This is a reflection of a number of factors:

- non-availability of whole classes either in 1992 or 1994;
- absences in 1992 or 1994;

11–13 Cohort

PHASE 1   1992   PHASE 2   1994

| 11 year olds (Year 7) in Leeds in 1992 about to start foreign languages *(n = 378)* | *13 year olds (Year 9) in Leeds in 1994 learning German (n = 371)* **(1992 + 94: n = 194)** |

+   +

| 11 year olds (Year 6) in Kiel in 1992 learning English *(n = 250)* | 13 year olds (Year 8) in Kiel in 1994 learning English *(n = 263)* **(1992 + 94: n = 204)** |

13–15 Cohort

PHASE 1 1992   PHASE 2   1994

| 13 year olds (Year 9) in Leeds in 1992 learning German *(n = 429)* | 15 year olds (Year 11) in Leeds in 1994 learning German *(n = 131)* **(1992 + 94: n = 115)** |

+   +

| 13 year olds (Year 8) in Kiel in 1992 learning English *(n = 246)* and in some cases French *(n = 77)* | 15 year olds (Year 10) in Kiel in 1994 learning English *(n = 209)* **(1992 + 94: n = 139)** and in some cases French *(n = 67)* **(1992 + 94: n = 42)** |

15–17 Cohort

PHASE 1   1992   PHASE 2 1994

| 15 year olds (Year 11) in Leeds in 1992 learning German *(n = 158)* | 17 year olds (Year 13) in Leeds in 1994 learning German *(n = 14)* **(1992 + 94: n = 13)** |

+   +

| 15 year olds (Year 10) in Kiel in 1992 learning English *(n = 190)* and in a few cases French *(n = 74)* | 17 year olds (Year 12) in Kiel in 1994 learning English *(n = 95)* **(1992 + 94: n = 59)** and in a few cases French *(n = 21)* **(1992 + 94: n = 8)** |

Figure 4.1 The two-phase approach: cohorts and numbers participating in the survey. (*In italics*: total number of pupils surveyed in Phase 1 (1992) and Phase 2 (1994). **In bold**: number of pupils surveyed in both Phase 1 and Phase 2)

- pupils opting out of German (especially between Years 9 and 11 (GCSE option stage) and Years 11 and 13 (A-level option stage);
- in the case of one school, pupils not being regarded as good enough at French to be able to take German;
- pupils transferring to a different school or leaving school;
- new pupils transferring into a survey school.

It also reflects the difference in provision of modern languages in each of the two cities at the time of the survey. In Leeds, pupils had the option of dropping German at the end of Year 9 and in some cases even earlier. In Kiel, English or a second foreign language is compulsory until pupils leave school. This applies to all pupils apart from those taking mathematics as a main *Abitur* (A-level equivalent) subject who may drop the foreign language in Year 13.

Some observations should be made on the numbers participating in the survey. In Leeds: the number of pupils in Year 7 of Phase 1 (378) indicates not the numbers taking German but rather those taking foreign languages. It should be remembered that these pupils were surveyed at the very beginning of their secondary school experience just as foreign language learning was about to become a feature of their curriculum. That this number is more or less maintained (371) in Phase 2 when these pupils are in Year 9 may reflect the implementation of 'diversification of first foreign language' programme in the four schools surveyed. Under this scheme pupils have the opportunity of taking German as their first foreign language or first equal foreign language with French (Chambers & Sheppard, 1993). The differences in the numbers in each school taking German within and between Phases 1 and 2 is a reflection of the extent to which diversification is being implemented and the structure of the diversification model adopted. Notable also is the drop in numbers taking German between Year 9 and Year 11 and again in Year 13. This is again a reflection of the option system whereby pupils have the opportunity to choose which subjects they wish to take for GCSE and for A-level. In spite of the fact that the study was conducted at a time in advance of the requirement to implement the National Curriculum for Modern Foreign Languages at Key Stage 4, in the schools participating in the survey all pupils, with few exceptions, were obliged to take a foreign language to the end of Year 11 and had the choice between French, German and in one case Russian. The very small number taking A-level is partly a reflection of pupils limited to between two and four subjects only in Years 12 and 13. Probably less significant is the fact that some pupils do not stay on at school to take A-level.

In Kiel/Neumünster a major drop in the numbers taking English is in evidence between Year 10 and Year 12 only. The reasons for the drop in

Year 12 are broadly the same as for Leeds although the number of subjects taken for the *Abitur* is greater than that for A-level, given that pupils take two main subjects and between five and seven subsidiary subjects. All pupils are obliged to take a foreign language. Most opt for English. Some pupils do not stay on to take the *Abitur* but leave at age 16 with the *Realabschluß*, a vocationally orientated qualification.

French is the second foreign language in the Kiel/Neumünster schools. Pupils can opt to take it at the option stage in Year 7. Numbers again remain fairly strong between years 8 and 10. This may be expected given that having opted for French in Year 7, pupils are, with few exceptions (i.e. those not staying to take *Abitur* in years 11–13; these pupils can opt out of the second foreign language at the end of Year 8), obliged to continue the course until the end of Year 10. In Year 12, however, when pupils have had the opportunity to opt for *Abitur* subjects, the number taking French drops considerably.

The data relating to French do not necessarily represent all pupils taking French in the two schools in Kiel. Only those taking French and English had the opportunity to contribute. It could well be the case, especially with 17 year olds, that some may have opted to take French rather than English and so would not have been present at the time when the questionnaires were filled in.

Important differences between Leeds and Kiel

A number of variables relating to differences between the systems of education in Leeds and Kiel and which may have more than a little significance, should be borne in mind to allow an accurate interpretation of the data which follows.

Age and year groups. It was felt important to compare pupils according to age group. Given that Germans start formal primary education a year later than UK pupils and join the secondary school after only four years, this leads to the discrepancies shown in Table 4.1 with the groups relevant to this study.

Table 4.1 Age and year groups: Leeds and Kiel

	Leeds	*Kiel*
11 year olds	Year 7	Year 6
13 year olds	Year 9	Year 8
15 year olds	Year 11	Year 10
17 year olds	Year 13	Year 12

Table 4.2 Model of foreign language provision and timetable allocation in four Leeds schools

	Model of foreign language provision	*Timetable allocation*
School 1	1992 and 1994 All pupils in Year 7 (11 year olds) take French and German as first equal foreign languages. Pupils have the opportunity to opt to take French and/or German at the end of Year 9 (13 years old) or drop both (pre-National Curriculum)	1992 and 1994 Year 7: 6 × 35 mins (3 × French; 3 × German) – 210 minutes Year 9: 1 × 70 mins + 1 × 35 mins – 105 mins Year 11: 2 × 70 mins – 140 mins Year 13: 4 × 70 mins – 280 mins
School 2	1992 and 1994 All Year 7 pupils (11 year olds) have a taster course in French and German in Term 1 and decide at the end of the term, with which language they would like to continue at least until the option stage at the end of Year 9. They do not have the opportunity to take a second foreign language.	1992 Year 7: 4 × 35 mins – 140 mins Year 9: 1 × 40 + 2 × 50 – 140 mins Year 11: 3 × 50 – 150 mins Year 13: n/a 1994 Years 7, 9, 11: 3 × 50 mins – 150 mins
School 3	1992 All pupils in Year 7 (11 year olds) take French. In Year 8 those who are assessed as 'good at French' are selected to take German (four lessons of French and two lessons of German. Opportunity to opt to take French and/or German at the end of Year 9 (13 years old) or drop both (pre-National Curriculum) 1994 In Year 7, eight forms take French and two forms take German. (Beginning of diversification programme.)	1992 and 1994 Year 7: 4 × 45 mins – 180 mins Year 9: 5 × 45 mins – 225 mins (3 × French and 2 × German for pupils taking both; French only: 4 × 45 mins – 180 mins) Year 11: 4 × 45 mins – 180 mins Year 13: 5 × 45 mins – 225 mins
School 4	1992 and 1994 In Year 7 five forms take French and four forms take Geman. In Year 8 pupils may opt to take Russian. Opportunity at the end of Year 9 to opt to take first foreign language (French or German) or Russian or both.	1992 and 1994 Year 7: 2 × 70 mins – 140 mins Year 9: 2 × 70 mins for first foreign language – 140 mins – and 1 × 70 mins + 1 × 35 mins if taking Russian. Year 11: 2 × 70 mins for first foreign language – 140 mins; 2 × 70 mins for Russian – 140 mins. Year 13: 4 × 70 mins – 280 mins

Table 4.3 Timetable allocation for English and French in two Kiel schools

	No. of English lessons (@ 45 mins)	No. of French lessons (@ 45 mins)
Year 6 (11 years)	6	n/a
Year 8 (13 years)	4	4
Year 10 (15 years)	4	4
Year 12 (17 years)	5 (English as main subject) 3 (English as subsidiary subject)	5 (French as main subject) 3 (French as subsidiary subject)

Age at which foreign language learning begins. It is possible that in Leeds and Kiel some foreign language teaching may go on in the primary school but not as a statutory requirement of the curriculum. In both cities foreign language teaching and learning formally begins in the secondary school. Pupils in Kiel therefore have a year's start on their Leeds counterparts given that English appears on their timetable from Year 5, when pupils are age 10. Leeds pupils tend not to start their formal foreign language learning experience until age 11.

First and second foreign languages. At the time of this study the situation in Leeds regarding the identity of the first foreign language in each of the four schools and the identity and timing of the introduction of the second foreign language was inconsistent. The Local Education Authority was in the midst of a reorganisation programme, which meant the closing down of middle schools and the conversion of 13–18 schools into 11–18 schools. Simultaneously a programme of diversification of first foreign language was being promoted (Chambers & Sheppard, 1993). The situation in each of the four Leeds schools involved in this study is shown in Table 4.2.

The situation in Kiel is much more clear-cut in that subjects taught and the timing of their introduction are determined by the Ministry for Education and therefore standard across the *Land* of Schleswig-Holstein. All pupils start with English in Year 5 (age 10) and have the opportunity to take a second foreign language, French or Latin, in Year 7 (age 12). Regarding timetable allocation, the Ministry again stipulates the number of lessons in each subject (see Table 4.3).

When a direct comparison of time allocated to each age group is made, a significant discrepancy becomes apparent (see Table 4.4).

Not until age 17 do *some* Leeds pupils get something approaching the same time allocation as their Kiel peers. Access to more foreign language teaching does not necessarily mean better foreign language learning and

Table 4.4 Difference in time allocated to modern languages between Leeds and Kiel

	Leeds	*Kiel*
Age 11	140–210 mins	270 mins
Age 13	105–180 mins	180 mins
Age 15	140–180 mins	180 mins
Age 17	225–280 mins	225 mins

better motivation for all pupils. Time allocated to foreign languages could nonetheless be a factor in motivation and also in performance.

The Questionnaires

The questionnaire for Year 7 pupils at Leeds and Year 6 pupils in Kiel/Neumünster differed slightly from those for the older pupils. (See Appendices 1–4 for sample questionnaires.) Eleven year olds in Leeds had just transferred from primary school and most had not yet had experience of foreign language learning. Rather than focusing, therefore, on current experience, attention was given to pupils' anticipation of the new experience of secondary school and subjects, with special reference to foreign languages. In the light of the Burstall *et al.* (1974) findings on primary school French, it was important to establish whether pupils had had experience of foreign languages and whether they had found this a positive experience. This was likely to have some bearing on their attitude of foreign language learning at their new school. Other batteries of questions on ethnocentricity, usefulness and home background remained the same. Questions on whether pupils would like to exploit their foreign language competence later were not included, given that they were but on the threshold of the language learning experience.

The questionnaire for Year 9 pupils in Leeds and Year 8 pupils in Kiel/Neumünster picked up on the question of anticipation targeted in the Year 7 version. Pupils were asked to what extent their expectation of school in general and of specific subjects had been met. This would perhaps offer some insight into whether motivation was on the wane as suggested by the findings of Barber (1994a). Otherwise the questionnaire for this age group was very much the same as for Year 11 pupils at Leeds and Year 10 pupils in Kiel/Neumünster.

In Phase 2 of the project the Year 7 (Leeds) and Year 6 (Kiel/Neumünster) questionnaire was no longer needed, given that the original 11 year olds had moved on to Years 9 and 8 respectively and no new Year 7 / Year 6 cohort was included in the second phase. Given the focus on any development of motivation over the two-year period, a new cohort of 11 year olds was not regarded as relevant.

The same questionnaires were re-used for Years 9 and 11 in Leeds and Year 8 and 10 in Kiel/Neumünster. The Year 11 (Leeds) / Year 10 (Kiel/Neumünster) version was used to a very large extent for Year 13 (Leeds) and Year 12 (Kiel/Neumünster).

References to GCSE (now in the past) were removed. In all of the Phase 2 questionnaires one question was added relating to pupils' perceptions of any change in how they felt about their foreign language learning experience over the two year period and possible reasons for it.

Motivational areas of focus

The areas of focus within this study may be grouped under the three headings of the model of Ajzen's 'Theory of Planned Behaviour'. References to the individual questions in the Phase 1 version of the questionnaires are provided.

Attitudes towards the behaviour

> The individual's positive or negative evaluation of performing the particular behavior of interest. (Ajzen, 1988: 117)

- *Pupils' enjoyment of school generally or in the case of Year 7, pupils' anticipation of enjoyment of secondary school generally.*
  Responses to this battery of questions would help tackle the problem of distinguishing between possible disaffection with German/foreign languages and the totality of the school experience. Keys and Fernandes (1993) focus on this area without specific reference to foreign language learning. Burstall *et al.* (1974), APU (1983–85) and OXPROD (1989–91) neglect learning in general and concentrate on the foreign language dimension.
- *Extent of pupils' enjoyment of individual subjects with special focus on German/foreign languages or in the case of Year 7, their anticipation thereof.*
  This would provide some subject specific information on the above questions; pupils may not like German/foreign languages but it could also be the case that they like German/foreign languages just as much/little as other subjects. One may argue that this may overlap significantly with the previous area of focus. This may be true but only insofar as pupils associate their like/dislike of school with school

subjects. It may also be the case that this is influenced by other factors such as social aspects of school life or non-subject related activities such as extra-curricular activities.

- *Pupils' perception of their effort.*
  This question is of interest not only for what it contributes to 'attitude towards the behaviour' but also for its relevance to what pupils think their teachers' perceptions of their effort are and therefore to 'subjective norm' (see Chapter 3, p. 41 ff). Especially in the case where the teacher is adopted as a 'significant other' or 'referent', the matching of a pupil's and a teacher's perception plays an influential role. Even in the case where the teacher is not viewed by an individual pupil as a 'significant other', the matching of perceptions may have a contribution to make to a healthy relationship between the two parties.

- *Pupils' views on the usefulness of subjects.*
  This battery of questions would help to indicate whether pupils regard German/foreign languages as a means to an end or an end in itself/themselves. Data may reflect whether they are instrumentally or integratively motivated (Gardner & Lambert, 1972). This may serve to counterbalance the intrinsic motivation, i.e. learning a foreign language because they enjoy the learning process, which may be accessed in the enjoyment of individual activities scale; the information was sought in various ways interspersed throughout the questionnaire.

  Pupils' perceptions of the usefulness of German may also be reflected in: (1) their intentions to use it in the near and not so near future; (2) in their response to the hypothetical situation where German is not available on the school curriculum; and (3) where they have the power to change school policy for German.

  These questions may arguably offer more detail than that provided by other UK-based studies and target the sort of information accessed by Gardner and Lambert in the Canadian and American contexts and Heuer (1983), Fengler and Fischer (1983), and Sol-mecke (1983) in the German context. It would be interesting to note how their theories of instrumental and integrative motivation apply in Leeds and Kiel.

- *Pupils' perception of the classroom experience.*
  These questions aimed to access pupils' views on teachers' methodology and related classroom activities, and the possible motivational role of the learning environment – the arrangement of the classroom, resources, media, textbooks, the teacher, etc.

- *Pupils' attitudes to the country and people of the languages they are learning: is ethnocentricity a significant factor (Gardner & Lambert, 1972; APU, 1983–85; OXPROD, 1989–91)?*
  Pupils were asked a battery of questions relating to foreign countries visited, their perceptions of those countries and other nationalities, whether they would consider working in those countries, their perceptions of Germans, French and the British. It was regarded as important to include pupils' perceptions of their compatriots, something neglected in the other studies, given that it was possible that they may have a low opinion of the Germans and French but an even lower opinion of the British. This would make an important contribution to the assessment the extent of any ethnocentricity. Information gleaned in earlier studies and the pilots regarding pupils' views of other nationalities was exploited in this section. Again this was thought to be a possible area of contrast between Leeds and Kiel/Neumünster pupils. Given the difference in geographical locations, was it not likely that German pupils would have travelled more with greater access to a wider range of European countries than their sea-bound UK peers?

Subjective norm

The person's perception of social pressure to perform or not to perform the behavior. (Ajzen, 1988: 117)

- *Pupils' perception of influence of parents and home background.*
  Within the primary school context, Burstall *et al.* (1974: 61) had put considerable store by home background and parental influence.This area was examined by OXPROD (Filmer-Sankey, 1989, 1991) but only to the extent to which parents were pleased that their child was learning a foreign language. Keys and Fernandes (1993) also included this area in their study on attitudes to school generally, with no specific focus on languages. This battery of questions may offer greater insight into parental influence and the form that this takes, as perceived by the pupils. It was also thought that this may provide an area of contrast between Leeds and Kiel/Neumünster pupils in that it was hypothesised that German pupils may have parents with more foreign language competence and greater access to English speaking guests and friends of the family.
- *Pupils' perception of teacher's assessment of their progress and effort.*
  (See previous section on pupils' perception of their effort, p. 65). In Chapter 3, p. 43, the importance of teacher and pupil sharing a view

of expectations and assessment of effort and progress was emphasised. Other areas of questions in the questionnaires (see p. 64 ff and
p. 67 ff (perceived behavioural control)) access pupils' perceptions of
their own effort and progress. The following questions would access
what they think their teachers' views are and allow comparisons
between perceptions to be made.

The findings of the pilot project suggested that a discrepancy in this area
could have a detrimental effect on pupils' motivation. This echoes the
findings of Gardner and Lambert's Connecticut study (1972: 57, 134) Other
UK studies do not go into this detail. Studies which focus on this area tend
not to have a foreign language learning/teaching dimension.

Perceived behavioural control

The perceived ease or difficulty of performing the behavior and it is
assumed to reflect past experience as well as anticipated impediments
and obstacles. (Ajzen, 1988: 132)

- *Pupils' evaluation of any previous foreign language learning experience.*
  In spite of the pressure caused by a crowded National Curriculum, a
  small number of primary schools offer pupils some foreign language
  learning experience. In the case where this experience is positive, this
  may fire pupils with enthusiasm to continue with French (the most
  common language taught at primary school). Where the experience
  is less than positive, however, this may already sow the seeds of a
  negative attitude to foreign language learning which pupils take with
  them to secondary school.
- *Pupils' assessment of their progress in German.*
  (See p. 65 on pupils' perceptions of teachers' assessment of their
  progress and effort.)
  These batteries of questions would not only offer insight into pupils'
  views on their progress in German but again contribute to the
  'subjective norm' dimension where the matching of teachers' and
  pupils' perceptions becomes relevant.
- *Pupils' views on how German teaching could/should be changed and/or
  enhanced.*
  It was thought that pupils who felt that circumstances (e.g. teacher;
  teaching style; resources) were militating against easier/faster progress in German, would be able to identify the problems and make
  suggestions accordingly. Again this had been a focus of attention in
  the other UK studies but not with quite the same emphases.
  Responses to these questions would offer, among other things,

valuable insight into possible intrinsic motivation and the activities which may stimulate it.

The Interviews

After an interval of approximately six to eight weeks, follow-up interviews were conducted with a selected sample of 10% of pupils surveyed in Leeds and Kiel/Neumünster. Pupils were selected on the basis of their responses in the questionnaire which indicated whether they felt positive about learning German/English (one-third of the 10% sample), negative (one-third of the sample) or neutral (one-third of the sample).

The purpose of the interviews was to get confirmation of the reliability and validity of the questionnaire and to probe rather more deeply into pupils' responses. The questions included:

- Do you enjoy going to school? What do you enjoy about it?
- *Which subjects do you enjoy most? Why?*
- *Which subjects do you enjoy least? Why?*
- *Do you enjoy learning foreign languages? Why?*
- *Do you enjoy learning German? Why?*
- *Do you enjoy learning French? Why?*
- *How could German lessons be improved?*
- *Which of these two subjects do you prefer? – paired subjects exercise – pupils were shown subjects written on card in pairs and asked to give their preference.*
- *Do you think it is important to learn a foreign language? Why?*
- *Do you think it is important to learn German? Why?*
- *Why are you learning German?*
- *If foreign languages were not on offer at the school, would you make any effort to learn them elsewhere, at an evening class or by reading magazines or listening to cassettes?*
- *If German were not on offer at the school, what would you do, if anything?*
- *Do you intend to continue/discontinue with German after GCSE? Why?/ Why not?*
- *Can your parents speak any foreign languages? Which ones?*
- *How much do your parents encourage you to do well at school? How do they encourage you (if they do)?*
- *Do your parents encourage you in specific subjects? Which ones?*
- *Do your parents encourage you in modern languages?*

The interviews were recorded on audio-cassette and subsequently analysed directly from the tape.

An identical process of survey by questionnaire plus follow-up interview was conducted with pupils in the same age groups in Kiel/ Neumünster.

The Schools

Careful consideration was given to the selection of the schools in Leeds and in Kiel/Neumünster. A key factor was the representativeness of the school population in terms of ability range, ethnic mix and socio-economic backgrounds. It was also vital to the study to select schools in Leeds with a model of foreign language provision where German was the first foreign language or first equal with French or in the process of becoming so.

Schools in Germany were sought which would allow a reasonable comparison of like with like in terms of school- and pupil-type. Schleswig-Holstein, the *Land* in which Kiel and Neumünster are located, has a developing comprehensive sector with schools not dissimilar to those in Leeds. Feasibility was also a factor. A sound link has existed between Kiel/Neumünster and Leeds since the mid-1980s. Healthy relationships and reliable lines of communication with colleagues in schools and teacher-training institutions obviated many of the potential organisational problems. This is in line with the philosophy of Green and Hecht:

> Researchers who do not have a ready-made relationship with the teachers whose pupils they wish to use as subjects should probably budget time for building up a relationship before administering any tests. (Green & Hecht, 1989: 96)

Models of foreign language provision in Kiel posed fewer problems as all schools in Schleswig-Holstein adopt the same model in accordance with Ministry of Education directives. (See p. 60 for details of important differences between the approach to teaching modern foreign languages in Leeds and Kiel.)

The Leeds schools

Four schools in Leeds were selected to contribute to the project:

School 1: an inner city, coeducational, multi-cultural comprehensive with 808 pupils, 54% of whom represented ethnic minorities and 48% of whom were eligible for free school meals: 16.3% of the pupils were identified as having special educational needs and 5.9% were statemented.

School 2: a coeducational, community high school on the periphery of Leeds with 1560 pupils. The catchment included a high proportion of children from local council estates; 3.3% of pupils represented ethnic minorities; 30.4% were eligible for free school meals; 12.8% of its pupils in Years 7–9 were identified as having special educational needs and 4.6% were statemented.

School 3: coeducational, multi-cultural comprehensive school on northern edge of the city with 1560 pupils, 13% of whom represented ethnic minorities; 2.7% pupils were statemented; 15.4% of pupils were eligible for free school meals.

School 4: coeducational, denominational high school with 1090 pupils, 13.4% of whom represented ethnic minorities; 11.5% pupils had special educational needs; 2.3% had statements; 7.3% were eligible for free school meals.

This selection would give access to information from pupils across a wide range of ability and cultures as well as diversity of teachers and teaching approach within the state, comprehensive sector.

The Kiel/Neumünster schools

Only two German schools were selected to contribute to the study. Comprehensivisation is in its early stages in Schleswig-Holstein and a wide range of schools from which a selection could be made was not available. The schools selected bore comparison with the Leeds schools, in terms of catchment area, cultural mix, pupil numbers and location on the periphery of the town. Regrettably the inner-city aspect of the German dimension could not be accessed. The proportion of pupils with special educational needs in the German schools is substantially lower than is the case in the Leeds schools. This reflects a difference in approach to provision for this category of pupil. In contrast to Leeds, Schleswig-Holstein still has a considerable number of Special Schools (*Förderschulen*), although a policy of integration is in the early stages of implementation.

School 1: a coeducational, multi-cultural comprehensive school on the outskirts of Kiel. It has a wide catchment area and a pupil population of 1111; 10% of these represented ethnic minorities. About 5% came from families eligible for income support and only 1% of pupils were identified as having special educational needs.

School 2: a coeducational, multi-cultural comprehensive school in Neumünster, about 25 miles from Kiel. It had 909 pupils, 8.5% of whom represented ethnic minorities. About 3% came from families receiving income support. There were only exceptional cases (about five) of pupils who could be described as having special educational needs.

Summary

This chapter provides a reminder of the purpose of this study and the methodology implemented with a view to accessing the relevant data. A breakdown of the batteries of questions and the information they target is also outlined. As was the case with the review of current literature, the three strands of Ajzen's 'theory of planned behaviour' are exploited as a structural model. The schools participating in the survey are described. Some insight is provided into the conducting of the survey as are early impressions of the limitations of the project methodology.

The backdrop has been set for the revealing of what the pupils said.

Chapter 5

Attitudes Brought to the Classroom

This chapter looks at pupils' perceptions of foreign language learning just as they enter the secondary school at the beginning of Year 7. What sort of experiential baggage may inform these perceptions? Have they learned any foreign languages at primary school? If so, what sort of influence may this have had on their views of the prospect of learning French/German/Spanish? What can we as teachers learn from what the pupils tell us?

Introduction

The prospect of maths at secondary school terrified me. Why should this be so? It was not because I found maths particularly difficult or because I had performed appallingly in tests up to this point. It was all Mrs Walker's fault. I always associate the learning of maths at primary school with her. My memories of her consist exclusively of her patrolling up and down the classroom as we pupils toiled over our hard sums. As she walked from the front of the room to the back and she caught me whispering to my neighbour, THWACK, she would smack me across the back of the head. If on the return journey from the back of the room to the front she spied my having completed a long division successfully, THWACK, she would smack me across the back of the head again, adding, 'Well done Gary'. I hated maths. I took all this fear and dread with me to secondary school where I declared my hatred of maths to my new friends. It was not until I met Mrs Purdey quite a few years into my secondary school experience and was taught with care, interest, sensitivity and a complete absence of gratuitous violence, that maths became not so bad after all.

What about newcomers to secondary school foreign language classes? What if any, experience of French/German/Spanish do they bring? Do they come full of fear and dread as I did with maths? If their learning experience has been positive, perhaps they come full of excitement at the prospect of yet further enjoyment. If they have not had any experience of foreign language learning, are they fearful of the prospect of this new subject area or attracted by the novelty value and the promise of a fresh start on an equal footing with most other pupils?

Previous Experience of Foreign Language Learning

How much experience of French, German and other languages have pupils had prior to transferring to secondary school? The responses of 11-year-old Leeds pupils reveal that 63.9% claim to have had some foreign language tuition, in 91.1% of these cases French. Only 1.6% claim to have learned some German. This predominance of French is hardly surprising given the position it has traditionally occupied as first foreign language on the vast majority of school timetables (Phillips & Filmer-Sankey, 1993: 32–3; TES/CILT Survey: 'Shortages prolong supremacy of French' in *Times Educational Supplement*, 2.2.96). If primary school teachers enjoy foreign language competence, it is more likely to be in French than not.

The duration of the foreign language experience varies between one (48.3%) and two years (46.7%). How intensive the experience may have been is not known, although anecdotal evidence suggests that it is likely to have taken the form of a taster course. There are areas of the UK, e.g. Scotland, Kent, Richmond, Gloucestershire, Cornwall and West Sussex, Manchester and North Yorkshire (Satchwell in Hawkins, 1997: 166 ff) where, in spite of National Curriculum pressures, foreign languages form a constituent part of the primary school diet. This, however, is not the case with this Leeds-based sample.

Extent of Enjoyment of Previous Foreign Language Learning Experience

When asked how much they enjoyed the foreign language learning experience, pupils' general response is positive, with 85.3% scoring it 3 or above on a scale of 1–5. While 46.6% of the sample of 11 year olds opt for the top scores of 4 and 5, a median of 3 (37.7%) and a mean of 3.57 indicates, however, that the experience was by no means exclusively positive but rather tempered in some cases (see Table 5.1).

Table 5.1 Percentages of Year 7 Leeds pupils in 1992 responding to the question: 'Did you enjoy learning the foreign language?'

I did not enjoy it		*It was OK*		*I enjoyed it very much*			
1	2	3	4	5	Sample	Mean	S.D.
8.2	6.6	37.7	15.6	32.0	122	3.57	1.23

What were the reasons for pupils' enjoyment or lack of enjoyment of any previous foreign language learning experience they may have had? When asked in open questions to justify their response, only 65.5% of 11-year-old beginners chose to do so. Of this number 45.8% identify the influence of the teachers and their teaching, 30% providing overtly positive, and 16.6% overtly negative comments; 21.2% also referred to enjoying learning a foreign language because it was something new and quite different from other subjects in their experience so far: 'I enjoy it because there are a lot of funny words in it like Farter [*sic*] which means father.'

Anticipation of German, French and Other Subjects

In the light or absence of foreign language learning experience, how did these Leeds pupils, on the very threshold of their secondary school experience in the first week of September, view the prospect of setting out on the odyssey towards French/German competence?

This presented an opportunity to access the attitudes and motivations which pupils brought with them to Key Stage 3 foreign language learning, before they were influenced by the teacher, the teaching, experience of success or failure, and other factors. They were not asked about German or French in isolation but as subjects amongst a number of others which were to form part of their school timetable. There was little to be learned from their claim to adore or loathe French, when this may apply to all other subjects too. More was to be gained from a picture of pupils' perceptions of a given subject (in this case French and/or German) within a context of their perceptions of learning in general (i.e. the other subjects taken in Year 7).

It is immediately striking that pupils adopt a generally positive outlook across all curriculum subjects. Pupils bring with them an enthusiasm for school and for learning. There is some evidence to suggest an enthusiasm for German and French specifically as they occupy laudable fourth and sixth places respectively in Table 5.2 behind art, PE and technology, with science splitting the two foreign languages.

When asked specifically how they felt about the prospect of learning a foreign language, again the response was positive; 81.6% were either 'excited' at the prospect or 'quite looking forward to it'. Only 11.6% were indifferent and 6.9% were either not looking forward to learning a foreign language or hated the thought of it. The picture of general enthusiasm for languages in Year 7 is corroborated. There was no statistically significant difference between the responses of boys and girls.

When asked to explain their answers, only 90% ($n = 194$) opted to do so; 25.9% provided answers which could not be categorised. Of the remainder

Table 5.2 Percentages of Year 7 Leeds pupils in 1992 responding to the question, 'How much are you looking forward to taking each of the following subjects at secondary school?'

	Not at all		Neutral		Very much			
	1	2	3	4	5	Sample	Mean	S.D.
Art	4.7	4.7	15.2	21.5	53.9	191	4.15	1.14
PE	8.4	4.2	15.8	18.4	53.2	190	4.04	1.27
Technology	5.3	3.7	21.9	24.1	44.9	187	4.0	1.14
German	8.2	5.5	23.1	20.3	42.9	182	3.84	1.27
Science	9.4	7.9	27.2	24.1	31.4	191	3.60	1.26
French	12.9	12.4	31.2	19.4	24.1	170	3.30	1.31
English	7.3	10.9	47.9	18.2	15.6	192	3.24	1.08
Music	14.9	13.3	37.2	14.9	19.7	188	3.11	1.29
Geography	12.5	13.0	41.8	17.9	14.7	184	3.09	1.81
Maths	17.2	10.9	38.0	15.1	18.8	192	3.07	1.30
History	18.9	12.6	33.2	16.8	18.4	190	3.03	1.34
RE	31.6	23.0	27.8	7.5	10.2	187	2.41	1.28

($n = 124$) the predominant justifications represented were (1) the novelty of a new subject ('I couldn't wait to learn a foreign language as I didn't do anything like this in junior and infant school', 'I'd never done a language before and my older friends could talk a language and it sounded really good. I couldn't wait to get a French homework'); and (2) the influence of previous experience (positive – 'I like singing French songs' – and negative – 'It's boring'); 13.8% regarded not having done foreign languages before in a positive light while 10.5% took the opposite view; 12.8% claimed always to have wanted to learn a foreign language and 14.6% and 11.4% respectively saw the utility of foreign language competence in terms of talking to people and going on holiday. Those who had little enthusiasm for the prospect of learning a foreign language based this response on their previous negative experience where they felt they were 'no good at it' (9.5%) or were bored (4.9%).

The data were analysed for gender difference using the chi-square test. Previous research (Whyte, 1981) reveals that in general boys show greater enthusiasm for science than girls, and regarding modern languages, girls feel more positively inclined towards French than boys do (Powell & Littlewood, 1983). Responses to the above question do not fully support the

Table 5.3 Cross-tabulation 'looking forward to German' by 'gender'

	Looking forward to German	1	2	3	4	5	Row total
Boys	Count	10	1	20	22	42	95
	Exp val	7.8	5.2	21.9	19.3	40.7	
Girls	Count	5	9	22	15	36	87
	Exp val	7.2	4.8	20.1	17.7	37.3	
	Column total	15	10	42	37	78	182

Table 5.4 Percentages of 11-year-old Leeds pupils (Year 7) in 1992 responding to the questions: 'Which subject are you looking forward to most of all?' and 'Which subject are you dreading most of all?'

Subject	Percentage (n = 194) looking forward to	Percentage (n = 194) dreading
Art	23.7	4.6
PE	16.5	7.2
German	15.5	5.2
Maths	9.3	21.6
Technology	8.2	0.5
English	5.2	1.5
French	5.2	6.2
Science	4.6	4.1

'traditional' findings. It is particularly interesting in relation to this study that no significant gender difference is apparent except for German (χ^2 = 9.61; df: 4; $p < 0.05$), where boys show more enthusiasm. On what can this male enthusiasm be attributed? It must be remembered that they have, in all likelihood, very little experience of German on which to base their positive response. Are they influenced by comics and war films (see O'Sullivan, E., 1990), the success of German sports stars (Klinsmann and Rösler in English soccer, for example) and teams, contact with German visitors? (See Table 5.3.)

The general enthusiasm for foreign languages, German in particular, is confirmed in pupils' responses to questions relating to which subjects they were looking forward to/dreading most of all (see Table 5.4).

Again it is hard to explain the very healthy response to German. Is it the novelty value? Pupils are unlikely to be attracted by the mellifluous flow of the language, any predominance of German songs in the pop charts (they

Table 5.5 Cross-tabulation: 'Have you been learning any foreign language up to now?' by 'How much are you looking forward to learning German?'

Experience of learning FL	Looking forward to German	1	2	3	4	5	Row total
No	Count	6	1	17	5	31	60
	Exp val	4.7	3.4	13.8	12.1	26.0	
Yes	Count	8	9	24	31	46	118
	Exp val	9.3	6.6	27.2	23.9	51.0	
	Column total	14	10	41	36	77	178

are too young to remember Kraftwerk, 'Auf der Autobahn' or Nena with her '99 Luftballons', (English version: '99 Red Balloons') or German-speaking role models. Pupils were given the opportunity to give reasons for their answers in an open question. In terms of both the subject they were most looking forward to and the subject they were most dreading, there appear to be the same two categories of justification for pupils' choice as was the case for Table 5.2, that is: (1) the novelty value of a subject (positive: 'I've always wanted to learn it' 18%; negative: 'I've never done it before' 7.2%;) and (2) judgement based on previous experience (positive experience: 'I like it', 'I'm good at it' 40.7%; negative experience: 'It's boring', 'I hate it', 'I'm no good at it' 72.2%.) In the case of German it appears that it has profited from pupils' lack of experience of the subject in advance of coming to secondary school. They seem to be looking forward to something new. The expectation is exciting. In this case ignorance (of the reality) may be bliss. It may also be argued that pupils' perception of German may be positively influenced by their experience of French at primary school; if it was positive then they may have a positive attitude towards learning foreign languages in general; if it was negative they may be looking forward to learning a completely different language.

In order to get closer to the existence of any relationship between the extent to which pupils look forward to learning German and whether or not they have already had experience of foreign language learning, these two variables were cross-tabulated and a chi-square test applied (see Table 5.5).

The chi-square confirms a significant relationship between the two variables ($\chi^2 = 11.95$; df: 4; $p < 0.05$). It seems that 11-year-olds look forward to learning German whether or not they have had previous language learning experience. There is a difference, however, in the level of enthusiasm displayed between those with and those without this experience. Those with experience of foreign language learning are less likely to

Table 5.6 Cross-tabulation 'previous enjoyment of foreign language learning' by 'extent to which German is being looked forward to'

Looking forward to German	*Enjoyment of previous FL learning*	*1*	*2*	*3*	*4*	*5*	*Row total*
1	Count	2	0	2	1	2	7
	Exp val	0.5	0.5	2.6	1.1	2.3	
2	Count	0	1	3	1	4	9
	Exp val	0.7	0.6	3.4	1.4	2.9	
3	Count	0	0	15	4	5	24
	Exp val	1.8	1.6	9.0	3.7	7.8	
4	Count	2	4	8	9	8	31
	Exp val	2.4	2.1	11.7	4.8	10.1	
5	Count	5	3	16	3	19	46
	Exp val	3.5	3.1	17.3	7.1	14.9	
	Column total	9	8	44	18	38	117

opt for the very top end of the scale (5: 39%) than those without (5: 52%). This may be an indication of the difference between expectation and reality. This conclusion is tempered, however, by the very similar response rates when scores for categories 4 and 5 are added: those with foreign language learning experience: 65.3%; those without foreign language learning experience: 60%

Taking the pre-secondary school foreign language learning experience a stage further, was there any relationship between the level of pupils' enjoyment of the experience and the extent to which they claimed to be looking forward to learning German? The data on these two factors were cross-tabulated (see Table 5.6).

The chi-square test does not facilitate comment on any significant relationship between the two variables, given the low expected frequency in some of the cells (<5: 72%). As a result of the uneven distribution of these cells, collapse of columns does not help to alleviate the problem. Table 5.6 serves to confirm that pupils are generally enthusiastic at the prospect of learning German, regardless of their previous learning experience, i.e. 65.8% of pupils are located in categories 4 and 5. Only 20.5% appear indifferent (category 3) and 13.7% in the negative categories 1 and 2. Of the 17 who claim not to have enjoyed their previous learning experience, only three are unenthusiastic about their forthcoming German experience. While not confirming the 'fresh start theory', these data may provide some tentative, evidential underpinning. It would be erroneous to jump to any conclusions, taking the data in isolation, however.

So What Happens to All That Enthusiasm?

The general picture provided by the Leeds sample of Year 7 pupils is of the majority of 11 year olds entering their foreign language learning classes for the first time full of enthusiasm and eager to learn. Does the picture remain the same after two years of the course? Is the level of enthusiasm maintained? Are the expectations of Year 7 met by the learning reality? Two years later the same pupils, now in Year 9, were asked to assess their school subjects in terms of how they measured against their expectations (see Table 5.7).

As far as modern languages are concerned, especially German, the picture does not appear at first to be quite as bright as it had been in Year 7. The mean score suggests that pupils in the main have had their expectations just about met by German. For those who had positive expectations this may present a positive response. For those who had been less than positive in their expectations, this is a less than encouraging result. The response for French is slightly more positive. Given that there are nine subjects to which pupils have given a positive rating (i.e. as reflected in a mean of more than 3.00), indicating expectations being bettered to varying

Table 5.7 Percentage of Year 9 pupils in 1994 responding to the question: 'Have individual subjects been as good/as bad as you expected they would be?'

	Worse than expected		Neutral		Better than expected			
	1	2	3	4	5	Sample	Mean	S.D.
PE	3.1	5.7	24.2	25.8	40.7	194	4.10	2.28
Technology	5.2	9.3	26.3	33.5	25.8	194	3.66	1.12
Art	7.3	9.3	28.5	29.5	25.4	193	3.57	1.18
English	7.7	12.4	35.6	27.3	17.0	194	3.34	1.13
Geography	7.3	15.0	37.3	19.2	21.2	193	3.32	1.17
French	9.8	13.4	39.3	22.3	15.2	112	3.20	1.15
Science	9.8	16.6	34.7	22.3	16.6	193	3.19	1.19
History	13.9	13.4	31.4	23.2	18.0	194	3.18	1.27
Maths	9.8	16.0	39.2	19.6	15.5	194	3.15	1.16
German	12.4	19.7	35.2	21.8	10.9	193	3.00	1.16
Music	16.8	21.1	34.7	14.2	13.2	190	2.86	1.24
RE	24.1	24.1	27.1	13.9	10.8	166	2.63	1.29

degrees, it may arguably be concluded that pupils' enthusiasm for German is not what it had been in Year 7. Application of the chi-square test and cross-tabulation reveals no significant gender difference for any of the subjects, including German.

The 13 year olds were given the opportunity in an open question to explain their feelings regarding German. The majority of answers do not provide much useful insight ('I like it' 55.7%; 'I don't like it' 22.7%). Insofar as other explanations are provided in numbers of any significance, teachers and their teaching appear to be important influences, positive and negative, for some pupils (around 11%):

> 'The teacher goes too fast.'
> 'I'm scared of getting shouted at if I can't do it.'
> 'We've had too many different teachers.'

Interview responses suggest that pupils who enjoy German do so because they appreciate its novelty as a new subject. Those who do not enjoy the subject tend to blame the teacher ('Teachers shout at you when you don't understand.' 'The teacher complains about my writing. You should see her worksheets.' 'When the teacher says, 'I thought we went over this in class,' it makes me mad.') or the degree of difficulty 'I am slow at learning and it's too hard.' 'It's hard to pronounce.' 'You don't understand what foreign people are saying.').

Summary

Given that modern foreign languages do not form part of the National Curriculum for Key Stages 1 and 2, it may come as something of a surprise that almost 64% of 11 year olds in 1992 claim to have had some experience of learning a foreign language. It is arguably all the more surprising, given that at the time of the survey, the National Curriculum was in the early stages of its introduction in primary schools and teachers were voicing concern at the lack of space on the timetable to meet its requirements (Campbell & Neil, 1994; Pollard *et al.*, 1994). It comes as less of a surprise that almost all of these pupils claim that their foreign language experience at primary school took the form of French. This almost certainly reflects the traditional position of French as the first foreign language in UK secondary schools. If a primary school teacher has any foreign language competence, it is most likely to be French.

Most pupils appear to have found their first taste of foreign language learning a reasonably positive experience, 46% scoring 4–5 on a scale of 1–5, although 38% were not prepared to commit themselves to the positive or negative side of the 3. When these data were cross-tabulated with variables relating to how much pupils were looking forward to German, the outcome suggested that whether 11-year-old pupils have had a foreign language experience or not, and whether any experience was positive or negative, they look forward to learning German.

Secondary school teachers of modern foreign languages rejoice. Secondary school teachers of German rejoice. The evidence provided by this small sample suggests that your Year 7 pupils are looking forward with enthusiasm to learning your subject. Some of them have learnt some French. Most of these quite enjoyed the experience and want more. Even those who did not enjoy the experience are positive about the prospect of learning more. Those who have not had any foreign language learning experience are equally keen. The scene is set for a very positive start.

Two years later, the picture is not quite so encouraging. It seems that pupils' expectations are not matched by the reality. The honeymoon is over. The enthusiasm is on the wane. Pupils appear disgruntled. Something has gone wrong. Why this may be so and what can be done about it, are issues taken up later in this book.

Chapter 6

Influence of Home Environment

Ajzen stresses the importance of the influence of 'significant others' in the strand of his model of planned behaviour which he calls 'subjective norm'. If parents are adopted as 'significant others', which is by no means guaranteed, they can play an important role in shaping the pupils' attitude and motivation to learn German.

This chapter reviews data relating to the influence of parents and the home, examining the influence of parental encouragement, the level of parents' target language competence as perceived by pupils, opportunities to hear the target language at home with relatives, guests and friends of the family and speakers of the target language known by pupils. All of these factors may affect the attitudes of learners to the language.

Introduction

Ryan hates German. Why can't he do something useful like more maths or English or science?

Briony can't stand French. I was exactly the same when I went to school. I used to tell her how boring the lessons were and how we played up with the teacher.

These excerpts from dialogues which took place on two separate parents' evenings in a Leeds school in 1996 reflect *inter alia*:

- the potential influence a parent's view may have on the attitude which the pupil brings to the foreign language lesson;
- yet another factor against which the teacher has to battle in her efforts to give modern languages the status they deserve and requires and to promote positive attitudes in her learners.

Milner (1981) provides a model of attitudinal influence to which three processes contribute:

(1) Direct tuition from parents.
(2) Indirect tuition, i.e. the attitudes of the parents are implicit in their behaviour.
(3) Role-learning, i.e. the behaviour of the children reflects the behaviour of those around them.

Within the context of foreign language learning, the success of these three processes may depend largely on: (1) positive attitudes of parents to learning in general and language learning in particular; (2) the level of parents' foreign language competence; and (3) their willingness to demonstrate this competence not only when helping with homework but also when in the company of native speakers of the target language. David Blunkett (then Shadow Education Secretary) stresses the importance of parental support: 'I think the most important thing has to be to make a personal commitment, to be willing to give some time and make a little bit of an effort' (Wilce, 1997).

Parental attitude towards foreign language learning and indeed learning in general may be influenced by educational, socio-economic, socio-cultural, ethnic and linguistic background. Feenstra and Gardner (1968: 52) suggest that learners with the most positive motivation towards learning foreign languages, in the case of French learners in Canada, tend to be integratively-orientated and to come from homes where parents have a basic integrative orientation in combination with pro-French attitudes. The situation in the UK tends to be rather different. UK foreign language learners do not live in an environment where a foreign language such as French is spoken as a first language by a substantial proportion of the population. As a result, evidence of integrative motivation is much harder to find. In the context of an island nation, it is possible that pro-French/German/Spanish, etc. attitudes may be outweighed by apathy, ignorance or in some areas negativity. This will do little to enhance the individual's perception of social pressure to perform (the 'subjective norm'). Arguably parents may have a key role in the shaping of this perception. In order to get some sort of view of this influence, pupils in Leeds were asked to answer a battery of questions relating to:

- the amount of encouragement they received from parents to learn German;
- their perception of their parents' German competence;
- the amount of contact they have with Germans and the German language at home.

The same pupils addressed the same issues two years later.

Encouragement from Parents

How prevalent is the attitude of the parents of Briony and Ryan? Such information was impossible to access with any validity in this study, given its emphasis on pupils' perceptions; parents were not addressed directly. Some insight may be gleaned nevertheless from pupils' thoughts on the encouragement they think their parents give (see Table 6.1).

With the exception of 13 year olds in Leeds in 1994, whose responses tend towards the negative side of the mean, and 15 year olds in 1992, who respond with greater enthusiasm, Leeds pupils' assessment of their parents' level of encouragement to learn foreign languages/German is quite positive. Why do 13 year olds in 1994 give a view which is more negative than that of others? Whether this is a result of a perception of lack of encouragement from home is open to question, especially given that their responses in most batteries of questions reflect this negativity. Convery *et al.* (1997) in their research into pupils' perceptions of Europe, found 1994 to be a particularly Eurosceptic year. Numerous events hit the headlines, especially crudely in the case of the tabloids: Maastricht debate in the House of Commons; BMW take over of Rover; World Cup without England; events in Bosnia and Chechnia; the rise of the Conservative right. It is interesting to note that when a t-test[1] was applied to the the responses of Year 7 pupils and the same pupils two years later in Year 9, the difference was statistically significant: $t = 6.12$; df = 176; $p < 0.001$. This was also true for the Year 9 to Year 11 cohort: $t = 2.27$; df = 107; $p < 0.05$. In the case of the 11–13 year old cohort, this may reflect the enthusiasm and positive mindset of new entrants to the secondary school in contrast to the more detached, 'cool', independent (of parents at least) teenagers into which they seem to develop two years later. For the older cohort the reverse may be true: the 'cool', detached teenager in Year 9 may grow to appreciate the support and

Table 6.1 Percentages of pupils responding to the question: 'How much do your parents encourage you to learn foreign languages/German?'

| Place/age/yr | Not at all | | A little | | Very much | | | |
	1	2	3	4	5	Sample	Mean	S.D.
Leeds 11/92	10.3	2.7	29.2	21.1	36.8	185	3.7	1.27
Leeds 13/94	20.5	16.2	25.4	24.3	13.5	185	2.9	1.33
Leeds 13/92	6.4	10.0	16.4	39.1	28.2	110	3.73	1.17
Leeds 15/94	10.6	8.0	23.0	43.4	15.0	113	3.44	1.16
Leeds 15/92	0.0	0.0	23.1	46.2	30.8	13	4.08	0.76
Leeds 17/94	7.7	0.0	23.1	46.2	23.1	13	3.77	1.09

encouragement of parents as GCSE examinations approach in Year 11. This hypothesis may be confirmed by the enthusiasm shown by 15 year olds in 1992. Bearing in mind the caveat that the sample for this age-cohort is small, these pupils are about to take their GCSE examinations and go on to take A-level German. It may be expected that this category would contain a higher proportion of pupils who get positively encouraged to do well in their chosen subjects than do the younger cohorts. Their responses to this question may be an indication, albeit a not terribly well substantiated indication, that pupils who get encouragement to do well at German are more likely to take it for A-level. Or do parents tend to encourage their children in those subjects for which they show enthusiasm? It is interesting to note that there was no statistically significant difference[2] between responses given by the 15 year olds in 1992 and the same pupils two years later. GCSE and A-level examinations may lead pupils to value the encouragement from parents in these crucial years.

These data are corroborated by the responses provided in interviews. Almost all interviewees in Leeds feel that their parents encourage them to do well at school. There is a fairly even divide between those who feel encouraged in particular subjects (usually mathematics and English) and those who simply feel encouraged generally. When asked what sort of indicators they had of parents' encouragement, most respondents referred to help provided with homework:

> My mum always asks me how much homework I have to do and, when I have finished it, has a look at it. (13 year old)

> My mum always asks me how things have gone at school. (15 year old)

> When I have a problem with my homework, I always ask my dad for help.

Other responses referred to help with revision, rewards for good results and reminders of the value of education: 'Take the chance when you can get it.' (15 year old). In the light of this apparent relationship between perception of level of encouragement and provision of help with homework, it will be interesting to note (see p. 87 ff) the proportion of parents who are regarded as having the foreign language competence (German in particular) to allow them to offer this support.

Usefulness of German and encouragement from parents to learn German

How much encouragement to learn German, or indeed any other foreign language, does Ryan's mum provide? Her comments suggest that she struggles to see the relevance of German to her son's needs. Ryan makes it very clear to his beleaguered teacher that he certainly struggles to see the

Table 6.2 Correlation coefficients: perceived usefulness of German by encouragement from parents (Leeds 13 year olds 1992)

	Usefulness of German	*Encouragement*
Usefulness of German	1.0000	0.5018
	(115)	(110)
	$p = .$	$p = 0.000$
Encouragement	0.5018	1.0000
	(110)	(110)
	$p = 0.000$	$p = .$

Table 6.3 Do your parents encourage you in specific subjects? If so, which ones?

	Year 7 (n = 34)	*Year 9 (n = 41)*	*Year 11 (n = 17)*
English	36.4	34.1	23.5
Maths	100	22.0	52.9
French	27.3	9.8	–
German	28.2	9.8	23.5

relevance of German to his needs. The 'chicken and egg' question arises. Is Ryan's negative attitude the product of his mother's negativity? Or is Ryan's mum negative because of her son's antipathy to German. Perhaps it is the case that there is a relationship between pupils' perception of the usefulness of German and the encouragement they claim to get from their parents. This was put to the test. The 13–15 cohort was the focus of attention, given the important decisions which have to be be made by these age groups regarding GCSE and A-level (see Table 6.2).

Table 6.2 suggests that one of the two variables accounts for 25% of the variance of the other. The direction of the influence, however, is uncertain. A cross-tabulation confirms the trend that the more encouragement pupils receive from parents to learn German, the more useful it is likely to be perceived. The opposite may also be true. Interview evidence suggests that the latter suggestion may be the more fitting, i.e. the more useful a subject is perceived to be generally, the more likely parents are to offer encouragement. Sadly for the teacher of modern languages, responses indicate that Leeds parents who offer encouragement in specific subjects tend to focus on mathematics and English rather than German or French. In Year 11 the response for German is not quite so disappointing. Pressure of GCSE may account for this (see Table 6.3).

Table 6.4 Cross-tabulation: perceived usefulness of German by encouragement from parents (Leeds 15 year olds 1994)

Encouragement	Usefulness of German	1	2	3	4	5	Row total
1	Count	3	2	2	0	0	7
	Exp value	0.2	0.3	2.2	2.7	1.7	
2	Count	0	1	6	2	2	11
	Exp value	0.3	0.4	3.4	4.3	2.6	
3	Count	0	1	6	6	5	18
	Exp value	0.5	0.7	5.6	7.0	4.3	
4	Count	0	0	15	21	7	43
	Exp value	1.2	1.6	13.3	16.8	10.2	
5	Count	0	0	5	14	12	31
	Exp value	0.8	1.1	9.6	12.1	7.3	
Column total		3	4	34	43	26	110

Does the picture alter two years later? (See Table 6.4.)

The trend shown in Table 6.4 is maintained two years later with the same group of pupils, although the significance of the relationship is somewhat reduced ($p < 0.01$) and the proportion of the variance accounted for amounts to only about 9%. This may be an indication of increased maturity and independence leading to a diminishment in the influence of parental encouragement. It is interesting to note, however, that interview evidence, albeit based on a much smaller sample, rather contradicts this (see Table 6.3).

Foreign language competence of parents

If pupils equate parental encouragement with the willingness and ability of their mum and dad to offer and provide them with help to do their homework, it may be interesting to ascertain how many pupils perceive their parents as being in a position to provide assistance with foreign language homework, German in particular. It may also be of interest to compare the position of the Leeds learner of German with the Kiel learner of English.

Pupils in Leeds and Kiel were asked to give their perceptions of their parents' German and English competence respectively. The trend is the same for all three age cohorts. The data for the 13–15 cohort is used to illustrate (see Table 6.5).

It is reassuring that there is no significant difference in the mean scores

Table 6.5 Percentage of 13–15 cohort in Leeds and Kiel responding to the question: 'How much German/English does your mother/father know?'

	None		Some		Lots			
	1	2	3	4	5	Sample	Mean	S.D.
Mothers of Leeds 13/92	47.7	18.3	17.4	8.3	8.3	109	2.09	1.34
Mothers of Leeds 15/94	57.9	19.3	13.2	3.5	6.1	114	1.81	1.17
Fathers of Leeds 13/92	53.6	23.6	13.6	3.6	5.5	110	1.83	1.15
Fathers of Leeds 15/94	46.5	20.2	18.4	8.8	6.1	114	2.08	1.25
Mothers of Kiel 13/92	27.0	13.9	35.0	13.9	10.2	137	2.66	1.29
Mothers of Kiel 15/94	26.5	19.9	32.4	14.7	6.6	136	2.55	1.22
Fathers of Kiel 13/92	22.3	12.2	25.9	23.7	15.8	139	2.99	1.38
Fathers of Kiel 15/94	24.5	14.4	25.2	23.7	12.2	139	2.85	1.36

relating to the responses given by the same pupils two years apart. This may confirm some consistency in pupils' answering of this question on the two occasions of the survey. It must be recognised, however, that the comparing of the means requires some circumspection, in that the criteria applied by pupils to their judgement of parents' competence could vary considerably. There is nonetheless some evidence to suggest that Kiel parents may be in a stronger position to offer help and support to their children than is the case for Leeds parents. When the chi-square test was applied to pupils' responses in Leeds and Kiel for 1992, the difference was found to be highly significant in relation to both mothers ($\chi^2 = 16.79$, df = 4, $p < 0.01$) and fathers ($\chi^2 = 48.39$, df = 4, $p < 0.0001$). (See Tables 6.6, 6.7.)

When, two years later, the same test was applied to the same pupils' responses to the same question, the difference again was highly significant:

regarding mothers: $\chi^2 = 32.82$, df = 4, $p < 0.0001$;
regarding fathers: $\chi^2 = 22.07$, df = 4, $p < 0.001$.

On what evidence do pupils base their response? Interview data suggest that some base their judgement on having heard their parents use the foreign language on holiday or on their capacity to help with homework. Given that Schleswig-Holstein has had a 'languages for all' policy for more than 30 years, English competence in Kiel should be more common among a larger proportion of parents than may be so for German in Leeds. This is corroborated in responses in interviews where well over half of the Kiel pupils claim that their parents could speak a foreign language, in the vast

Table 6.6 Chi-square test on relationship between Leeds and Kiel pupils with regard to the variable: 'How much German/English does your mother know?'

	1 (%)	2 (%)	3 (%)	4 (%)	5 (%)	Total (%)
Mothers/Leeds/92	47.7	18.3	17.4	8.3	8.3	44.3
Mothers/Kiel/92	27.0	13.9	35.0	13.9	10.2	55.7
Total	36.2	15.9	27.2	11.4	9.3	100

Table 6.7 Chi-square test on relationship between Leeds and Kiel pupils with regard to the variable: 'How much German / English does your father know?'

	1 (%)	2 (%)	3 (%)	4 (%)	5 (%)	Total (%)
Fathers/Leeds/92	53.6	23.6	13.6	3.6	5.5	44.2
Fathers/Kiel/92	22.3	12.2	25.9	23.7	15.8	55.8
Total	36.1	17.3	20.5	14.9	11.2	100

majority of cases, English. Only around a third of Leeds pupils interviewed regard their parents as having foreign language competence, usually in French rather than German (see tables 6.8, 6.9).

Correlation coefficients were examined to ascertain whether a relationship exists between pupils' perception of the encouragement they received from their parents and the level of target language competence they thought their mother and father had. In the case of Leeds 13 year olds in 1992 the correlation is significant ($p < 0.05$) but the score is weak, accounting for less than 9% of the variance.

The same methodology was applied to Kiel pupils in the 13–15 cohort. The outcome was very similar to that in Leeds. Cross-tabulation reflected a tendency for pupils to feel more encouragement, the higher the level they perceived their parents' English competence to be. This would tie in with the suggestion above that pupils equate parental encouragement with the ability to provide help, especially with homework..

Kiel pupils seem to enjoy a considerable advantage over their Leeds peers. (See also Chapter 10.) English has been an obligatory subject on the school curriculum in Schleswig-Holstein for more than 30 years. A foreign language has been compulsory in Leeds (and UK) schools only since the advent of the National Curriculum (1992), and even this requirement is

Table 6.8 Percentages of Leeds pupils responding to the interview question: 'Which foreign language/s does your mother speak?'

	Year 7 (n = 34)	Year 9 (n = 41)	Year 11 (n = 17)
French	29.4	31.7	11.8
German	20.6	9.8	17.6
Other	8.8	2.4	17.6

Table 6.9 Percentages of Leeds pupils responding to the interview question: 'Which foreign language/s does your father speak?'

	Year 7 (n = 34)	Year 9 (n = 41)	Year 11 (n = 17)
French	26.5	17.1	17.6
German	17.6	14.6	23.5
Other	8.8	7.3	29.4

being diluted with the introduction of short courses (1996). Still further dilution is on the cards in the review of the National Curriculum currently being carried out by the Qualifications and Curriculum Authority (QCA), (see Pyke, 1998). As a result, Kiel pupils are far more likely to have mums and dads, brothers and sisters with English competence than are Leeds pupils whose family members are seen as being able to provide little support. If Leeds relatives have any foreign language competence, it is more likely to be in French than anything else.

What is the position in Schleswig-Holstein for a language which may not enjoy the high status of English, French for example? Given the traditional status of French and German as second foreign languages in Germany and the UK respectively, a comparison of the data for both within the area of perceived competence of parents may reveal some interesting insights (see Table 6.10).

The data confirm the picture of French with all the features of the second foreign language and bear considerable resemblance to responses provided for Leeds parents. Pupils learning French in Kiel are at much the same disadvantage as pupils in Leeds learning German. In Kiel where English is the first foreign language, fewer parents have French competence. The same is true in Leeds where French has traditionally dominated as the first foreign language and so parents with German competence are few. The sad truth, however, appears to be that in spite of the dominance of French

Table 6.10 Percentage of Kiel pupils learning French (13–15 cohort) responding to the question: 'How much French does your mother/father know?'

	None		Some		Lots			
	1	2	3	4	5	Sample	Mean	S.D.
Mothers of Kiel 13/92	54.8	7.1	14.3	19.0	4.8	42	2.12	1.38
Mothers of Kiel 15/94	(54.8)	(9.5)	(16.7)	(14.3)	(4.8)	(42)	(2.05)	(1.32)
	62.5	0.0	25.0	12.5	0.0	8	1.88	1.25
	(62.5)	(0.0)	(37.5)	(0.0)	(0.0)	(8)	(1.75)	(1.04)
Fathers of Kiel 13/92	61.9	7.1	21.4	4.8	4.8	42	1.83	1.21
Fathers of Kiel 15/94	(54.8)	(23.8)	(14.3)	(4.8)	(2.4)	(42)	(1.76)	(1.03)
	57.1	0.0	28.6	14.3	0.0	7	2.00	1.29
	(75.0)	(12.5)	(0.0)	(12.5)	(0.0)	(8)	(1.50)	(1.07)

in Leeds (and UK) schools, pupils appear not to perceive their parents as having competence in this foreign language or indeed any other.

Opportunity to hear German/English/French at home

Do pupils in Kiel also have more opportunities than their Leeds peers to see the practical application and value of foreign language competence at home? In theory, pupils who hear their parents and friends at home interacting in a foreign language with guests at home, may have more appreciation of the usefulness of the target language than those who do not have this opportunity (see Table 6.11).

The difference between Leeds and Kiel pupils at age 11 is highly significant: $\chi^2 = 131.36$, df = 1, $p = 0.0001$. Kiel pupils claim to have had more occasion than their Leeds counterparts to hear the target language used with friends of the family (be it English or French); 74% of 11 year olds in Kiel claim to have heard English used in context, while only 16% of pupils of the same age in Leeds respond positively. At the older end of the scale only two of the 13 Leeds pupils taking A-level German have had this opportunity, in contrast to 57% of the 56 Kiel 17 year olds.

Pupils do not provide much evidence on the nature of the opportunities. The restricted data provided by the open questions suggest that English is heard in use most commonly on holidays or when relatives are visiting. Regarding Kiel pupils learning French, exchange visits attract the most support. Leeds pupils' opportunities to have heard German barely change in the course of the two years. Very few Leeds pupils reveal any source for hearing German in the open questions, except for 15 year olds in 1992, 53.8% of whom identify exchange visits. The difference between the response of

Table 6.11 Percentage Leeds and Kiel pupils responding to the question: 'Have you ever had the opportunity to hear German/English used with friends of the family?'

Response	Age/Year	Percentage: Leeds	Percentage: Kiel/English	Percentage: Kiel/French
No	11/92	84.4 ($n = 158$)	26.4 ($n = 193$)	n/a
	13/94	82.2 ($n = 180$)	66.7 ($n = 193$)	n/a
	13/92	68.2 ($n = 110$)	64.3 ($n = 129$)	65.0 ($n = 40$)
	15/94	70.2 ($n = 114$)	59.0 ($n = 136$)	52.5 ($n = 40$)
	15/92	61.5 ($n = 13$)	47.4 ($n = 57$)	16.7 ($n = 6$)
	17/94	84.6 ($n = 13$)	42.9 ($n = 56$)	33.3 ($n = 6$)
Yes	11/92	15.8 ($n = 158$)	73.6 ($n = 193$)	n/a
	13/94	17.8 ($n = 180$)	33.3 ($n = 193$)	n/a
	13/92	31.8 ($n = 110$)	35.7 ($n = 129$)	35.0 ($n = 40$)
	15/94	29.6 ($n = 114$)	38.1 ($n = 136$)	47.5 ($n = 40$)
	15/92	38.5 ($n = 13$)	50.8 ($n = 57$)	83.3 ($n = 6$)
	17/94	15.4 ($n = 13$)	57.1 ($n = 56$)	66.7 ($n = 6$)

11 and 15 year olds in Kiel and Leeds respectively in 1992 and the same pupils in 1994 is bizarre, as is that for Kiel 15 year olds learning French in 1992. It can only be concluded that pupils either overstated their response as 11/15 year olds or understated it as 13/17 year olds. It may also be possible that their definition of 'knowing' altered. Nevertheless it again seems that Kiel English learners (and certainly with regard to this question French learners too) enjoy an important instrumental advantage over the Leeds learners of German (and although relevant data are not provided, quite possibly French too).

Authentic use of German/English/French

What about opportunities beyond the household? Do Leeds and Kiel offer pupils openings for authentic application of their foreign language competence? (See Table 6.12.)

The discrepancy between Leeds and Kiel is considerable. Not only do more Kiel pupils respond positively in 1992 and 1994 but the rate of increase, which one expects with experience of holidays, exchanges, visitors, etc., is also greater in Kiel than in Leeds. (The decrease for 13 year olds in 1992 and the same pupils as 15 year olds in 1994 is difficult to explain.) Interview responses of Leeds pupils reveal some other interesting situational contexts:

Table 6.12 Percentages of pupils in Leeds and Kiel responding to the question: 'Have you ever been in a situation where it would have been useful to be able to speak German/English?'

Response	Age/year	Percentage: Leeds	Percentage: Kiel/English	Percentage: Kiel/French
No	11/92	79.4 ($n = 160$)	54.1($n = 194$)	n/a
	13/94	71.0 ($n = 183$)	37.3 ($n = 201$)	n/a
	13/92	45.5 ($n = 101$)	27.4 ($n = 124$)	29.7 ($n = 37$)
	15/94	55.3 ($n = 114$)	10.9 ($n = 137$)	19.5 ($n = 41$)
	15/92	23.1($n = 13$)	7.1 ($n = 56$)	12.5 ($n = 8$)
	17/94	23.1($n = 13$)	0.0 ($n = 59$)	0.0 ($n = 8$)
Yes	11/92	18.8 ($n = 160$)	45.9 ($n = 194$)	n/a
	13/94	27.9 ($n = 183$)	62.7 ($n = 201$)	n/a
	13/92	54.5 ($n = 101$)	72.6 ($n = 124$)	70.3 ($n = 37$)
	15/94	44.7 ($n = 114$)	89.0 ($n = 137$)	80.5 ($n = 41$)
	15/92	76.9 ($n = 13$)	92.9 ($n = 56$)	87.5 ($n = 8$)
	17/94	76.9 ($n = 13$)	100.0 ($n = 59$)	100.0 ($n = 8$)

'Our teacher doesn't speak much English.' (13 year old)
'When Stuttgart fans came to Elland Road.' (15 year old)

By the time pupils reach Year 13 (age 17) in Leeds, three-quarters (10/13) have found themselves in an authentic German-speaking situation, most commonly on holidays or, as they progress through the school, on exchange visits. By the same age all Kiel pupils in the survey have been in an authentic situation to speak English, again usually on holidays or when encountering tourists at home. Being able to practise their foreign language competence even on an irregular basis must, one might assume, make pupils aware of its usefulness and therefore do much to enhance their instrumental and possibly their intrinsic motivation. Again this is a great advantage enjoyed by Kiel teachers of English which Leeds teachers of German appear to be denied.

Speakers of German/English/French who pupils know

The same discrepancy between Leeds and Kiel is found in relation to the question on German/English speakers known to pupils (see Table 6.13).

Again Kiel pupils (and their teachers) enjoy a favourable learning context. The situation for Leeds pupils improves a little in the course of the two years, certainly for 13–15 year olds, and again for the 15–17 cohort. (It

Table 6.13 Percentages of Leeds and Kiel pupils responding to the question: 'Do you know any people who speak German/English/French as their mother-tongue?'

Response	Age/Year	Percentage: Leeds	Percentage: Kiel/English	Percentage: Kiel/French
No	11/92	73.4 ($n = 173$)	48.6 ($n = 183$)	n/a
	13/94	78.3 ($n = 179$)	51.7 ($n = 201$)	n/a
	13/92	71.7 ($n = 106$)	41.0 ($n = 122$)	18.9 ($n = 37$)
	15/94	55.0 ($n = 111$)	31.7 ($n = 129$)	17.9 ($n = 39$)
	15/92	50.0 ($n = 12$)	27.8 ($n = 54$)	0.0 ($n = 7$)
	17/94	0.0 ($n = 13$)	8.6 ($n = 58$)	33.3 ($n = 6$)
Yes	11/92	26.6 ($n = 173$)	51.4 ($n = 183$)	n/a
	13/94	21.8 ($n = 179$)	48.3 ($n = 201$)	n/a
	13/92	28.3 ($n = 106$)	59.0 ($n = 122$)	81.1 ($n = 37$)
	15/94	45.0 ($n = 111$)	61.2 ($n = 129$)	82.1 ($n = 39$)
	15/92	50.0 ($n = 12$)	72.2 ($n = 54$)	100.0 ($n = 7$)
	17/94	100.0 ($n = 13$)	91.4 ($n = 58$)	66.7 ($n = 6$)

is interesting to note that the sample interviewed revealed a small number of pupils (8%) in this cohort who named their teachers (non-native-speakers) as the Germans they knew.) The rate of improvement for Kiel pupils is slow but starts from a much higher base-line. It would be erroneous to claim that the Leeds pupils win over the advantage at age 17. The size of the much smaller Leeds sample must be borne in mind. Some bizarre responses appear with this question as for the preceding one (e.g. 11 year olds in Leeds and Kiel (learning English) and 15 year olds in Kiel (learning French) in 1992 and the same pupils two years later). The same reasons may apply.

In terms of the number of target language speakers known, the median in both locations (for German and English) is between one and two, increasing slightly for the 15–17 cohort. The data for French are rather different with most pupils claiming to know 20 target language speakers (an exchange group?) in the 13–15 cohort and 10 (or more) in the 15–17 cohort.

The hypothesis that Leeds pupils who hear the target language spoken at home and who claim to know people who speak the target language as their mother-tongue, may be more aware of the usefulness of the target language, was tested by applying the chi-square test. Surprisingly, perhaps, the test reveals no significant relationship between the variables. Cross-tabulation suggests little difference between those pupils with experience of German heard at home and those without, and those who claim to know German native speakers and those who do not. This is difficult to explain.

May it be the case that the influence of the position of English and the world language and pupils' relative lack of experience of foreign language use in authentic contexts seduces them away from the perception of German/ foreign language competence as something useful? This contrasts considerably with the language learning context of Kiel pupils who appear not to be able to escape the usefulness of English competence, given that the 'world language' seems to be all around them and its importance is emphasised by its status as an entrance qualification to the world of further study and work and as a social tool.

Summary

Leeds pupils feel encouraged to learn foreign languages by their parents, especially in the early years. As they get older, they feel less encouraged, apart from those few who go on to take A-level German. The reasons for the perceived diminishment in encouragement are unclear. Some possibilities have been outlined above and may relate to maturation of pupils and the foreign language competence of parents. If Leeds parents have a foreign language, it is more likely to be French than German. This limits the amount of language-specific help which can be offered. Leeds pupils enjoy little access to speakers of German in the home context and few opportunities to practise their competence in authentic situations.

Kiel pupils (and their teachers) enjoy so many advantages: parents with English competence; contact with speakers of English/French; more authentic contexts for use of English. This must enhance their awareness of the utility and relevance of the target language and enhance their motivation, be it instrumental, integrative, extrinsic or intrinsic or a blend of all of these, to learn it.

There is little doubt that the Leeds (and UK) teacher of foreign languages is up against it. The next chapter will investigate how tough aspects of her job are.

Notes
1. A non-parametric test was applied in the first instance, since the assumption of equal interval data is questionable. It was thought, however, that, given the large sample, a parametric test would be adequately robust. It was found that both the parametric and non-parametric approaches led to precisely the same conclusions.
2. Given that the sample is small in this case, a non-parametric test was applied.

Chapter 7

Pupils' Perceptions of People from Other Countries

Have Leeds learners of foreign languages had the opportunity to visit target language and other countries? What are their attitudes towards other nationalities? What, if any, influence do these have on their attitude to foreign language learning? Is it the case that those pupils with more experience of travel are more likely to be conscious of the advantages of foreign language competence and therefore more motivated to learn German/French? Some results are compared with responses of German pupils from Kiel to the same questions to test the hypothesis that Kiel learners of English may feel more positively motivated to learn a foreign language because, as a consequence of living on the European mainland, they have more immediate access to and possibly greater experience of foreign countries.

Introduction

Andrew came to German lessons with a very positive attitude. He claimed to love Germany. He liked the Germans enormously. He also claimed to love German. It all seemed to be connected. He had been on a German exchange and had enjoyed the experience hugely. He got on extremely well with his exchange partner whose family treated him like a son. In Cologne he found so much to do which interested him. He was not bored for an instant.

Sarah came to German 'with attitude'. She claimed that she hated Germans. She hated German. She had no intention of ever going to Germany. Again this all seemed connected. Her older sister has been part of the German exchange. Her exchange partner, Bettina, had spent a week with her family in Leeds. Sarah, unlike her sister, did not get on with the German guest at all. They had nothing in common. Sarah thought that Bettina was really rude. She seemed abrupt and held her knife and fork in a strange way. Sarah's mum had felt obliged to change all their usual meals to suit Bettina. Sarah was so glad when the week came to an end.

Do travel and experience of other peoples, their culture, food, language and *modus vivendi*, affect pupils' attitude to foreign language learning in a positive manner? Do pupils like Andrew feel they wish to learn the language because they want to experience more? Or can these experiences have a negative influence? What if experience of other countries and peoples been less than enjoyable? Does it teach some pupils, like Sarah, to feel happier with what they know and with all things familiar? Do some pupils lack the need for access to the unknown and unfamiliar? If so, why would they need foreign language competence?

Are the perceptions of pupils on the European mainland, Germany for example, any different? Are they likely to have a more positive view of other countries and peoples? It may be the case that their views are influenced by relatively easy access to a large number of other countries, in that they do not need to cross a substantial channel of water in the manner that UK pupils do.

Leeds Pupils' Experience of Travel Abroad

Does a positive attitude to foreign language learning relate to experience of travel abroad and interaction with peoples of other nations? Eleven year old Leeds pupils were asked whether or not they had already visited a foreign country. Of the 191 asked, 67.5% responded positively. This increased to 78.3% two years later when the pupils were 13 years old. The picture in Kiel is significantly different. 89.7% of 11 year olds there have already been abroad ($\chi^2 = 31.63$; df = 1; $p = 0.0001$), increasing to 93.6% two years later ($\chi^2 = 23.68$; df = 1; $p = 0.0001$). For the 13–15 cohort of Leeds pupils the gap narrows a little with 86.1% and 87.8% responding positively, as compared with 94.9% and 97.1% for Kiel pupils of the same age. The difference is still significant, however, in each case: 13/92: $\chi^2 = 3.92$; df = 1; $p = 0.05$; 15/94: $\chi^2 = 8.26$; df = 1; $p = 0.005$. The gap disappears completely for the 15–17 cohort in which all Leeds pupils ($n = 13$) claim to have been to a foreign country.

Table 7.1 Percentages of 11-year-old pupils in 1992 and the same pupils aged 13 in 1994 in Leeds and Kiel responding to the question: 'Have you ever been to a foreign country?'

Response	Year	Leeds	Kiel
No	11/92	31.9 ($n = 160$)	9.8 ($n = 191$)
	13/94	21.7 ($n = 183$)	6.4 ($n = 189$)
Yes	11/92	67.5 ($n = 160$)	89.7 ($n = 191$)
	13/94	78.3 ($n = 183$)	93.6 ($n = 189$)
I don't know	11/92	0.5 ($n = 160$)	0.0 ($n = 191$)
	13/94	0.0 ($n = 183$)	0.0 ($n = 189$)

Which countries do pupils claim to have visited? Those pupils who have travelled abroad seem to have visited quite a range of countries. Of the 11 year olds in Leeds, 38.0% claim to have visited various European countries and 17.1% various countries all over the world. Where pupils are specific in naming a single country, Spain is the most common (16.3%). France and Germany are mentioned specifically by only 4.6% and 1.0% respectively. The actual numbers having visited Germany and France are likely to be considerably higher, given that they are probably included in European and world countries visited. Two years later the percentage visiting various countries across Europe (45.9%) and the world (23.6%) increases as does that for France (8.8%) and Germany (2.0%). The number mentioning Spain decreases to 6.1% however.

For the 13–15 cohort this trend remains the same but with larger numbers of pupils specifically mentioning France (1992: 17.2%; 1994: 13.7%). Germany continues to receive little support (2.00% and 1.00%).

The 13 representatives in Leeds in the 15–17 cohort are equally non-specific, nine claiming to have visited a number of European countries and three a number of countries across the world. Only one specifically mentions France. Germany is not mentioned at all, although it could be included in the European experience of some pupils.

Would data from Kiel confirm the hypothesis that German pupils are likely to be more widely travelled across Europe possibly because of ease of access? Pupils in the 11–13 cohort in Kiel do seem to have visited their European neighbours more (1992: 54.9%; 1994: 59.2%) than Leeds pupils but have less experience of world travel (1992: 3.3%; 1994: 10.5%). Denmark (1992: 17.4%; 1994 13.6%) is the country nominated by those who specify one country visited only. This comes as no surprise, given Kiel's proximity to the Danish border. This pattern of response is maintained for the 13–15 and 15–17 cohorts in Kiel.

Given the non-specificity of pupils claiming to have visited foreign countries in their identification of those countries, one cannot be seduced by the attractive thought that pupils who have visited Germany and France are more likely to be positive about learning German and French. It was worth considering, however, whether experience of travel abroad in general enhanced pupils' awareness of the usefulness of foreign language competence, German in particular. (See Holec *et al.*, 1996 and Goethe-Institut, 1998, for insights into potential negative effects of travel to just one foreign country but the benefits of visiting several.) Cross-tabulations and the chi-square application were used to investigate this question. Results indicate that having been abroad or not appears to have little influence on a pupil's perception of the usefulness of German. Although it does not have a diminishing effect, which is of course possible, this is still a rather disappointing outcome which raises the question of the value of foreign travel as a means of heightening pupils' consciousness of the importance and relevance of foreign language competence.

Desire to Visit Other Countries

There may be some evidence to suggest that travel may not serve to stimulate and motivate Leeds pupils in terms of foreign language learning. What about the reverse? May it be the case that foreign language learning serves to stimulate and motivate in terms of travel to other countries, with special reference to those where the target language is spoken? Given that Leeds pupils are learning German at school, there may be the possibility that they would become interested in visiting German-speaking countries. This could be a reflection of simple curiosity, of a motivation to put into practice what they had learnt or even of Gardner and Lambert's 'integrative motivation' (1972: 147), actually to become part of the target language community. Pupils were therefore asked which other countries they would like to visit. They were asked the same question two years later (see Table 7.2).

The trend of responses in the 11–13 and 13–15 cohorts is very similar. Immediately apparent is the popularity of America and Australia. Attractions such as Disneyland and the pop-culture are powerful factors in favour of the USA. In response to the open question relating to the reason(s) for their choice of country (see Table 7.3), 22.6% of Leeds 13 year olds in 1992, for example, put attractions at the top of the list, 34% of whom make specific reference to Disney. Pupils are also clearly influenced by what they hear from friends, relatives and others (applies to 34.8% of 13 year olds in 1994) and it may be assumed that some of this will relate to Disneyland ('I'd love

Table 7.2 Percentages of 11–13 cohort in Leeds responding to the question: 'Which other country would you like to visit?'

Country	11/92 (n = 170)	13/94 (n = 152)	13/92 (n = 103)	15/94 (n = 103)	15/92 (n = 13)	17/94 (n = 13)
America	28.8	30.9	28.2	27.2	30.8	7.7
Australia	12.4	9.2	10.9	10.7	0.0	15.4
Germany	8.2	5.9	10.0	7.8	30.8	30.8
France	7.1	2.0	2.7	1.0	0.0	0.0
Spain	7.1	3.3	0.0	0.0	0.0	
Italy	4.1	7.9	0.0	0.0	23.1	7.7
Canada						15.4

Table 7.3 Percentages of 11, 13 and 15-year-old Leeds pupils in 1992 and the same pupils in 1994 responding to the question: 'Which other country would you like to visit? *Why*?'

Reason	11/92 (13/94) (n = 194)	13/92 (15/94) (n = 115)	15/92 (17/94) (n = 13)
Attractions	19.1 (5.7)	22.6*	7.7** (7.7)
Relatives	10.3 (6.7)	7.8	7.7
Hearsay	9.8 (18.1)	20.9 (34.8)	7.7 (53.8)
Weather	8.8 (7.7)	16.5 (9.6)	7.7
Scenery	8.2	14.8	7.7
Novelty		12.2	23.1
To learn/practise the language	7.7 (2.1)	7.8 (6.1)	7.7 (23.1)
Culture	3.1 (10.3)	(7.8)	(15.4)
Other	28.9 (14.9)	(22.6)	
No response	4.1 (34.5)	0.0 (19.1)	

* 7% mention Disney specifically
**7.7% mention Disney specifically

to go to Disneyland'; 'My stepdad took me to Disneyland when I was 10. I'd love to go again'), and other attractions too.

Interview responses indicate that the influence of the television soap operas from Australia is very strong:

> 'I'd love to live in Australia. I've seen it on "Neighbours". When they go to the beach and go surfing and swimming, it makes me want to go there.' (13-year-old Leeds pupil in 1992)
>
> 'If I had the money I'd go to Australia. The kids in "Home and Away" don't seem to get as much homework as we do.'
>
> 'The boys are gorgeous!' (13-year-old Leeds pupil in 1994)

Pupils get their 'daily fix', seem seduced by the sunshine, beautiful people and different life-style and want to experience it for themselves. Although the numbers wishing to visit Germany are comparatively small, at least the target language country does feature. Sadly the number drops two years later, in keeping with the general drop in enthusiasm for German between Years 7 and 9. It is interesting to note that 'to learn/practise the language' is offered by Leeds pupils as one of the eight most common justifications for their choice of preferred destination. It is more than likely that they have Germany/France/Spain in mind. It is encouraging that this justification is common across the cohorts.

The data for the 15–17 cohort deserve special attention (see Table 7.2). America and Australia remain on pupils' list of countries to be visited but are seriously challenged by Germany. Given that pupils are doing German for A-level, that 3/13 would like to study German at university, and 5/13 (1992) and 4/13 (1994) are interested in working there one day, one should expect the target language country to be quite strongly represented. It is also pertinent that 'to learn/practise the language' represents the second most popular justification (equal with 'Novelty') for choice of preferred destination after 'Hearsay'. Are 17 year olds becoming ever more aware of the advent of the examination season and the need to enhance their competence and hone their skills?

The Leeds teacher of German may well cherish the hope that her pupils would feel some need, however superficial, curiosity-driven perhaps, to visit the country where the language of interaction in their classes three times a week has its natural home. Sadly it appears to be a vain hope. Does the Kiel teacher of English suffer the same disappointment? When Kiel pupils in the 11–13 cohort were asked which country they would most like to visit, America (1992: 28.7%; 1994: 31.6%) and England (1992: 14.9%; 1994: 12.8%) are the only countries nominated in significant numbers. Responses in interviews suggest that America holds the same attractions for Kiel pupils as for Leeds pupils:

'Dort kann man Aktivitäten machen, die hier nicht möglich sind.' *'You can do things there which aren't possible here.'* (13 year old in 1992)
'Disney muß man mal erlebt haben.' *'You have to have experienced Disney.'* (15 year old in 1994)
'Man hört nur gutes davon und einmal muß man sich das mal angucken.' *'You only hear good things about America and you have to see it for yourself some time.'* (15 year old in 1994)

The influence of the pop-culture in England is also a feature of pupils' answers:

Table 7.4 Percentages of Kiel pupils responding to the question: 'Which other country would you like to visit?'

Country	11/92 (n = 195)	13/94 (n = 196)	13/92 (n = 133)	15/94 (n = 133)	15/92 (n = 56)	17/94 (n = 58)
America	28.7	31.6	42.9	39.1	37.5	34.5
England	14.9	12.8	16.5	6.8		
Australia			4.5	13.5	12.5	15.5

Table 7.5 Percentages of 11, 13 and 15-year-old Kiel pupils in 1992 and the same pupils in 1994 responding to the question: 'Which other country would you like to visit? *Why*?'

Reason	11/92 (13/94) (n = 204)	13/92 (15/94) (n = 139)	15/92 (17/94) (n = 59)
General interest	22.1 (10.3)	25.2 (22.3)	25.4 (35.5)
Wildlife / Countryside	18.6 (5.9)	19.4 (10.8)	28.8 (18.6)
Attractions	17.6 (5.4)		
The people	13.7 (2.9)		
Way of life	(2.5)	17.3	(22.0)
To learn language better	(2.5)		
Weather	9.3 (1.5)	7.2	
Hearsay	8.3 (3.4)		
Relatives	(2.5)		32.2
Other	4.0 (44.5)	19.4 (47.9)	6.8 (20.5)
No response	6.4 (18.6)	11.5 (19.0)	6.8 (3.4)

'Weil in England Mark Owen wohnt.' *'Because Mark Owen lives in England.'* (13 year old in 1994)

There is some evidence in response to the open question relating to the justification of the choice of preferred destination that other factors too are held to be important, such as wildlife, the countryside and the way of life (see Table 7.5).

Topping the list of justifications is 'general interest' which could cover any number of possible reasons. One of these may be the opportunity for England pupils to visit the places they have read about in their textbooks and to practise their English *in situ*. An additional country in the responses of the 13–15 cohort is Australia. This may reflect the advent of Australian soap operas on German television and how they became popular between 1992 and 1994. In addition, 4.5% of respondents in 1992 wish to visit Australia; this increases to 13.5% in 1994. Pupils in the 15–17 cohort withdraw any significant support for England on their list of countries to be visited and replace it largely with increased nominations for America (up to 38%) and Australia (up to 16%). France, the second foreign language of some of the respondents, does not feature significantly in the data relating to any of the cohorts. Does this reflect lack of interest or the likelihood that pupils will already have visited their near neighbours?

What an enviable motivational advantage the Kiel teacher of English appears to enjoy over her Leeds German-teaching colleague. What an enviable motivational advantage the teacher of English in almost any non-English speaking context is likely to enjoy over her foreign language-teaching colleague in the UK and arguably other parts of the English-speaking world. How ideal, how absolutely perfect for the teacher of English, that pupils with ambitions to travel most commonly identify English-speaking countries as chosen destinations. Germany wins some but few nominations from pupils in Leeds. The potential motivational difference between the Leeds and Kiel pupils, insofar as they believe that their ambitions to travel can be realised, must be huge. It is difficult to see how this situation can be turned around for Leeds pupils and their beleaguered German teachers. It seems that on the basis of this sample other countries cannot compete with Disneyland and pop stars in America and England and the soap operas of Australia. British television did its best to spread abroad a version of the culture of Germany when it ran the series *Schwarzwaldklinik* in the early 1990s. Sadly the programme did not attract many viewers. BBC Education is currently making laudable efforts to provide young language learners with an attractive, entertaining and informative view of today's Germany with a 'grown-up' approach in a number of series dealing with topical issues of import to the youth culture, e.g.: 'Fünf Wochen im Herbst'; 'Leute von heute'; 'Alltag'; 'Brennpunkte'. Germany too has its own version of Disneyland, *Phantasialand*. It is not on a scale, however, to rival its American counterpart. On this basis, America seems to hold the upper hand with Australia also playing an influential role.

Willingness to Learn Language of Country to be Visited

An attempt was made to take pupils' thoughts on travel a stage further in order to gain some insight into any ethnocentric and/or monolinguistic attitudes they may harbour. They were asked whether they would make efforts to learn the language of the country they would like to visit, should that language not be English, or in the case of Kiel pupils, German (see Table 7.6).

Pupils aged 11 in Leeds and Kiel respond with similar enthusiasm (no statistically significant difference) in their declared willingness not to depend on their mother-tongue. Two years later, however, Leeds pupils become significantly less willing to learn the foreign language (Wilcoxon Test: $Z = -3.41; p < 0.001$). The number providing a resounding 'No' doubles in the case of 13 year olds in 1994. To what can this be attributed? It may be a reflection of the general drop in the level of enthusiasm as reflected in other aspects of the findings for this cohort of pupils. It may have been easier at age 11 to say 'Yes' when little was known about the language learning process. After two years of formal teaching, the reality of foreign language learning may no longer seem so attractive. This idea would be more convincing, were not the trend for the 13–15 cohort similar. These Leeds 13 year olds already have experience of the language learning process yet respond with a resounding 'Yes' (81.5%) in 1992. Resounding 'Yes', but still significantly different from the very positive response of their Kiel peers: $\chi^2 = 8.18$; df = 2; $p < 0.05$. The 13 year olds in Kiel are only slightly less positive than they were two years before, with a higher proportion not sure whether they would learn the foreign language or not. But 15-year-old Kiel pupils are more decisive: 76.6% say 'Yes' (as opposed to 85.2% responding positively in 1992 at age 13) and 21.9% say 'No'.

As was the case for the Leeds 13 year olds in 1994, responses from 15 year olds in the same year reflect a drop in this figure to 67.6%. (It is interesting to note that at this age there is no statistically significant difference between the answers of Leeds and Kiel pupils.) What is clear is a general diminishment in enthusiasm over the two-year period. The difference in the two age cohorts is interesting. The 13–15 cohort appears

Table 7.6 Percentages of Leeds and Kiel pupils responding to the question: 'If the language of that country was not English (*Kiel: German*), would you try to learn it before you went?'

Response	Age/yr	Percentage: Leeds	Percentage: Kiel
No	11/92	18.9 ($n = 148$)	12.1 ($n = 190$)
	13/94	37.6 ($n = 149$)	3.5 ($n = 200$)
	13/92	17.6 ($n = 108$)	8.6 ($n = 128$)
	15/94	29.6 ($n = 108$)	21.9 ($n = 137$)
	15/92	23.1 ($n = 13$)	20.7 ($n = 58$)
	17/94	15.4 ($n = 13$)	44.1 ($n = 59$)
I don't know	11/92	4.7 ($n = 148$)	2.1 ($n = 190$)
	13/94	2.7 ($n = 149$)	20.5 ($n = 200$)
	13/92	0.9 ($n = 108$)	6.3 ($n = 128$)
	15/94	2.8 ($n = 108$)	1.5 ($n = 137$)
	15/92	0.0 ($n = 13$)	1.7 ($n = 58$)
	17/94	0.0 ($n = 13$)	5.1 ($n = 59$)
Yes	11/92	76.4 ($n = 148$)	85.8 ($n = 190$)
	13/94	59.7 ($n = 149$)	76.0 ($n = 200$)
	13/92	81.5 ($n = 108$)	85.2 ($n = 128$)
	15/94	67.6 ($n = 108$)	76.6 ($n = 137$)
	15/92	76.9 ($n = 13$)	77.6 ($n = 58$)
	17/94	84.6 ($n = 13$)	50.8 ($n = 59$)

to have had a much more positive start to their language learning experience in the years preceding the survey and so feel able to give a more enthusiastic response in the first round of questioning. The 11–13 cohort appears to have lost its enthusiasm at a more accelerated rate. Does this reflect a deterioration in teaching? A deterioration in learning conditions (which arguably could be linked with the added pressure concomitant with the National Curriculum and/or the reorganisation of schools which took place in Leeds around the same time)? A general malaise in the younger generation of secondary school pupils of today?

Pupils in the 15–17 cohort appear to be less put off by the reality of the language learning process (if that is where the problem lies). Between 10/13 and 11/13 over the two years declare a willingness to learn the foreign language if need be. This is hardly surprising given that these pupils have opted to take at least one foreign language at A-level. They share this positive view with their Kiel counterparts, with no significant difference in their responses.

When asked to justify their response, Leeds and Kiel pupils provide similar information (see Tables 7.7, 7.8).

The majority of those who would be prepared to learn the foreign language (e.g. 45.2% of Leeds 13 year olds and 54% of Kiel pupils the same age), see the utilitarian advantages of being able to communicate, to carry out basic transactions ('Because you don't want to get conned.' Leeds 13 year old in 1992; 'Um nicht ganz ausgetrickst zu werden' Kiel 13 year old in 1992 with exactly the same view) and in some cases (13–14% of 11 and 13-year-old Leeds pupils and 6.8% of 15-year-old Kiel pupils in 1992) 'to make friends'. A small number of pupils regard it as polite to make the effort. The minority claiming not to be prepared to learn the language would generally find it too much trouble (e.g. 14.8% Leeds 15 year olds and 7.8% of Kiel 13 year olds in 1994). The perception of pupils in Leeds and Kiel that everyone speaks English is a significant contributory factor to this response:

'They speak better English than I do.' (13 year old)
'Englisch als *lingua franca* genügt.' *'English as the lingua franca is sufficient.'* (13 year old)
'Englisch ist ja überall die 2. Sprache auf der Welt.' *'English is the second language all over the world.'* (15 year old)

As many as 20.3% of Kiel 17 year olds adopt this position. While this is rather disappointing in terms of pupils broadening their education and communicative competence, it confirms their appreciation of the importance of English. It does little to help the teacher of German in Leeds, however.

Table 7.7 Percentages of 11, 13 and 15-year-old Leeds pupils in 1992 and the same pupils in 1994 responding to the question: 'If the language of that country was not English, would you try to learn it before you went? *Why? /Why not?'*

Reason	11/92 (13/94) (n = 194)	13/92 (15/94) (n = 115)	15/92 (17/94) (n = 13)
Utility	30.4 (19.1)	45.2 (23.5)	69.2 (100.0)
To make friends	13.9	13.0	
Too much trouble/ Everyone speaks English	5.7 (7.8)	15.7 (14.8)	23.1 (7.7)
I don't like learning languages		6.1	
Other	12.9	(37.4)	7.7
No response	37.1 (77.3)	27.0 (24.3)	

(Some pupils provide responses appropriate to more than one category)

Table 7.8 Percentages of 11, 13 and 15-year-old Kiel pupils in 1992 and the same pupils in 1994 responding to the question: 'If the language of that country was not German, would you try to learn it before you went? *Why?/Why not?'*

Reason	11/92 (13/94) (n = 204)	13/92 (15/94) (n = 139)	15/92 (17/94) (n = 59)
Utility	64.2 (40.2)	54.0 (37.4)	50.8 (23.7)
To make friends			6.8
I like learning languages	3.4		
English is sufficient for all countries	2.9 (5.9)	(7.2)	8.5 (20.3)
Too much trouble	(7.8)		11.9
Other	7.4	23.0 (9.4)	10.1 (45.8)
No response	22.1 (21.6)	23.0 (46.0)	11.9 (10.2)

(Some pupils provide responses appropriate to more than one category)

Job in a Foreign Country?

Pupils' interest in the target language country, their curiosity and the extent of their 'integrative motivation' may be reflected yet further in their response to the question relating to any wish to work abroad (see Table 7.9).

Table 7.9 Percentages of pupils in Leeds and Kiel responding to the question: 'Would you consider trying to get a job in a foreign country when you leave school?'

Response	Age/yr	Percentage: Leeds	Percentage: Kiel
No	11/92	57.8 (n = 185)	33.7 (n = 199)
	13/94	51.9 (n = 162)	37.1 (n = 202)
	13/92	40.2 (n = 112)	33.1 (n = 139)
	15/94	44.2 (n = 113)	31.9 (n = 135)
	15/92	7.7 (n = 13)	22.8 (n = 57)
	17/94	38.5 (n = 13)	15.3 (n = 59)
I don't know	11/92	5.4 (n = 185)	5.5 (n = 199)
	13/94	6.8 (n = 185)	6.9 (n = 202)
	13/92	2.7 (n = 112)	9.4 (n = 139)
	15/94	4.4 (n = 113)	3.0 (n = 135)
	15/92		15.8 (n = 57)
	17/94		
Yes	11/92	36.8 (n = 185)	60.8 (n = 199)
	13/94	41.4 (n = 185)	55.9 (n = 202)
	13/92	57.1 (n = 112)	57.6 (n = 139)
	15/94	51.3 (n = 113)	65.2 (n = 135)
	15/92	92.3 (n = 13)	61.4 (n = 57)
	17/94	61.5 (n = 13)	84.7 (n = 59)

Leeds pupils do not find the prospect of working abroad unattractive and become more interested in the idea as they get older. Of the 13 pupils in the 15–17 cohort, 12 respond positively in 1992 and eight in 1994. Kiel pupils respond positively in higher numbers than those in Leeds in all age groups apart from age 15 in 1992. The difference is significant for 11 year olds in 1992 in Leeds and Kiel and the same pupils two years later (1992: χ^2 = 23.62; df 2; p < 0.05; 1994: χ^2 = 8.33; df 2; p < 0.05). The gap tends to narrow as pupils get older. There is no significant difference between the Leeds and Kiel cohorts 13/92, 15/94, 15/92 or 17/94.

While these data in themselves are interesting, the teacher of foreign languages may also be interested in the identification of the countries where the pupils would opt to work (see Table 7.10).

For the 11–13 cohort of Leeds pupils America holds sway over the target language country, although there are signs on the basis of this sample that Germany is becoming inceasingly attractive, certainly more attractive to 13 year olds in 1994 as a place of work than Spain and France. For the 13–15

Table 7.10 Percentages of Leeds pupils responding to the question: 'Which foreign country/countries (would you consider trying to get a job in)?'

Country	11/92 (n = 65)	13/94 (n = 66)	13/92 (n = 110)	15/94 (n = 103)	15/92 (n = 13)	17/94 (n = 13)
America	27.7	18.2	7.8	11.9		
Europe: various	9.2	10.6	29.7	16.9	41.7	12.5
Germany	7.7	12.1	10.9	10.2	23.1	50.0
France	4.6	6.1	18.8	20.3	8.3	37.5
Spain	12.3	10.6		10.2		
World: various	6.2	13.6	17.2	22.0		

cohort America is no longer as attractive as Europe with increasing interest shown in France and Germany. In terms of the response from the 15–17 Leeds cohort, America no longer features as a target country but is replaced by various European countries, Germany and France. So why these countries?

Generally Leeds learners of German choose not to justify their choice of country. Between 73.7% of 13 year olds and 30.8% of 17 year olds in 1994 offer no response. The expectation that responses would be much the same as for the question relating to justification for the choice of country pupils

Table 7.11 Percentages of 11, 13 and 15 year old Leeds pupils in 1992 and the same pupils in 1994 responding to the question: 'Would you consider trying to get a job in a foreign country when you leave school? In which country? *Why this country?*'

Reason	11/92 (13/94) (n = 194)	13/92 (15/94) (n = 115)	15/92 (17/94) (n = 13)
Availability of jobs	6.2 (6.7)	6.1 (13.0)	23.1
Attractions of foreign country	7.2 (5.7)	5.2	(30.8)
Dislike of England	2.6		
I speak the foreign language	(5.7)	14.8 (24.3)	38.5 (38.5)
They speak English		2.6	7.7
Weather		4.3	
Other	18.5 (8.2)	18.3 (15.7)	
No response	65.5 (73.7)	48.7 (47.0)	30.8 (30.8)

would like to visit was not met. Pupils who did respond give 'availability of jobs' as a justification. Notable are the percentages who are attracted to work in a given foreign country because they 'speak the foreign language' (e.g. of those providing a response 28.8% ($n = 59$) of 13 year olds in 1992; 45.9% ($n = 61$) of 15 year olds in 1994; 44.4% (i.e. 4/9) of 15 year olds in 1992 and 17 year olds in 1994). This offers some encouragement to the Leeds teacher of foreign languages that at least some pupils see this subject area as having some relevance to their future.

The idea that the language learning experience may contribute something to the arousal of interest in the target language country to seduce pupils away from the attractions of America and Australia is alluring. Responses suggest that as Leeds pupils learning German get older they appear more attracted to working in Europe and Germany and less in America and Australia. It is an idea which may lift the spirits of the teacher of German in Leeds but would need much closer investigation before any conclusions could be drawn. It must also be remembered that the small sample of Leeds 17 year olds consists of 13 pupils who have chosen German as one of their three or four A-level subjects.

The data provided by the Kiel pupils offer few surprises. Two target language countries, America and England, are by far the most attractive working contexts for Kiel pupils in all age groups. It is interesting to note that the interest in England drops from 23.3% for 13 year olds in 1992 to 5.7% for the same pupils in 1994. This seems to be replaced by an increasing interest in world travel (12.8% in 1992; 30.7% in 1994). Interest in England revives in the 15–17 cohort and even outstrips America in the case of 15 year olds in 1992.

Do Kiel pupils choose to nominate America and England for reasons other than linguistic? Pupils were asked to justify their response. As was the case for Leeds pupils, many chose not to answer and those who did provided such a wide range of justification that categorisation proved very difficult. The most popular justifications were general interest (e.g. 22.3% of 13 year olds in 1992), and the beauty of the country (e.g. 13.6% of 17 year olds in 1994). The ability to speak the language of the chosen country (quite likely to be English for the majority of pupils) appears also to be a factor across the cohorts (e.g. of those providing a response 21.3% ($n = 108$) of 11 year olds in 1992; 17.6% ($n = 68$) of 15 year olds in 1994; 15.7% ($n = 51$) of 15 year olds in 1992).

Whatever the reason for pupils' choice of England, America or Australia, the Kiel teacher of English is likely to enjoy the benefit of more highly motivated pupils in the classroom than is the case for her colleague teaching German in Leeds. The Kiel teacher of French, however, in the absence of specific references from pupils to that country, may empathise rather more with her Leeds colleagues.

Attitude to the Germans, French and British

Having accessed pupils' views on countries they would like to visit and possibly work in, an attempt was made to gain insights into their perceptions of the peoples of other countries. If they liked and disliked German/French people, this may perhaps have an influence on their attitude to German/French lessons (see Gardner & Lambert, 1972: 14ff.). Following the example of Gardner and Lambert's battery of ethnocentricity questions (1972: 132) Leeds pupils were asked to describe each of German, French and British people on two occasions two years apart. The same applied to Kiel pupils. It was felt appropriate to ask the Leeds and Kiel pupils what they thought of their own peoples, given the opportunity this offered them to provide nationalistic views or indeed a dislike for their own people which may replicate or contrast with their views of other nationalities. It was noted whether pupils completed the sentence 'I think German/French/British people are . . . ' with a positive or a negative adjective or indicated that people were varied, in that some were nice, for example, and some not so nice. The inter-rater reliability for independent classification of a random sample of 30 responses was 29/30 or 96%. The categories of description were transformed into numerical data (0 = negative; 1 = non-committal; 2 = positive) to allow the application of the Wilcoxon Matched-Pairs Signed-Ranks Test (see Table 7.12.).

More than half the Leeds 11 year olds are positive about German people and around one-third negative. Responses two years later indicate that Leeds pupils become more positive and less negative about German people as they get older. This trend is reversed with results from the 13–15 cohort of pupils (where the difference is significant: $Z = -2.61$; $p < 0.05$). Interview responses indicate that this may be as a result of having met Germans on exchange visits either in Leeds or Germany and having found the experience less than positive.

> 'Germans talk too fast.' (11 year old)
> 'All Germans are like auntie.' (11 year old in 1992)
> 'The country is in a very bad state and I don't like the government.' (13 year old in 1992)
> 'I hate Germans.' (13 year old in 1994)
> 'They wear weird clothes and ride bikes.' (15 year old in 1994)

All pupils in the 15–17 cohort regard Germans either positively or as 'varied'.
Interviewees were asked on what experiential basis they made their

Table 7.12 Percentage of pupils who completed the sentence: *I think German people are* . . .

I think German people are . . .	Age/Year	Percentage: Leeds	Percentage: Kiel
Negative	11/92	31.3 ($n = 163$)	45.9 ($n = 185$)
	13/94	28.6 ($n = 175$)	52.5 ($n = 200$)
	13/92	15.3 ($n = 111$)	46.4 ($n = 125$)
	15/94	23.2 ($n = 112$)	53.0 ($n = 134$)
	15/92	0.0 ($n = 13$)	66.1 ($n = 56$)
	17/94	0.0 ($n = 12$)	74.1 ($n = 58$)
I don't know	11/92	11.0 ($n = 163$)	1.1 ($n = 185$)
	13/94	6.3 ($n = 175$)	6.5 ($n = 200$)
	13/92	8.1 ($n = 111$)	0.0 ($n = 125$)
	15/94	15.2 ($n = 112$)	6.0 ($n = 134$)
	15/92	0.0 ($n = 13$)	3.6 ($n = 56$)
	17/94	0.0 ($n = 12$)	3.4 ($n = 58$)
Positive	11/92	52.8 ($n = 163$)	37.3 ($n = 185$)
	13/94	55.4 ($n = 175$)	28.5 ($n = 200$)
	13/92	70.3 ($n = 111$)	39.2 ($n = 125$)
	15/94	49.1 ($n = 112$)	25.4 ($n = 134$)
	15/92	69.2 ($n = 13$)	16.1 ($n = 56$)
	17/94	83.3 ($n = 12$)	6.9 ($n = 58$)
Varied	11/92	4.9 ($n = 163$)	15.7 ($n = 185$)
	13/94	9.7 ($n = 175$)	12.0 ($n = 200$)
	13/92	6.3 ($n = 111$)	14.4 ($n = 125$)
	15/94	12.5 ($n = 112$)	15.6 ($n = 134$)
	15/92	30.8 ($n = 13$)	14.3 ($n = 56$)
	17/94	16.6 ($n = 12$)	15.5 ($n = 58$)

judgement of the Germans. On the basis of the 10% sample, visitors to the school appear to be the most likely source of influence for 11 year olds. As pupils get older, however, they are more likely to base their judgement on meeting Germans on exchange and holidays both in Germany and in other countries.

Some 11 year old pupils in Kiel are very critical of their own people. This self-criticism increases over the two years between 1992 and 1994 and is reflected also in the responses of the 13–15 cohort and even more in the 15–17 cohort. The difference between 1992 and 1994 for each cohort is not significant however. Perhaps the negative response is not surprising in an age where pupils in Germany engage in examination of the country's history of the last 60 years and more recently where the Right has been becoming increasingly active and vociferous and attacks on ethnic minorities have become more numerous and more vicious. (See 'Lessons to curb rise of neo-Nazi extremism' in *Times Educational Supplement*, 3.7.98.)

Year 11 Leeds pupils seem a little more fond of the French than they are of the Germans. Their view changes significantly, however, two years later ($Z = -2.47$; $p < 0.05$). This is also the trend with the 13–15 cohort ($Z = -2.46$; $p < 0.05$). Again interview responses suggest that this may be as a result of exchange visits but in this case where the experience has been less than positive. Pupils in the 15–17 cohort are more positive about the French than the Germans at age 15 (eight out of these 13 pupils take French as well as German), but also opt for the 'negative' option rather than 'varied'. Aged 17 they are slightly less positive. Not too much should be read into this difference, given the small sample.

Kiel 11 year olds and 13 year olds in 1992 are significantly more positive than their Leeds counterparts ($\chi^2 = 24.56$; df 3; $p < 0.0001$) but change their views significantly after two years ($Z = -3.04$; $p < 0.05$) whilst maintaining the difference between them and Leeds: $\chi^2 = 31.04$; df 4; $p < 0.0001$. The percentage describing the French in negative terms increases from 9.3% to 23.0% between 1992 to and 1994. Similarly the figure for a positive response drops from 73.1% to 53.5% in the case of the 11–13 cohort of 1992/94 and 79.3% to 49.6% for the 13–15 cohort of the same years. This too represents a significant difference ($Z = -3.95$; $p < 0.0001$). Again the statistically significant difference in the reponse of Kiel and Leeds pupils is maintained, showing signs of diminishing as pupils get older: 13/92: $\chi^2 = 25.37$; df 3; $p < 0.001$; 15/94: $\chi^2 = 9.79$; df 4; $p < 0.05$. In the 15–17 cohort the positive response is halved significantly between 1992 (63.5%) and 1994 (32.7%) years ($Z = -2.65$; $p < 0.05$). There is no significant difference between the responses of Leeds and Kiel pupils.

Can the experience of French people in the course of the two years really have been so dreadful? ('Ich war letztes Jahr in Paris. Es war einfach schrecklich!' *'I was in Paris last year. It was simply dreadful.'* Year 10 pupil. 'Die Franzosen sind total langweilig. Ich war eine Zeitlang in Frankreich. Da war überhaupt nichts los.' *'The French are completely boring. I was in France for a while. There was absolutely nothing going on there.'* Year 6 pupil.) Or are there other/additional factors to which the difference can be attributed? ('Die Franzosen sind langweilig. Das sind nur Vorurteile.' *'The French are boring. These are merely prejudices.'* Year 10 pupil. 'Die Franzosen sind nett und freundlich – das weiß ich aus Erzählung her und vom Fernsehen und Nachrichten.' *'The French are nice and friendly. I know this from hearsay and from television and the news.'* Year 8 pupil.) May it be the case that they no longer like their French lessons and/or their French teacher and transfer this mindset to all things French? ('Französisch kann ich nicht leiden. Die

Lehrerin auch nicht!'. *I can't stand French. I can't stand the teacher either!* Year 8 pupil.) There is also the tendency for Kiel pupils to be rather more hesitant to offer a view than is the case with Leeds pupils of the same age. ('Das kann ich nicht beurteilen. Ich kenne keine Franzosen.' *'I can't judge. I don't know any French people.'* Year 8 pupil.) (See Table 7.13.)

In terms of self-criticism, Leeds pupils regard themselves in a much more positive light than Kiel pupils do. There is evidence of little change in view over the two years of the survey, the only difference manifesting itself in the form of an increase in the 'varied' category.

Kiel pupils are more positive about the British than they are about the French. Responses in interviews suggest that pupils base their judgement on their knowledge of English people that they know ('Ich habe Verwandte in England.' *'I have relatives in England.'* Year 10 pupil) as well as experience

Table 7.13 Percentage of Leeds and Kiel pupils who completed the sentence: *I think French people are . . . .*

I think French people are ...	Age/Year	Percentage: Leeds	Percentage: Kiel
Negative	11/92	26.8 ($n = 168$)	9.3 ($n = 182$)
	13/94	38.2 ($n = 173$)	23.0 ($n = 200$)
	13/92	26.5 ($n = 113$)	8.3 ($n = 121$)
	15/94	36.6 ($n = 112$)	21.4 ($n = 131$)
	15/92	15.4 ($n = 13$)	19.2 ($n = 52$)
	17/94	23.1 ($n = 13$)	38.2 ($n = 55$)
I don't know	11/92	8.9 ($n = 168$)	15.9 ($n = 182$)
	13/94	4.6 ($n = 173$)	20.5 ($n = 200$)
	13/92	2.7 ($n = 113$)	6.6 ($n = 121$)
	15/94	8.9 ($n = 112$)	13.7 ($n = 131$)
	15/92	0.0 ($n = 13$)	7.7 ($n = 52$)
	17/94	0.0 ($n = 13$)	16.4 ($n = 55$)
Positive	11/92	58.9 ($n = 168$)	73.1 ($n = 182$)
	13/94	48.6 ($n = 173$)	53.5 ($n = 200$)
	13/92	54.0 ($n = 113$)	79.3 ($n = 121$)
	15/94	35.7 ($n = 112$)	49.6 ($n = 131$)
	15/92	76.9 ($n = 13$)	63.5 ($n = 52$)
	17/94	61.5 ($n = 13$)	32.7 ($n = 55$)
Varied	11/92	5.4 ($n = 168$)	1.6 ($n = 182$)
	13/94	8.7 ($n = 173$)	3.0 ($n = 200$)
	13/92	16.8 ($n = 113$)	5.8 ($n = 121$)
	15/94	18.8 ($n = 112$)	15.3 ($n = 131$)
	15/92	7.7 ($n = 13$)	9.6 ($n = 52$)
	17/94	15.4 ($n = 13$)	12.7 ($n = 55$)

Table 7.14 Percentage of Leeds and Kiel pupils who completed the sentence: *I think British people are . . .*

I think British people are . . .	Age/Year	Percentage: Leeds	Percentage: Kiel
Negative	11/92	20.9 ($n = 182$)	4.8 ($n = 186$)
	13/94	22.4 ($n = 183$)	12.6 ($n = 199$)
	13/92	26.3 ($n = 114$)	3.2 ($n = 126$)
	15/94	21.2 ($n = 113$)	10.5 ($n = 133$)
	15/92	38.5 ($n = 13$)	19.6 ($n = 56$)
	17/94	38.5 ($n = 13$)	24.1 ($n = 58$)
I don't know	11/92	1.6 ($n = 182$)	11.3 ($n = 186$)
	13/94	0.0 ($n = 183$)	15.1 ($n = 199$)
	13/92	1.8 ($n = 114$)	7.9 ($n = 126$)
	15/94	1.8 ($n = 113$)	9.8 ($n = 133$)
	15/92	0.0 ($n = 13$)	5.4 ($n = 56$)
	17/94	0.0 ($n = 13$)	10.3 ($n = 58$)
Positive	11/92	63.7 ($n = 182$)	83.3 ($n = 186$)
	13/94	53.6 ($n = 183$)	66.8 ($n = 199$)
	13/92	42.1 ($n = 114$)	81.7 ($n = 126$)
	15/94	41.6 ($n = 113$)	68.4 ($n = 133$)
	15/92	30.8 ($n = 13$)	66.1 ($n = 56$)
	17/94	30.8 ($n = 13$)	41.4 ($n = 58$)
Varied	11/92	13.7 ($n = 182$)	0.5 ($n = 186$)
	13/94	23.5 ($n = 183$)	5.5 ($n = 199$)
	13/92	29.8 ($n = 114$)	7.1 ($n = 126$)
	15/94	35.4 ($n = 113$)	11.3 ($n = 133$)
	15/92	30.8 ($n = 13$)	8.9 ($n = 56$)
	17/94	30.8 ($n = 13$)	24.1 ($n = 58$)

of visits to England ('Interessant. Ich war mal in London. Es war einfach toll da.' *'Interesting. I was in London once. It was simply brilliant there.'* Year 10 pupil). As was the case with the French, however, something happens in the course of the years between 1992 and 1994 to dampen their positive response which drops significantly, for example, from a most enthusiastic 83.3% at age 11 to a more conservative 66.8% at age 13 ($Z = -2.03$; $p < 0.05$). What are the reasons for this? Can it be the case that getting to know native speakers and visits to the target language country can have such a negative influence? Or does perhaps a developing maturity bring a more critical view?

There is nothing in the data to suggest that the Leeds learners of German or Kiel learners of English are ethnocentric in their views. On the basis of these results (a limited basis admittedly) there may even be a hint that Kiel pupils are quite the antithesis of ethnocentric in that they are extremely critical of the German people. Whether this has a positive effect in terms of motivation to learn other languages is open to question. It is interesting that as Leeds pupils' enthusiasm for learning German diminishes, so does their positive estimation of the Germans (and the French). It would be foolish to conclude that the two are connected, however, not only in the presence of numerous other factors in the equation but also in the light of a similar trend among German pupils for a diminishing positive response to the British and French but the contrasting trend of maintained and even enhanced enthusiasm for learning English.

Summary

It would probably be erroneous to base the enthusiasm which 11-year-old Leeds pupils bring to the foreign language learning classroom on their experience of travel and certainly not on their first-hand experience of Germany. Over a third of Year 7 pupils claim never to have been in a foreign country. The remaining pupils are more likely to have visited Spain than Germany. The proportion with experience abroad increases as pupils get older as does the number who have visited Germany, albeit slightly, insofar as one can judge. How beneficial such visits are in terms of heightening awareness of the usefulness of German, on the basis of these data, is open to question.

Concomitant with the youthful enthusiasm for foreign languages which 11 year olds bring is their liking of peoples of other nations, certainly the Germans and the French. It is a little disturbing, however, that increased experience of travel and of exchange visits between the age of 11 and 13, and again between 13 and 15 seems to have a slightly negative influence on this and also the willingness to learn the languages of other countries. This appears to have less to do with a developing ethnocentric attitude and rather more with an awareness of what language learning entails. Why submit oneself to all that hard work when it is possible to get by in English, almost regardless of where one is in the world? The above trend is reversed, as one might expect, in the 15–17 cohort.

America and Australia are the countries which Leeds pupils generally wish to visit, although a small but increasing number over the two years show interest in Germany, especially in the 15–17 cohort. For Leeds teachers of German this may be a case of too little interest, too late. If pupils' justifications for their choice may be taken as reliable indicators, the advent of the Australian soap opera to British and German television appears to be influential. Should this be the case it is to be regretted that *Schwarzwaldklinik*, a German soap opera shown on British television for a short time, failed to attract many viewers. What may be needed to contribute to the enhancement of the status of Germany and the Germans in the minds of secondary school pupils, is a television series set in the target language country and dealing with situations of interest to teenagers and of relevance to their reality. Teachers of German would almost certainly welcome the motivating potential of a television programme with the possibility of exploitation in the classroom. The BBC is currently doing its best to facilitate them with their new breed of language programmes. (See p. 103) It is also collaborating with the Goethe-Institut in delivering workshops on how teachers and pupils can use the programmes in the classroom. (See the *Programme of Events September-December* 1998, published by the Goethe-Institut.)

Kiel pupils have more experience of travel abroad, certainly within Europe, at an earlier age than their Leeds peers. They are very positive about other nationalities but extremely negative about themselves. Leeds teachers of German must look at their colleagues who teach English in Kiel with some envy in that the countries which Kiel pupils in these age groups wish to visit are the countries where English is spoken. Germans are unlikely to get by easily with their own language in America and England. In theory, at least, extrinsic motivation should not be a problem in English lessons for a significant number of learners. Having said that, Kiel pupils also reflect the Leeds trend of diminishing enthusiasm for learning a new language. In spite of the fact that they are less likely to get by with their mother-tongue than their Leeds peers, they become increasingly negative as they get older. They too may be painfully aware of the amount of work involved and of the fact that they too are likely to get by with English, albeit their first foreign language.

Pupils' level of interest in getting a job in a foreign country, having left school, may provide some indication of the extent to which they feel inextricably tied to their mother country. The prospect of working abroad is attractive to only about a third of Leeds pupils at age 11 and this proportion increases to over a half at age 13 (1992) and again at age 15 (1994). It may be expected that 11 year olds feel put off by the prospect of prolonged periods far from home. By the age of 13 and 15, however, some may have had some/more experience of travel abroad and/or exchange visits. Increasing maturity and consciousness of current affairs may bring an awareness of the importance of finding meaningful, gainful employment which may not always be available on the doorstep. Kiel pupils are more enthusiastic with only a third across the age groups preferring to work at home. Working abroad for Kiel pupils may mean only a drive of a few hours between home and the workplace. The stretch of water between the UK and the European mainland may make working abroad an altogether more daunting prospect.

The questions relating to how Leeds learners of German and Kiel learners of English (and French) feel about the Germans, French and British provide some interesting insights. Generally Kiel pupils are more positive about the British and the French than Leeds pupils are about the Germans and the French. This may be as a result of the potential for more immediate contact with other European mainlanders than may be the case for Leeds pupils. The latter may fall victims to the propaganda of the popular press. (See Chapter 3, p. 45.) Pupils become less positive about other peoples as they get older. Experience (of visitors to the school; exchanges; holidays) or a difference in the criteria they apply for judging other peoples leads to a generally more negative response in 1994 than was the case in 1992. This applies to both Leeds and Kiel pupils and is particularly apparent with the 13–15 cohort. May this be an indicator of a negative consequence of exchange programmes? On the basis of these data, it may be the case that pupils meet Germans and French of the same age, be this in France/Germany, Leeds or elsewhere, and make a negative assessment of the experience. The reality fails to meet up with the expectation and the pupils generalise from the one experience. An exception to this negative development in judgement of German people is of course the 15–17 cohort of Leeds learners of German. None of these 13 pupils makes a negative judgement on the German people. They judge the Germans either positively or as varied as any other nation. Perhaps the more cautious view of the 13–15 cohorts should not give grounds for concern. Bjørg (1988) conducted a study involving 170 foreign students in Norway, which examined the hypothesis that it was important for students in a foreign country to have a sound and critical but not hostile attitude to the host people. The findings of the study suggest a relationship between a balanced and critical attitude to the target language people and proficiency in the target language.

Leeds pupils tend to judge German people more positively than the French. This may perhaps be expected in a survey which focuses on learners of German. The general trend of a negative development between 1992 and 1994 is maintained with the difference tending to be more significant in the case of Kiel pupils than for Leeds. This again may be an indication of a negative influence of exchanges and the risk of expectations and reality not meeting.

Kiel pupils are extremely negative in their judgement of the Germans and this becomes more acute as pupils get older and in the interim between the survey points in 1992 and 1994. Leeds pupils tend to be less self-critical with only 20–26% in the 11–13 and 13–15 cohorts offering a negative view of British people. In the 15–17 cohort the trend is more negative with 5/13 providing a negative adjective. The response of Kiel pupils may reflect the times in which they are living. Reunification of Germany brought with it an influx of foreign asylum seekers, increased pressure on the economy, increased unemployment and with it the rise of the Right and numerous racist attacks, some resulting in fatalities. This forces German secondary school pupils to look at themselves as a race and debate the crucial issues. To this should be added that part of the school curriculum which covers the history of two world wars. In the light of this it is perhaps hardly surprising that the self-assessment is less than positive.

By contrast, Leeds pupils see themselves in a positive light, decreasingly so as they get older. Rather than select the negative option as opposed to the positive, increasing numbers choose to describe the British as 'varied'. It is perhaps a little surprising that pupils with an awareness that some British people can be described positively and some negatively, do not think it appropriate to apply this to other peoples too. Why should they be inherently different? Leeds pupils have perhaps had less opportunity to indulge in self-examination with a negative outcome, certainly in terms of the history curriculum. Perhaps as a result of the difference in the histories of the last 60 years, racist incidents in the UK have not had the national and international coverage in the media which might stimulate a negative response from Leeds pupils on the same scale as from those in Kiel.

Leeds teachers of German must long to share a 'level playing field' with their English teaching Kiel colleagues. Kiel pupils perceive more opportunities to use English than do their Leeds peers with regard to German; more Kiel pupils claim to intend to use their English competence later in the world of work; Kiel pupils wish to visit English-speaking countries; Leeds pupils would prefer to visit English-speaking countries (America and Australia) than Germany. In the relative absence of extrinsic factors such as those above to motivate their German learning pupils, Leeds teachers must endeavour to provide a positive in-school experience to compensate. Pupils' views of their learning experience will be the focus of attention in the following chapter.

Chapter 8

The Pupils' Perspective from the Classroom

This chapter provides an insight into pupils' views of the in-school foreign language learning experience. They provide information on their likes and dislikes, the factors which influence their opinions and are also given the opportunity to make suggestions as to how they feel their experience could be improved. Based on this evidence, broad suggestions are made as to those areas to which teachers should perhaps be giving attention in their classroom-based foreign language provision.

Introduction

> Why do I have to learn German? I want to be a car mechanic. I'll never go to Germany. What do I need German for? (13 year old boy in Leeds comprehensive school)

How do you answer this pupil's perfectly reasonable question? He is unlikely to appreciate references to job opportunities in the wider European Community, tolerance, understanding, insights provided into a foreign culture or the transferable skills which foreign language learning develops. (Council of Europe 1996: 6)

'Disaffected', 'demotivated', 'switched off' pupils provide a major challenge for their teachers – and not only those of modern foreign languages! How often do conversations take place over coffee in staffrooms on the topic of how a given pupil in Year 9 was so sullen, uncooperative and disinterested, when in Year 7 she had been so full of enthusiasm and vitality? Around the age of 13 things seem to start going wrong for some pupils. The eagerness to learn, the commitment, the thirst for knowledge appears to dissipate. Barber (1994b) found that 'more than 70% of 13–14 year olds say they count the minutes to the end of a lesson'. Sue Harris (in O'Connor, 1994) also found disaffection setting in around this age as Year 8 pupils articulated their resentment at what they saw as restrictive rules and regulations.

The number of in-service courses (Mill Wharf; Goethe-Institut; Leeds and Bristol Comenius Centres; CILT), conferences on the subject (the author has given papers on the subject of motivation and foreign language learning at a dozen different conferences between 1992 and 1998) and publications on how to tackle the problem (Alison, 1993; Chambers 1993, 1994; Convery & Coyle, 1993; Crookes & Schmidt, 1991; Evans, 1993; Maley & Duff, 1994 provide an interesting and comprehensive overview of research into motivation in mainstream education but in a non-UK, non-subject specific context) seem to reflect a niche in the market catering for teachers of languages. Teachers of German at a Goethe-Institut conference in Leeds ('Motivation im Deutschunterricht', 21 March 1994) argued that they felt more challenged than their colleagues in other subject areas as they had to deal not only with the attitudinal and social problems associated with motivation to learn, but also felt an obligation to spend the lion's share of their time interacting with the pupils in the target language rather than English.

The multifarious factors which contribute to a pupil's motivation to learn can be crudely allocated to two very broad categories: perceived usefulness; perceived enjoyment. The teacher has a contribution to make in both areas but cannot be held solely responsible for the vast spider's web which constitutes motivation. Society, government, parents, friends, the media, self-esteem, success, failure, *inter alia*, are also influential. These influences have a bearing on the mindset which the foreign language learner brings to the classroom. Arguably this is the context where the teacher has most control. She provides and/or facilitates the learning experience. Some form of quality control has to take place to determine whether the provision is appropriate. Level of performance may be one measure of quality. The nature of pupil response to the learning experience may be another. The latter suggested measure is the focus of this chapter.

Plus ça change?

What do secondary school pupils think of their in-school experience? What can we learn from their views? Not that pupils' views have been neglected. The work of the Assessment of Performance Unit (APU) (DES/DENI/WO 1985, 1986 and 1987; see Chapter 3, p. 31 ff) provides useful insights into pupils' likes and dislikes in the foreign language learning classroom. They liked 'listening to French on the tape-recorder' but disliked 'answering the teacher's questions in French about a tape . . . ' They liked 'talking to the French assistant', although over half the pupils surveyed had never had such an opportunity. The most unpopular of any of the speaking and reading activities was 'Reading aloud in French to the

Table 8.1 Most liked activities

	Boys (%)	Girls (%)	All (%)
Playing games or doing puzzles	46	42	44
Drawing pictures, maps, diagrams	44	32	39
Watching a film, slides about France	26	16	22

Table 8.2 Most disliked activities

	Boys (%)	Girls (%)	All (%)
Learning verbs	30	38	34
Reading aloud in French to the class	26	30	28
Learning lists of French words	19	25	22

class'. (DES/DENI/WO, 1986: 221–2). It still goes on. The 1985 report (DES/DENI/WO, 1987: 63–4) drew up tables for the top three most liked and disliked activities (see Tables 8.1, 8.2).

These findings are for the most part the same for today as they were for the mid-1980s. The only feature which may reflect a certain 'datedness' is the absence of any reference to computers. (See Chambers, 1994 and Phillips & Filmer-Sankey, 1993 for pupils' likes and dislikes.) At the time of the APU survey, computers were less common in the home, in schools and did not form part of any pupil-entitlement on the school curriculum. (The APU surveys pre-date the introduction of the National Curriculum.) Improved user-friendliness of hardware, sinking prices and a glut of entertaining and educational software have increased computer availability in the home while the National Curriculum requires greater accessibility in schools.

Pupils are always likely to enjoy games and puzzles as they divert them from the grind of what they may perceive as work. Drawing is similar in that it is different from the 'normal' foreign language learning diet of practising the four skills/attainment targets of listening and responding, speaking, reading and responding, and writing (with the emphasis predominantly on listening and speaking). Some teachers will confess – off the record – to resorting to 'colouring-in' tasks on wet Friday afternoons; the pupils may learn little French/German/Spanish but at least they are quiet.

Watching films, now conveniently on video, and television programmes

Table 8.3 Activities not perceived by pupils as part of formal lessons

Activity	% responding 'Not done'
Talking to the French assistant	58
Making a recording of yourself speaking French	54
Doing a project on France	45
Watching a television or video programme in French	38
Singing French songs	37
Reading French magazines or storybooks by yourself	36
Talking in English about a French story you have read	30
Watching a film or slides about France	30
Writing in French about something you did	29
Writing a made-up story in French	28
Writing a letter in French	27

are still enjoyed but mostly, I suspect, because of novelty value. Slide-shows rarely feature in the modern languages classroom of the 1990s.The reference to this activity in Table 8.3 as 'Not done' suggests that this may have been the case in the 1980s as I suggest it is today. A GCSE syllabus driven by transactional language and the National Curriculum demand for interaction in the target code leave little room for lessons devoted to cultural awareness (Wright, 1996). Do you remember how much you enjoyed your teacher's anecdotes about her year abroad as an English language assistant? I still remember Dessie Johnstone (now HMI for Modern Languages in Northern Ireland) telling us about his adventures on a scooter travelling through France and Germany.

The major feature which contrasts this table with the preceding one is the predictable shift of emphasis from fun to work. Which pupils of any era are going to vote for work rather than fun? Learning verbs and vocabulary are a *sine qua non* for the long hard slog towards foreign language competence. (Michel Thomas would dispute this, *The Knowledge*, BBC2, 23 March 1997.) I would like to be in a position to suggest that the communicative era has seen the demise of reading aloud as a common feature of the language learning experience. Sadly this appears not to be the case (Chambers, 1994). Individual pupils are still invited to read aloud texts which they do not understand or which they may not even have seen before. Other pupils are subjected, more often than not, to an excruciating listening experience. Pupils, be they readers or listeners, still hate it. No change here. What does anyone gain from this?

The APU report (DES/DENI/WO, 1987: 63) also reveals interesting insights into potentially useful and enjoyable activities which pupils claim not to experience in French. Is it an eternal truth that pupils/children/people invariably enjoy most that which they do not do or do least? Pupils surveyed by the APU appear to be asking for a learning experience which includes a real reason to speak, access to technology, the opportunity to work independently and learn autonomously, and more reading and writing which is meaningful to them. Is this a case of *plus ça change*? Have pupils' views changed in the interim? Have the communicative approach and the advent of the National Curriculum altered pupils' perceptions of their in-school language learning experience?

What the Pupils Think

In Chapter 5 (p. 79 ff) there was some evidence to suggest that the enthusiasm which pupils brought with them from primary school for foreign language learning and German in particular was rather dampened by the reality of the first two years of the experience in the secondary school. This view is supported by answers given in 1994 by Leeds pupils, now 13 year olds in Year 9, to the question on how much they liked German compared to other subjects. Although not part of the 11–13 cohort, results relating to 13 year olds in 1992 (13–15 cohort) are also provided because of the interesting differences, not least between the Leeds pupils (see Table 8.4).

The mean of 2.73 for 13-year-old Leeds pupils again provides a less than encouraging picture. The data for the 1992 13 year olds are significantly more positive, however (Mann-Whitney non-parametric test for two independent samples: $Z = -5.6$; $p < 0.0001$). Why this discrepancy? Reasons for one group of 13 year olds being more positive than another are open to speculation. A potential contributory factor, but one lacking in substantial evidence to support it, may be the different models of modern language provision of the schools in which the pupils learn German, in the light of the promotion of a programme of diversification in Leeds schools (see Chapter 4, Table 4.2). Given that diversification was in a very early phase

Table 8.4 Percentages of 13-year-old (Year 9) Leeds pupils in 1992 and 1994 indicating how much they liked German compared to all other subjects

	Not at all		Neutral		Very much			
Place/year	1	2	3	4	5	Sample	Mean	S.D.
Leeds/94	15.5	21.8	41.5	16.6	4.7	193	2.73	1.06
Leeds/92	1.8	10.5	41.2	37.7	8.8	114	3.41	0.86

in 1992, 13 year olds in two of the schools in that year had only one year's German experience on which to base their responses to survey questions. It may well be the case that the novelty of learning a new language, a factor to which pupils attach importance in responses to open and interview questions, may not have worn off. Thirteen year olds in 1994, however, in three out of the four schools, had at least two full years' experience. Perhaps by the end of the second year of German the novelty was starting to wear off as the emphasis shifted from the 'fun' element and more towards the rigour of grammar and development of linguistic sophistication and diversity.

Given the apparent diminution in enthusiasm, pupils were asked a battery of questions on their perceptions of the in-school foreign language learning experience. What were their likes and dislikes? What were the factors which influenced their views on what goes on in the classroom? How did they feel the in-school experience could be enhanced? They were asked the same questions again after two years. Could this help identify what it is that leads to the apparent diminution in enthusiasm for learning (languages) after Year 7 or 8 (pupils aged 11/12 years)?

Pupils in the 13–15 and 15–17 cohorts were asked to consider a range of foreign language learning activities and rate them on a scale of 1–5. They were also given the opportunity in open questions and interviews to add to and justify their responses. (The 11–13 cohort is not included here. The 11 year olds were surveyed at the very beginning of their secondary school experience and so were not in a position to give an informed response to questions on the language learning experience which they were yet to have. They were in a position to respond two years later. These data have been omitted, however, given that no comparison can be made between two sets of responses two years apart, which is the case for the other two cohorts.) (See Table 8.5.)

In six out of the seven categories in which answers are provided in both years there is a drop in the mean. When the paired samples t-test[1] was applied, it was found that in four of the categories the difference was statistically significant:

group work: $t = 2.71$, df = 78, $p < 0.05$
writing: $t = 3.88$, df = 112, $p < 0.001$
reading: $t = 2.86$, df = 93, $p < 0.05$
speaking: $t = 3.68$, df = 113, $p < 0.001$

It is interesting that these should include three out of the four basic skills or 'Attainment Targets' (ATs) (listening and responding; speaking; reading and responding; writing). Whether pupils' experience of German learning

Table 8.5 Percentage of Leeds pupils (13–15 cohort) who responded to the question: 'How much do you enjoy the following activities in German lessons?

Activity	Age/yr	I do not like this at all 1	2	I don't mind this 3	4	I enjoy this 5	Not done[a]	Sample	Mean[b]	S.D.[b]
Computer	13/92	0.9	3.5	0.9	3.5	7.9	83.3	114	3.84	1.39
	15/94	1.7	1.7	0.9	1.7	5.2	88.7	115	3.61	1.61
Pair work	13/92	0.0	6.1	15.7	31.3	43.5	3.5	115	4.16	0.92
	15/94	0.0	0.0	20.9	38.3	40.0	0.9	115	4.19	0.76
Group work	13/92	0.0	4.4	19.3	28.1	32.5	15.8	114	4.05	0.91
	15/94	1.7	5.2	29.6	22.6	24.3	16.5	115	3.75	1.02
Project/ Coursework[c]	13/92 15/94	5.3	5.3	11.4	8.8	1.8	67.5	114	2.89	1.15
Speaking	13/92	7.0	10.5	34.2	24.6	23.7	0.0	114	3.47	1.17
	15/94	10.4	15.7	44.3	22.6	7.0	0.0	115	3.00	1.04
Reading	13/92	3.5	9.6	35.1	24.6	13.2	14.0	114	3.40	1.01
	15/94	7.0	14.9	43.0	21.9	4.4	8.8	114	3.02	0.96
Listening exercise	13/92	9.6	17.5	41.2	21.1	10.5	0.0	114	3.05	1.10
	15/94	11.3	20.9	43.5	20.9	3.5	0.0	115	2.84	0.10
Writing exercise	13/92	6.2	8.8	40.7	30.1	14.2	0.0	113	3.37	1.04
	15/94	9.6	12.2	53.9	20.0	4.4	0.0	115	2.97	0.94

[a] 'Not done' – to indicate activities which pupils feel they do not engage in in class.
[b] Includes only those pupils who claim to participate in activities, i.e. excludes those under 'not done'.
[c] 13 year olds in 1992 were not asked about project/coursework, as this was not considered to be part of their language learning experience. It is included two years later as the result of greater emphasis on a modular approach, flexible and independent learning.

becomes less enjoyable or whether they become more critically aware as they get older is open to question.

Do pupils provide any insights into grounds for a downward shift in satisfaction, especially regarding those areas of activities which represent the meat and drink of the language learning experience?

Speaking can be a source of embarrassment for some pupils: 'I feel scared to answer. If I make a mess, people laugh at me.' (13 year old)

When pupils are younger they have fewer inhibitions, are less image-conscious and are more prepared to 'play the language-learning game' by indulging in suspension of reality and making the shift in imagination from the classroom in a UK comprehensive to an ice-cream parlour near Cologne cathedral. As they get ever deeper into adolescence, however, this all changes. Being seen as 'cool' by the peer group seems to take precedence over the learning opportunities provided by make-believe.

Those who do not enjoy writing sometimes fail to see the point of it all: 'We just copy and copy and copy. Sometimes all we seem to do is copy out things we do not understand.' (13 year old)

Is this a reflection of a teacher struggling to provide a meaningful writing task where pupils have a real reason to write, e.g. for a wall display, a class magazine, a letter to the class link in the target language country, or of a teacher struggling to maintain/regain order in a generally disruptive class? In the reality of today's classroom the teacher is forced to strike a balance between provision of meaningful, enjoyable learning activities for the pupils on the one hand and maintenance of order and retention of sanity on the other. Any judgement must be made in the reality of the teaching context. Teachers are often constrained in terms of what they can do. The range of activities at their disposal is often determined by the pupils and their behaviour.

Pupils are generally unenthusiastic about listening exercises. Pupils complain of unclear recordings, defective equipment, foreigners speaking too fast, inappropriate tasks and, obliquely, the inauthentic nature of the activity ('I can't watch their lips', 15 year old). The major dilemma for the teacher here is how to transform the listening activity from a test into a learning experience. Of course pupils do need practice in tests of the GCSE variety but surely this does not need to be the norm. Does the testing syllabus have to be the teaching syllabus? Again 'meaningfulness' and something approaching 'authentic' or plausible activities deserve serious consideration if pupils are to value and exploit to the full the listening texts with which they are provided.

Reading too suffers a similar statistically significant slump in mean from a comparatively dizzy 3.40 to a worrying 3.02. Arguably as worrying as the drop in the mean is the claim by 14% and 8.8% of pupils respectively that reading does not form part of their language learning experience. Turner (1997) shares this concern that pupils do so very little reading beyond the snippets on adverts in newspapers and magazines and posters. The advent of the communicative era and the concomitant transactional GCSE syllabus appear to have sounded the death-knell for entire lessons spent reading stories with a beginning, a middle and an end. Teachers now appear to become anxious and conscience-striken if they are not seen to be the all-singing, all-dancing focus of their pupils' attention. How sad that they have been forced into this mindset. How regrettable that their pupils are denied this real learning opportunity.

One should not be misled by the above comment that a purely teacher-centred approach is the norm. Pupils' responses confirm that this is not the case. Pair work and group work are popular, although not all pupils engage in the latter. (See Littlejohn, 1983 and Long & Porter, 1985.) This may be because the risk factor – more noise; more opportunity for pupils to speak English; greater likelihood for pupils to wander away from the subject onto last night's football match or the disco at the weekend; more chance of disruption – is less with pair work than may be the case with group work. Pupils' comments suggest that both approaches have advantages and disadvantages. In the case of pair work there is the value in collaboration: 'You learn from each other' (15 year old). Image-conscious teenagers are also spared the potential perceived humiliation of speaking in a strange tongue before an audience of 25+ peers: 'You don't get embarrassed' (13 year old). The downside (from the quality of learning point of view) is reflected in the delegation of work to one's partner: 'You don't have to work. I let my partner do it all' (15 year old).

The above also applies to group work. In addition, pupils confirm the temptation to wander off-task: 'We have the chance to chat about other things' (13 year old). They value, however, the mutual support which can be provided: 'Your friends understand your problems better' (15 year old). (See Figure 8.1)

Immediately striking is that among the most enjoyed activities are those which do not form a part of the learning experience in German of a substantial number of pupils. (See APU findings above (p. 122) which also reflect the tendency of the activities 'not done' to be the most enjoyed.) The figures for computer-related activities (83.3% and 88.7%) are particularly disturbing, not least in the light of the emphasis placed on this in the *National Curriculum for Modern Foreign Languages* (DFE/WO 1991, 1995). (See also *The Times* 22.7.96 'British schools lead the world in teaching information technology'.) The very few pupils who claim to have taken part in computer-based learning say they have thoroughly enjoyed the experience. It is disconcerting that access has been provided to such small numbers. Possible reasons for this are discussed later (p. 120ff).

Results for project work and coursework (this applies only to the pupils in 1994, aged 15) are also quite alarming but for different reasons. It appears to be done by comparatively few pupils (32.5%), in spite of the opportunity it provides for them to engage in teamwork, to learn autonomously and to work at their own pace with short-term objectives and rewards. These are some of the transferable 'life-skills' sought by employers. (See *The Independent* 11.7.96, 'A range of skills will pave the way to a job'.) Galloway

% Not done

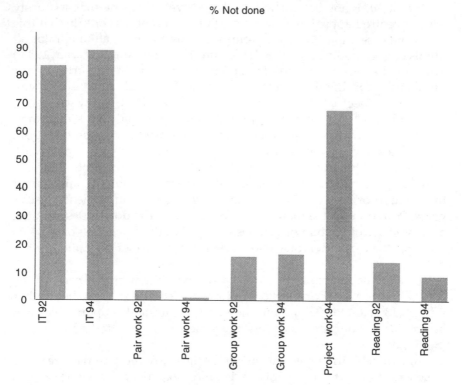

Figure 8.1 Percentage of Leeds pupils who responded to the question: 'How much do you enjoy the following activities in German lessons?' by indicating they were 'Not done'.

et al. (1998: 96) suggests a link between the diminishment in autonomous tasks between primary and secondary school and a concomitant diminishment in motivation. In contrast to computer work, however, the few who have had experience of project work, are not effervescent in their enthusiasm for it (mean score: 2.89).

One pupil is less concerned about the enjoyment of activities than the outcome:

> I'm not bothered what the teacher does to learn [*sic*] us; it onestly [*sic*] dosent [*sic*] matter how he does it as long as we learn it. (13 year old)

This boy's comment suggests the importance of success as a motivational factor in the foreign language learning process. If only all pupils shared his view. The truth remains, however, that most pupils do have preferences in how they learn. Some learn through visual activities; some benefit more from aural tasks; some learn kinesthetically (see Bruner, 1966). What an enormous challenge the teacher faces in meeting the needs of the various learner types within the class. (See Chapter 9.)

Other Influential Factors

There may well be other extrinsic factors which affect the pupils' motivation to learn German. Views were sought on what these might be and the extent of their influence (see Table 8.6).

Leeds pupils identify the following factors as most influential contributors to a positive view of their foreign language learning experience:

- the teacher;
- the textbook;

Table 8.6 Percentage of 13–15 Leeds cohort responding to the question: 'How important to you are the following in German lessons?'

Factors	Age/Yr	Unimportant 1	2	Reasonably important 3	Very important 4	5	Sample	Mean	S.D.
Teacher	13/92	3.5	9.6	25.2	23.5	38.3	115	3.84	1.15
	15/94	0.9	2.6	16.5	29.6	50.4	115	4.26	0.89
Textbook	13/92	2.6	6.1	28.7	38.3	24.3	115	3.76	0.98
	15/94	2.6	7.8	40.9	35.7	13.0	115	3.49	0.91
Equipment	13/92	4.4	8.8	41.2	25.4	20.2	114	3.48	1.05
	15/94	6.1	19.3	41.2	24.6	8.8	114	3.11	1.02
Teacher-made materials	13/92	0.9	11.3	48.7	31.3	7.8	114	3.29	0.97
	15/94	3.5	14.0	43.9	27.2	11.4	114	3.29	0.97
No. of pupils	13/92	19.3	15.8	28.1	26.3	10.5	114	2.93	1.27
	15/94	13.0	15.7	33.0	26.1	12.2	115	3.09	1.20
Exchange	13/92	15.5	25.5	30.0	20.0	9.1	110	2.82	1.19
	15/94	26.5	33.6	23.9	15.0	0.9	113	2.30	1.05
Computers	13/92	22.5	28.8	24.3	12.6	11.7	111	2.62	1.29
	15/94	42.9	29.5	13.4	8.0	6.3	112	2.05	1.21
Penpals	13/92	24.3	27.9	30.6	11.7	5.4	111	2.46	1.14
	15/94	33.3	28.8	24.3	9.9	3.6	111	2.22	1.12
Classroom	13/92	35.7	31.3	19.1	7.0	7.0	115	2.18	1.20
	15/94	38.3	27.8	25.2	2.6	6.1	115	2.10	1.14

- the equipment;
- teacher-made materials.

That the teacher should top the list should come as little surprise. Interview comments and responses to open questions tend to focus on the negative:

'The teacher goes too fast' (13 year old)
'I'm scared of getting shouted at if I can't do it' (13 year old)
'We've had too many different teachers' (15 year old)

The textbook is second on the list for Leeds and attracts mostly negative comments: 'Most of the pictures are from the 1960s and are boring' (13 year old). This seems surprising, given the attractive, colourful publications currently on the market. (See O'Sullivan, A., 1990; and Shirey & Reynolds, 1988 on the role of teaching materials in motivation.)

As for the remaining activities, low scores indicate that Leeds learners of German attach little importance to computers (given that they claim to use them so little, it is perhaps predictable that they will view them as unimportant), the way their classroom is furnished, or penpals. They tend not to regard the influence of exchanges as important. This may come as some surprise given that an exchange visit represents an opportunity to target a short-term goal and put into practice what has been learnt. Although the data suggest that Leeds pupils are not too concerned about class-size, two 13 year olds observe:

I can't learn German because the group is too big.
We should have a bigger room and two teachers.

One may have been forgiven for predicting higher status given to the issue of class-size given its enduring topicality (see, for example, 'Revealed: how 10,000 teachers disappeared' in *The Independent*, 28 September 1995; 'Class sizes up again' in *Times Educational Supplement*, 5 July 1996), as budget cuts demand more pupils per class and fewer teachers per school.

Penpals are clearly not as popular in the UK as they once may have been. This is regrettable, given the opportunities they provide for authentic writing and reading tasks (see 'Répondez s'il vous plaît' *Times Educational Supplement*, 7.3.97), quite apart from the establishing of international contacts and relationships. There is some evidence to suggest, however, that the pendulum may swing back to the popularity of such contacts with the spread of e-mail in schools. (See 'Cross-cultural collaborators', *Times Educational Supplement*, 7.3.97.)

For the 15–17 cohort the response is largely the same apart from that relating to equipment: this loses its importance and is replaced by the number of pupils in a class.

Suggestions As to How Learning Could Be Enhanced

Given that pupils' response to the German learning experience over the two years reflected a general tendency towards the negative, or certainly towards the less than positive, it was thought that the opportunity to suggest ways in which German learning could be enhanced might provide some useful feedback (see Table 8.7).

Many pupils opted not to answer the question posed in Table 8.8. Does this indicate general apathy? Or is it more an indication of pupils' struggle to identify and articulate what they really want and need? The few who do respond suggest that there should be no change (13/92: 16.5%; 15/94: 17.4%). Whether this reflects general satisfaction or an appreciation of a need for change but an inability to identify what the change should be is open to speculation. For those pupils who do have suggestions, the proposal that 'more interesting teaching methods' should be adopted, attracts the support of 30.4% of 13 year olds in 1992. Perhaps this advice was accepted, as two years later this percentage has dropped to 7.8%. More exchange visits (13/92: 8.7%; 15/94: 3.5%) and a change of teacher (13/92: 7.8%; 15/94: 10.4%) are other suggestions represented.

The pupils' suggestions provide little of real substance to help teachers meet perceived needs. In very general terms teachers are faced with the response: 'We are not particularly happy with what you provide but we are struggling to tell you what we want so that you can make things better'.

Table 8.7 Percentages of 13 and 15 year old Leeds pupils in 1992 and the same pupils in 1994 responding to the question: 'If you had the opportunity to change the way German in taught in your school, what would you do?'

Suggestion	13/92 (15/94) (n = 115)	13/94 (n = 194)	15/92 17/94 (n = 13)
No change	16.5 (17.4)	19.6	30.8 (46.2)
More interesting teaching methods	30.4 (7.8)	10.8	30.8
Change teacher	7.8 (10.4)	2.6	15.4 (15.4)
More exchange visits / penpals	8.7 (3.5)		
More computer work	3.5		
More oral work	(8.7)	3.1	
Better books and equipment			23.1 (46.2)
Other	(24.4)		
No response	71.3 (27.7)	45.9	

Responding to Diminishing Enthusiasm

On the basis of this sample, there is some evidence to suggest diminishment in enthusiasm for the in-school experience of German learning between Year 7 and 9 and again between Year 9 and 11. (See also Chapter 4.) To what may this apparent diminishment in enthusiasm for German be attributable? Helpful information provided by the pupils which may contribute to an improvement in the situation is limited. They tell us that only a few activities are enjoyed and these tend to be the very activities to which they claim to get little or no access. Computer-based tasks are experienced by only small numbers of pupils. The same applies to project work. Why is this so? Should computer- and project-related activities not form part of a rich and varied (foreign language) learning experience? Is variety not the spice of life? The data relating to the four attainment targets are also disturbing. Listening, speaking, reading and writing are the basic ingredients of the foreign language learning dish. If the basic ingredients are off, is it any wonder that the dish is less than palatable?

The purpose of the sections which follow is to make some tentative suggestions as to why that which is enjoyed is not on the menu and what is being done to spoil the basic ingredients of the dishes which are on the menu.

Computer-based tasks

Much of the National Curriculum documentation stresses the importance and benefits of the implementation of information technology (IT) in the foreign languages classroom. This includes wordprocessing, e-mail, software packages relating to creative writing, learning of vocabulary, practising of grammar and other exercises. Information technology gives pupils the opportunity to work with a medium which many of them have at home and enjoy, to work independently and at their own pace and to create documents which can be corrected neatly without the need for the teacher's dreaded red pen. Much has been written about the potential of IT for motivating pupils, especially the less able (Atkinson, 1992; Brown, 1993; Martin & Hampson, 1991; White & Wacha, 1992). Research by West et al. (1997) suggests that 7 year olds like working on computers better than anything else they do at school. In spite of this, however, in excess of 80% of pupils in the 13–15 cohort claim not to experience computers as part of their German learning reality. The few pupils who have had the experience, claim to enjoy it enormously. (See also Clark & Trafford, 1995: 321.)

Why should computer-related activities be the exception rather than the rule? Poor access to hardware (Chambers & Higham, 1993) is a major problem. In many schools other subject areas such as business studies, computer studies and mathematics, tend to block-book the computer room. (See also McKenna & McKenna, 1999.) The typical modern language department has one or two computers on a trolley which can be used by groups of up to three pupils at a time. This limits the computer to being used as part of a carousel of activities. These conditions do little to make the teacher's life easy. It is hardly surprising that she does not often feel inclined to make the considerable effort needed to make IT part of the regular German learning/teaching provision.

A common problem is the tendency for teachers to feel they lack the necessary IT competence (Chambers & Higham, 1993; see also Gunn, 1998: ' . . . teachers lacked the training and support to be effective in the use of IT.'). A certain degree of confidence in one's own ability and familiarity with the hard- and software are necessary before basing a lesson for up to 30 pupils on an IT package. It may indeed be a positive learning experience for the pupil who is enlisted to help the teacher struggling with the computer's sudden lack of memory or apparent crash. It takes a very confident teacher, however, not to feel embarrassed and inadequate by her own perceived computer-illiteracy.

As a result of these among other problems, it must often appear less trouble for teachers to stick to the methodology which they feel works and with which they are familiar, rather than introduce a medium which they may perceive as having the potential to create more problems than it might solve. The problem of consumer-dissatisfaction, however, is exacerbated by the provision of a diet which has become all too familiar and may not have been very enjoyable or satisfying in the first place.

Project work/autonomous/flexible learning

Autonomous and flexible approaches to learning were born of an effort to meet the diverse needs of the range of pupils within a class, including the 'disaffected'. They give pupils the opportunity to set short-term, achievable goals, to work at the pace which best suits them and to work independently, as part of a pair or of a group. This has the potential not only to enhance the subject-specific learning experience, whether the subject is German or any other, but also of giving the pupils access to life skills, much demanded by employers. (See Schofield, 1996.) As is the case with ICT, however, experience of project work and coursework which may form part of a flexible/autonomous learning package, is the exception rather than the rule in the German classroom.

Again teachers may have various justifications for not adopting the flexible/autonomous approach. Evans (1993) poses pertinent questions:

How is the teacher who has always adopted a didactic and serial mode of teaching to elicit this kind of autonomy from his or her pupils? It will surely not be enough to rely on the occasional session of group work to nurture this kind of competence. What systematic ways are there of monitoring independence and how can a teacher balance a necessary diet of centrally directed 'teaching' with structured access and use of multiple resources allowing for increased pupil independence in the work scheme for a given class? (Evans 1993: 19)

Evaluation of projects in learner centred course design (see Drew & Ottewill, 1998; Hurd, 1998; McDevitt, 1997; Remmert, 1997) has tended to show that clear and manageable targets play a major role in renewing and maintaining learners' motivation. A report on one scheme at Balcarras School (O'Connor, 1993) reflects enhanced enthusiasm, motivation and improved behaviour. It has also been suggested, however, that teachers do not always find it easy to move off centre-stage to allow pupils to take more responsibility:

> ... approaches designed to maximise the individual's responsibility for her own learning sometimes founder on the reluctance of teachers to relinquish control of the learning process or to change their over-dominant teaching style. (Stradling *et al.*, 1991: 47)

In addition, the autonomous approach is relatively new and comparatively untried and teachers may feel uncomfortable with a concept which gives pupils responsibility for their own learning. They may harbour fears that pupils may not set themselves targets which are demanding enough. What may be the implications for this in an age of 'league tables' for schools? A flexible/autonomous approach demands much of the teacher in terms of preparation. If pupils are to work independently with any degree of success, then the teacher has to provide an adequate stock of appropriately differentiated materials. Assessment also poses a challenge in that not all pupils will be ready to submit themselves for tests at the same time and at the same level. Having an accurate grasp on who is doing what is a source of concern for some teachers. They may fear that they simply do not have the capacity to retain an overview of up to 30 (or more) pupils striving to meet their own targets.

Within a teaching reality which is becoming ever more stress-filled and where administration and bureaucracy almost reduce teaching of pupils to a necessary inconvenience, it must surely appear simpler and better for the teacher's psychological well-being, to stick to the known and, while recognising the potential benefits of the unknown, to leave that to the enthusiastic, energetic and imaginative NQT (newly qualified teacher) or trainee teacher.

The four attainment targets

Listening and responding (AT 1), speaking (AT 2), reading and responding (AT 3) and writing (AT 4) get a mixed review from pupils. Some reasons for this are revealed in pupils' responses in the interviews and open questions. (See p. 123ff) Should consideration be given to an adjustment to teaching methodology to meet needs common to many pupils? (For articles dealing with teaching the four ATs see for example: Elston, 1991; Fawkes, 1993; Klapper, 1992a,b, 1993; Mitchell & Swarbrick, 1994).

Attainment Targets 1 (listening) and 3 (reading): the 'receptive skills'

- To what extent are listening and reading activities *testing* rather than *learning* experiences? (Chambers, 1996; Klapper, 1993)
- How much effort is made to establish overtly what the learners *know* (e.g. 'Underline all the words you understand' – a positive, success-orientated approach) as opposed to what they *don't know* (e.g. 'Underline all the words you don't understand' – a negative, failure-orientated approach)?
- Is enough effort made to contextualise and to access pupils' 'knowledge of the world' (i.e. pupils' experience of life; see Council of Europe, 1996: 37) or of the language relating to the given topic before tackling the text?
- How often are pupils given a *real* reason (access to needed information; interest; enjoyment) to read (Turner, 1997)/listen (Chambers, 1996)? How often are target language speakers or the class link with the school in Germany/France/Spain exploited for this purpose?

. . . in the field of reading – which is now often limited to scanning for information and skimming for the phrase that will enable the fumble-fingered editorial assistant to match up the magazine readers' letters with the agony aunt's replies. (Wringe, 1994)

How often are target language speakers or the class link with the school in Germany/France/Spain exploited for this purpose?

- Are pupils given the opportunity to infer and predict – skills which they apply in their mother tongue? This involves an element of risk-taking as pupils have to fill in the missing word, i.e. infer the meaning of the word/s which they may not understand. For example: 'Serious xxxxxxxx on the M1'. They infer the meaning of the unknown word from the words which they do know.

- Listening – how often do teachers over-use the pause-button in an effort to help the pupils, but by so doing, deny them the opportunity to hear enough known language to be able to contextualise and infer unknown language? (See 'M1' example above.) Are pupils given adequate opportunities to control the number of times they hear the text (in its totality and/or in parts)?

  > Every time I press the play-back button in front of the class, I am condemning the whole class to work at an identical speed. (Elston, 1991)

- Reading – how often are pupils given the opportunity to read for pleasure and/or choose what they wish to read? How much *real* reading do pupils do in preparation for GCSE? Are they not offered 'an odd mixture of signs and snippets' (Turner 1997) as opposed to texts of any real substance?

  > If we have no purpose in meaning (as often happens in the foreign languages classroom), we can bring no understanding to the text and it will therefore be meaningless. (Klapper, 1992)

- How much reading of any kind is done in the classroom of the 'communicative era'? Is reading not more of a required adjunct as the GCSE examination approaches? (Turner, 1997)
- Is enough care taken with choice of texts and preparatory activities (e.g. arousing pupils' curiosity (see Crookes & Schmidt, 1991: 488); establishing the context; knowledge of language; knowledge of the world) to allow pupils to read fluently?
- How often do teachers give pupils the opportunity to discuss their strategies for working out the meaning of unknown words?

Attainment Targets 2 (speaking) and 4 (writing): the 'productive skills'

- How often are castles built in the sand? How often do teachers expect the language to come out before it has been properly put in (i.e. inadequate presentation and practice)? Wringe (1994) notes the consequences of this in the context of a survey on birthdays:

  > Having started off amid great enthusiasm, the activity may quite quickly fall apart because numbers have not been revised before-hand, or those above 20 not even taught.

- How often are role-plays and writing tasks set up without pupils being given enough models upon which to base their creation?
- How often are pupils given a *real* reason to speak (an authentic audience) and write (an authentic readership)?

The Teacher: The Key Factor

Of other factors which may contribute to a pupil's positive or negative evaluation of a subject, the teacher comes out on top for all cohorts in Leeds. (This was also found in the OXPROD study, Filmer-Sankey,1989, 1991. See also Clark & Trafford, 1995: 318, 321.) The teacher is a factor which permeates almost every issue investigated in the survey relating to pupils' feelings about learning German and 'in-school' issues. The responses to the open questions where pupils have the opportunity to explain their views are particularly revealing. Again and again the teacher is named as the reason, for example, why they like/dislike German, why their learning experience has improved/deteriorated. The teaching methodology, the textbook, the computers available count for little if the teacher–pupil relationship is lacking. (See Chapter 3, p. 35ff.) The teacher carries an enormous burden of responsibility. She holds all the strings. Her approach to teaching, her personality, her power to motivate, make learning meaningful and provide something which pupils refer to as 'fun', represent the real foundation upon which pupils' judgement of the learning experience is based. How this tall order may be realised is discussed in Chapter 9.

Summary

This chapter merely touches upon one tiny part of what is a vast motivational carpet made up of legion interlocking threads. Pupils' views on their learning experience should be noted and, while accepting the limitations of their general applicability, teachers should bear them in mind in their evaluation of foreign language provision. There remains much to be done in the area of pupils' motivational perspectives of the foreign language learning experience. Crookes and Schmidt (1991: 499–500) rightly identify the need for research into motivation from the teacher's point of view and the issue of long-term reward. Only when these and other related areas become the focus of attention via a range of methodologies beyond questionnaire and follow-up interview, can the problem of motivation in the UK foreign language learning classroom context be tackled with any seriousness and hope for some degree of resolution.

Notes

1. A non-parametric test was applied in the first instance, since the assumption of equal interval data is questionable. It was thought, however, that given the large sample a parametric test would be adequately robust. It was found that both the parametric and non-parametric approaches led to precisely the same conclusions.

Chapter 9

The Teacher's Hats

This study and most other research (Campaign for Learning, 1998;
Clark & Trafford, 1995; Galloway et al., 1998; OFSTED, 1993; Phillips
& Filmer-Sankey, 1993) confirms that the teacher has a key role to play
in the motivational and attitudinal perspectives of pupils. This chapter
focuses on Leeds pupils' perceptions of the influence of their teacher on
their learning experience and provides some insights into the diversity
of the teacher's role, responsibilities and the challenges she faces
within and beyond foreign language teaching.

Introduction

Why are you looking forward to learning subject X at secondary school?
Why are you dreading subject Y at secondary school?
Why are you (not) looking forward to learning a foreign language?
What do you enjoy most about school?
What do you enjoy least about school?
Why do you think subject X is the most useful?
Why do you like French?
Why do you not like German?
How would you change the way German is taught?
Whose fault is it that there is a drug problem in our society?
Whose fault is it that the number of single, teenage mums is on the increase?
Whose fault is it that there is a hole in the ozone?

The answer to the above questions is the same in each case: *the teacher*. All
but the last three questions are taken from the interview schedule and open
questions relating to the Leeds study. The last three are confected but could
easily have been taken from British newspapers in the last five years. The
teacher seems to be the target of blame for every ill which befalls society.
(See Professor Ted Wragg: 'We all know who to blame' in *Times Educational*
Supplement, 18 September 1998.) She is also the target of blame for almost
every negative school learning experience. When 4245 11–16 year olds were
polled by MORI (Campaign for Learning, 1998) on their attitudes to
learning, 77% identified poor teaching as an impediment to their learning.

They also identified teachers who do not understand how children learn as a problem (72%). Mercifully the balance is redressed to some extent in this study as some pupils also laud their teacher for the enjoyment and fulfilment brought to the classroom. The shaping of a pupil's mindset starts early on in her school career. When, as part of this survey, 11-year-old pupils were asked to give reasons as to why they enjoyed or did not enjoy any previous foreign language learning experience they may have had, of the 65.5% who chose to justify their response, 46% identified the influence of the teachers and their teaching (about 50% more positive comments than negative).

The teacher's burden of responsibility is considerable. A trace of Sir Christopher Ball's influence on Tony Blair ('Education, education, education') may be identified in his speech at the North of England Education Conference in 1995:

> There are only three things of importance to successful learning: motivation, motivation and motivation . . . any fool can teach students who want to learn.' (Ball, 1995: 5)

A teacher's shoulders have to be strong and her skin thick. The number of hats she is required to wear is legion. Reisener (1992) uses the terminology of the theatre to describe the complexity of the role: the teacher is the writer, director, actor, prompter, props-person, technician. Within these various roles she has to encourage, drive on, hold back, scold, correct and so much more. And it is not as if the pupils in her charge are all the same; they are many and varied with a whole range of needs, interests and backgrounds. Tim Brighouse in an address at the UCET Spring Conference in 1998 described this aspect of the challenge and how the teacher endeavours to meet it in the following terms:

> Each morning 30 youngsters bring in different sets of baggage and the teacher immediately displays a variety of positive techniques as she silently marks the register. 'Did the match go well Shane? . . . Any chance of you giving me a hand with the music at dinner time Sian?

The relationship that the teacher has with her pupils plays a crucial role in the atmosphere created in the classroom and the nature of the interaction which goes on. If the relationship is poor, pupil- and for that matter teacher-motivation are unlikely to be good.

How Important a Factor is the Teacher?

In Chapter 8 the primacy of the teacher on the list of factors influencing pupils' attitudes to learning foreign language was established. That the

Table 9.1 Correlation coefficients for extent to which German is liked and the perceived importance of the teacher in German lessons (Leeds 13 year olds, 1994)

	Liking of German	*Importance of teacher*
Liking of German	1.0000	0.2391
	(192)	(191)
	$p = .$	$p = 0.001$
Importance of teacher	0.2391	1.0000
	(191)	(193)
	$p = 0.001$	$p = .$

teacher should top the list should come as little surprise. In other research, foreign languages-specific and non-subject specific, this too has been the outcome. Galloway stresses the importance of the teacher in research into school effectiveness:

> There is general agreement that although the differences in effectiveness between schools are educationally and socially important, the differences between teachers are greater than the differences between schools. . . . The implication here is clear: while the quality of the leadership and other organisational factors are critically important, the classroom teacher also plays a crucial part in determining the quality of pupils' learning experiences in school. (Galloway, 1998: 80)

With reference to this study, how significant then is the relationship between the importance rating given to the teacher and the extent to which pupils claim to like German? It is interesting that correlation coefficients reveal a significant relationship between the teacher and the extent to which German is liked for one age group only, that is 13 year olds in Leeds in 1994. Even in this case the correlation is relatively weak, accounting for only 4% of the variance. Given the lack of relevant data, grounds for this puzzling outcome are open to speculation. Does this suggest that although pupils acknowledge that the teacher is a very important factor, there are other factors which determine how much they like German, e.g. a perception of its status on the curriculum (as low) or of its level of difficulty (as high)? (See Table 9.1.)

In order to get closer to the identification of any such factors, 13-year-old Leeds pupils in both years of the survey were given the opportunity in an open question to explain their feelings regarding German. The majority of answers do not provide much useful insight ('I like it': 67.8% (13/92) / 55.7% (13/94); 'I don't like it': 13.1% (13/92) / 22.7% (13/94)). The remainder relate to the teachers and their teaching with a fairly even split between positive and negative comments:

'It's nice to be treated like an adult.'
'It's good fun.'
'We have to work hard but Mr X has a laugh with us as well.'
'The teacher goes too fast.'
'I'm scared of getting shouted at if I can't do it.'
'We've had too many different teachers.'
'The lessons are so boring.'
'The teacher complains about my writing. You should see her worksheets!'

Most pupils seem able to identify on a scale their like or dislike for a subject but struggle to explain what it is that influences their evaluation. This ties in with the view of Little (1985) who found that when young pupils were asked to give the reason for a given perception, they provided a description of the perception rather than the cause, e.g.:

Question: *Why do you feel this way about German?*
Answer: *I don't like it.*

Do Pupils' Perceptions Change? If So, Why?

Fifteen year old respondents (11 and 13 year olds were not asked, given that they did not have two years' experience on which to base their answers) to the question on whether their perceptions of learning German had changed in the course of the two years of the survey and grounds for their perception, are fairly evenly split on whether any perceived change has been for the worse or for the better. As pupils get older, they seem more prepared to express a view than not. How refreshing for the much maligned teacher that more positively inclined pupils are prepared to offer grounds for this than their more negatively inclined peers:

German gets more interesting.'
'I feel more enthusiastic.'

Pupils identify having 'a better teacher' as the reason for their enhanced perception of their learning experience:

'It's better because of the teacher.'
'It's more fun.'

In those cases where the change has been for the worse and the pupils are prepared to articulate a reason for this, the outcome for the Leeds German teacher is all too predictable:

'It's worse because of the teacher.'

'I've lost interest.'

What about those 17 year old pupils who have opted to take German for A-level? It seems reasonable to expect responses reflecting a positive change as pupils get to grips with a subject to which they have committed themselves voluntarily, working with a small group of like-minded peers, allowing them the opportunity to forge a closer relationship with their teacher than may have been the case earlier in their school experience. Six out of the 13 students confirm their perception of a change. Surprisingly perhaps, three find German less interesting than had been the case pre-A-level. (Is this not amazing given the difference between the very limited, restrictive, transactional GCSE syllabus and the world of opportunity which the A-level syllabus offers?) Four now find the subject 'more challenging'; whether this is seen as a positive or negative influence is not known. Three appreciate the improved resources and only one identifies the teacher as being a (positive or negative?) force for the perceived change.

How Can the Learning Experience be Made Better?

There is a striking quality to fine classrooms. Pupils are caught up in learning, excitement abounds; and playfulness and seriousness blend easily because the purposes are clear, the goals sensible and an unmistakable feeling of well-being prevails. (Rubin, 1985: v in Galloway, 1998: 142)

If only it were like this all of the time. Something rather less perfect tends to be the norm. We all wish we could change things to make our lives more fulfilling and enjoyable. Pupils were given the opportunity to suggest ways in which their German learning could be enhanced. Leeds pupils opted either not to answer this question (e.g.: 13/92: 27.7%; 15/94: 71.3%) or suggested that there should be no change (13/92: 16.5%; 15/94: 19.6%). Whether this reflects general satisfaction or an appreciation of a need for change but an inability to identify or articulate what the change should be is open to speculation. Of the remainder of pupils only the suggestion that 'more interesting teaching methods' should be adopted, attracts the support of more than 10.5% of respondents (13/92: 30.4%; 13/94: 10.8%). More exchange visits (13/92: 8.7%) and a change of teacher (13/92: 7.8%; 13/94: 10.4%) were other suggestions represented. The 15–17 cohort (n = 13) were more precise, placing emphasis on either 'no change' (15/92: 30.8%; 17/94: 46.2%) or 'better books and equipment' (15/92: 23.1%; 17/94: 46.2%). These findings are corroborated to a large extent in interview responses where the focus seemed to be on more group work, role-play, drama and more opportunities to visit Germany. Less emphasis was placed on the teacher and more on the teaching.

An optimistic fool I may be, but so many pupils opting out of answering the question on how they would change things may be an indicator that German lessons may not be all that bad. Were they abolutely horrendous, one would expect pupils, especially in the 13–15 age group, to have no end of suggestions. Perhaps, in spite of harbouring feelings of dissatisfaction, they struggle to come up with anything which may be better. Or is it a question of apathy and/or general indolence brought on by the stresses and strains of adolescence? Such a suggestion is surely too depressing to warrant consideration.

Is the Teacher Thinking What the Pupil is Thinking?

An important aspect of the in-school experience targeted in the survey was the learners' perceptions of the effort and progress they were making and the sharing of the same perception with their teachers (see Chapter 3, p. 43ff). This was thought to be a key factor in the nature and quality of the teacher–pupil relationship. Where the pupils' perceptions and that of their teachers are the same, there is less likelihood of conflict and greater likelihood of a healthy relationship. Where perceptions differ, the relationship may be at risk. Given that this study focuses on the pupils' views, it was not felt appropriate to access the teachers' views directly. This may have provided a more balanced picture of what the teachers thought but not necessarily an accurate impression of whether the pupil felt informed of this view.

Pupils were therefore asked for their views on: (1) their assessment of their own effort and progress; and (2) what they thought their teacher's perceptions of their effort and progress were. It is acknowledged that the data reflect only what the pupils are willing to report. It is nonetheless in keeping with the aim of the book.

Pupils' perceptions of their progress in German

A potentially important aspect of the in-school experience and pupils' positive attitude towards it is their awareness that they are making progress. Leeds pupils were therefore asked to estimate the progress they thought they were making in German (see Table 9.2).

Most 13 year olds in Leeds in 1994 regard themselves as doing well (55.7%) with 32.8% opting for 'making satisfactory progress'. Few pupils opt for the extremes of 'making excellent progress' (5.2%) and 'making poor progress' (5.7%).

Thirteen year old Leeds pupils in 1992 are even more positive about their

Table 9.2 Percentages of Leeds pupils responding to the request to tick the statement which applied to them regarding how much progress they were making in German

	I am making poor progress	I am making satisfactory progress	I am doing well	I am making excellent progress	Sample
Leeds 13/94	5.7	32.8	55.7	5.2	191
Leeds 13/92	0.0	21.9	70.2	7.9	114
Leeds 15/94	7.0	43.5	42.6	7.0	115
Leeds 15/92	0.0	7.7	84.6	7.7	13
Leeds 17/94	0.0	46.2	53.8	0.0	13

progress, although this drops significantly two years later (paired sample t-test: $t = 5.24$; df $= 113$; $p < 0.001$). This may be an indication of assessment being given a higher profile as GCSE examinations approach and pupils become more conscious of the true as opposed to the estimated standard to which they are working as reflected in grades.

Pupils in the 15–17 cohort too seem quietly confident about their progress, although their response is more positive in Year 11 than it is in Year 13. This may be predictable given the difference in degree of difficulty between GCSE and A-level. In addition, two of the pupils claim not to have been trying very hard (see Table 9.4), which may have had a decelerating effect on progress. In spite of this lack of effort however, none of the Leeds Year 13 pupils feel that they are making less than satisfactory progress.

How much can be read into these data is open to question, given that they reflect only the pupils' view of the progress they are making without reference to any solid basis on which to make the judgement, such as test results. It is nonetheless a source of some concern that pupils' estimations drop significantly within the 13–15 cohort. This may be as a result of pupils' heightened awareness with the approach of GCSE as suggested earlier, not least in the light of possible feedback from teachers which may be more functional or realistic (or may indeed become available for the first time in the opinion of the pupils). If this is so, it must be questioned, however, why it takes until this stage for them to have a realistic insight into what their progress is. Could it be the case that in spite of Records of Achievement, pupils do not feel informed by their teacher of what she thinks? (See Table 9.3.)

Table 9.3 Percentages of Leeds pupils responding to the request to tick the statement which best applied to them regarding how much progress they thought their teacher estimated they were making

	Age /Yr	S/he thinks I am making poor progress	S/he thinks I am making satisfactory progress	S/he thinks I am doing well	S/he thinks I am making excellent progress	I don't know what s/he thinks[a]	Sample
Pupil re:	13/94	4.7	14.7	23.0	3.7	53.9	191
Teacher	13/92	1.8	30.0	52.7	10.9	4.5[b]	110
	15/94	7.0	18.3	27.0	4.3	43.5	115
	15/92	0.0	7.7	76.9	7.7	7.7[b]	13
	17/94	0.0	23.1	23.1	0.0	53.8	13

[a] The 'I don't know' option was offered to Leeds pupils in the 1994 questionnaire only
[b] Percentage of pupils in 1992 articulating this view even though it was not given as an option

The most significant aspect of these data is that around half the pupils in 1994 claim not to know what their teacher thinks. Unreliable evidence it may be, but the fact that a number of pupils in the 13/92 and 15/92 cohorts indicate that they do not know what their teacher thinks, in spite of this not being an option available on the questionnaire in this particular year, may be an indicator that they were representatives of a larger number sharing this view. Pupils' lack of awareness of the teacher's opinion may at worst be damaging to a working relationship and at best may do little to enhance it. This is very disturbing much less for the fact that it makes it well nigh impossible to draw any conclusion about the symmetry of pupils' and teachers' views but much more because extremely important information is not being shared between teachers and learners, not least in their year of their GCSE or A-level examination. This is surprising in an age when such emphasis is placed on transparency and so much time spent on Records of Achievement and the target-setting and planning for personal development which are at their core. (Anecdotal evidence suggests that Records of Achievement are becoming a thing of the past with the advent of League Tables and the concomitant pressures on teachers and their pupils to achieve GCSE grades A*–C.)

Pupils' perceptions of their effort in German

What is pupils' assessment of the amount of effort they put into their German learning? Do they have a perception of what their teacher thinks? (See Table 9.4.)

Table 9.4 Percentage of Leeds pupils responding to the request to tick the statement which applied to them regarding how hard they try in German lessons

Age/Year	I don't really try at all	I try quite hard	I try very hard	Sample
13/94:	9.3	63.2	27.5	193
13/92:	2.6	58.8	38.6	114
15/94:	10.5	66.1	23.5	115
15/92	0.0	69.2	30.8	13
17/94	15.4	46.2	38.5	13

Less than 10% of Leeds 13 year olds in 1992 and again in 1994 claim not really to try at all. The 1992 13 year olds lose a little of their appetite for work as do 15 year olds in 1994 as the percentage for this category creeps to a statistically significant 10.5% ($t = 3.90$; df = 113; $p < 0.001$). Well over half in the 11–13 and 13–15 cohorts say they try quite hard, although there is an indication of a lessening in effort within each of these cohorts as pupils get older. This is a little surprising, given that 15 year olds are soon to take GCSE examinations.

One would expect pupils in the 15–17 cohort to be making considerable effort given that German is their chosen subject and that they are in their GCSE or A-level examination year. There is little suggestion of this, however, especially from 17 year olds in 1994, when two even admit to not really trying at all.

These data suggest a trend of pupils making less effort as they get older, or at least of pupils claiming that this is the case. Why should this be so? Is it not reasonable to assume that pupils would try harder as they get older, especially as they enter the crucial GCSE and A-level years? Perhaps the enthusiasm of youth stimulates them to make more effort lower down the school and as they get older peer pressure to 'look cool', to fit in and not be seen as a boffin, forces them to make less effort or give the impression of making less effort. Galloway *et al.* found a similar trend in their research:

> . . . feeling good about school seems to be increasingly associated with getting away with doing as little as possible. (Galloway, 1998: 98)

The results are broadly the same for the question relating to pupils' views on their teachers' perception of their progress (see Table 9.3). That around half the pupils do not know what their teachers think is disturbing.

Table 9.5 Percentages of Leeds pupils responding to the request to tick th
statement which best applied to them regarding how hard they thought
their teacher estimated they tried in lessons

	Age/Yr	S/he thinks I don't really try at all	S/he thinks I try quite hard	S/he thinks I try very hard	I don't know what s/he thinks	Sample
Pupil re:	13/94	8.4	26.2	9.4	56.0	191
Teacher	13/92	63.6	25.5	4.5	4.3[a]	114
	15/94	8.7	32.2	10.4	48.7	115
	15/92	0.0	61.5	30.8	7.7[b]	13
	17/94	0.0	46.2	7.7	46.2	13

[a] The 'I don't know' option was offered in the 1994 questionnaire only
[b] Percentage of pupils in 1992 articulating this view even though it was not given as an option

The Problem of Feedback

One can only speculate as to the reasons for the pupils' perception that
they remain uninformed on what the teacher thinks about their progress
and effort. Given the comparatively low status of foreign languages in the
minds of the pupils (see Chapter 10, p. 160ff), it may be the case that
German/French/Spanish do not occupy much space on the agenda which
they bring (or don't bring) to the Records of Achievement discussion or
other discussions on progress with their teacher, for example. Perhaps it is
discussed but for the reason given above, pupils do not take much note of
it. Perhaps the foreign languages teacher, given the plethora of other jobs
she is required to do, in spite of recognising the importance of pupils and
teacher having a shared understanding of where the pupil stands, and in
spite of every good intention, does not manage to find the opportunity to
provide meaningful feedback to individuals. (See p. 149ff.)

Even when time is found, even when foreign languages do have their
proper place on the agenda for discussion between teacher and pupil,
provision of feedback is far from easy. Teachers are aware of the
inextricable link between motivation and learning:

> No-one can make you learn, you have to want to. (Campaign for
> Learning, 1998: 20)

UK-based teachers of foreign languages are arguably more conscious of
this than teachers of other subjects. Self-esteem is an important motivational factor (see Chapter 3, p. 42ff). Pupils who feel good about themselves
are more likely to have a more positive mindset towards the subject and
related classroom activities than those who do not. (As with most aspects

of motivation generally, this is a difficult idea to substantiate. A pupil may feel good about himself and manifest this by being overtly uncooperative in class.) Teachers therefore wish to do all they can to maintain and enhance levels of self-esteem. This does not necessarily mean that they mislead the pupils into thinking they are doing well at the subject when they are not, but that they may struggle to come out with the total truth. They may use statements like, 'You're nearly right but . . . '; 'That's a really good try but . . . '; 'Have another little look at this.' They may ignore some mistakes. They may give a mark which in truth is more a reflection of the effort rather than the quality of the product. The GCSE marking scheme enables pupils to score very well in spite of making mistakes. All of this may lead pupils to believe that the teacher is quite satisfied with their performance but given that a focused discussion has not taken place where 'cards are put on the table', they cannot be sure.

Perhaps feedback on 'effort' poses fewer difficulties here than 'progress'. Effort is an 'unstable cause' (Weiner, 1986; see Chapter 2, p. 15ff). A pupil can do something about this. She may recognise that a poor performance in a test can be put right by trying harder. A problem arises when a teacher articulates the view that the pupil has not been working very hard and the pupil, in contrast, feels that she cannot work any harder. 'Progress' may be more problematic, especially when it is linked to 'ability', a 'stable cause'. If poor performance is linked to ability, where does the pupil go next? Where does the teacher go? The teacher finds herself in the position where she may feel the need to say: 'I know you are doing your best. I know that your marks are not very good. We just have to accept this because you happen not to be very able in this subject. Things are unlikely to get any better.' True this may be, and it may not do much for the pupil's self-esteem, but the implications are arguably fewer if the news is broken in the last year of the five year course to GCSE. What if this is the message at the end of the first or second year of the course? Galloway *et al.* (1998) identified these problems in their research into motivating 'the difficult to teach':

> The problem does not simply lie in the difficulties in manipulating teachers' feedback to pupils. A much more serious problem is the professional judgement needed in deciding what feedback to give. Simplistic panaceas like attributing failure to lack of effort rather than to lack of ability collapse under the reality that a child may have been making a credible effort on a task that is simply too difficult . . . (Galloway *et al.*, 1998: 133)

The motivational implications of this realisation may be serious both for pupil and teacher:

If children believe they have failed on a task due to lack of ability their motivation to attempt the same task again is likely to be low. If teachers believe children have failed due to lack of ability, *their* motivation to encourage children to continue working on similar tasks is likely to be low (Galloway, 1998: 31)

The Teacher's Motivation

The teacher of foreign languages in the UK context faces challenges on every front. A Lingua funded project (Wringe, 1996) gave teachers from a number of EU countries the opportunity to visit each others' schools and observe teaching. It was concluded that the status and working conditions of teachers in Britain were inferior to those in other European countries. Notably language teachers in the other countries enjoyed greater opportunities to get on with their teaching, freed from the pastoral and other responsibilities which took up so much of the time of their UK counterparts. And the above findings do not include the special problems posed by motivation in the context of foreign language learning in UK schools: English is the world language; English is the language of business and of the pop-culture; English is the language of the countries most young people wish to visit (see Chapter 7, p. 98ff).

It may be argued that foreign languages pose some problems not generally found in other subjects:

- *The target language is taught in a mother-tongue/non-target language environment*
  The teacher may do all she can to recreate the atmosphere of France/Germany/Spain in the classroom with appropriate wall displays, a French/German/Spanish corner full of attractive realia, music and even food and drink. At the end of the 40 minute lesson, however, the pupils return to an English-speaking environment and may not have another foreign language lesson for anything up to a week.
- *Target language as the language of interaction*
  The National Curriculum Non-Statutory Guidance (National Curriculum Council 1992, section C) encourages teachers to use the target language as the medium of interaction as much as possible. This is a considerable challenge: finding the appropriate level of language; applying appropriate pace; using appropriate visual support; maintaining pupils' attention and motivation when their understanding may be restricted – in what may well be a group including pupils of a considerable range of ability. Which other subjects are taught in a foreign code?

- *AT1   AT2   AT3   AT4*
  The teacher must include work on all four attainment targets: listening
  and responding; speaking; reading and responding; writing. This has
  implications for careful lesson planning and preparation (see *'Media'*
  below) and includes the challenge of implementing a range of
  activities within one lesson and ensuring smooth transitions between
  them.

- *Spiral memory*
  Learning a foreign language is not a linear process. Two steps back
  have to be taken before the next step forward can be considered. It is
  necessary to revise the 'known' before building the 'unknown' onto
  this foundation.

- *Intensity of practice*
  For consolidation to take place it is necessary to practise the same
  language and/or structure again and again and again, in a myriad of
  different ways, ensuring that motivation and interest are maintained
  and boredom does not creep in. The teacher is challenged to package
  what may in fact be 'drilling' in the form of a game or quiz.

- *Complexity (sound – spelling)*
  Some languages are more challenging in this respect than others.
  Compare for example *qu'est-ce que c'est* (French for: 'What is that?')
  with *Was ist das?* (German version). The teacher must consider
  carefully the timing of the introduction of the written version of a
  phrase; rather than support the pupils' remembering of the word or
  phrase, the complex spelling of a sound which they may have been
  practising orally with some degree of confidence and competence,
  may present an unwelcome distraction. Introduce the written form
  too early and mother-tongue interference may become a negative
  influence; leave it too late and the problem of memory overload has
  to be faced.

- *Abstraction*
  Young foreign language learners come to the classroom with a
  knowledge of what things are and a command of what they are called.
  They are now required to come to grips with a whole list of alternative
  names, many of which sound and look completely different from
  what they have become used to; some items may require two or more
  words rather than one, in order to identify them in the foreign code;
  others may have no equivalent at all in the foreign code.

- *Media*
  The challenge of motivation, catering for the spiral progression in
  learning and providing the appropriate intensity of practice in all four

attainment targets, make the teacher of foreign languages readily identifiable in the midst of other teachers. She is invariably the one setting off for the first two lessons of the day armed with flashcards, audio- and video-cassettes, role-play cue-cards, CD-ROMs and supermarket bags full of railway timetables and *bien fait* stickers. She probably looks rather more tired and stressed than teachers of other subjects.

- *Suspension of reality*
  So much of what is done in the foreign languages classroom depends on a suspension of reality. Pupils have to pretend they are on a ferry or checking into a hotel (at the age of 12) or buying petrol (at the age of 13) or asking the man at the petrol station to check the tyres and oil (how long has it been since one was able to have this done at a petrol station?). They have to be willing 'to play the game'. Sometimes they do not want to play because they find it all so childish, especially when they are dealing with language content (*My name is . . . Do you have any pets?*) which they thought they had left behind in primary school. They may also have been through all this before when learning their first foreign language.

- *Reward – long term*
  How long do pupils have to wait until they experience any real pay-off for their investment of time and effort? The exchange at the end of Year 9? GCSE results at the end of Year 11? In the world in which pupils live, patience is a rare quality. They want and expect (and in some cases and contexts demand) immediate gratification. How does the teacher cope with this? Goethe-Institut stickers and the occasional French breakfast are useful and help enormously but in a limited way for a restricted period of time.

The teacher's world beyond the modern languages classroom also poses challenges. Constant innovation and government policy have done little to enhance the teachers' motivation. The place of modern foreign languages is under threat (see DfEE Circular 3/98). They have enjoyed foundation status on the National Curriculum since 1991; pupils then were given the option of taking a language as a short course (DFEE/WO, 1995) and rumours abound at the time of writing that the QCA review of the National Curriculum may return modern languages to the status of the bad old days when they were optional. This does little to enhance teachers' morale. Add to this the reaction of the government and the media to the trend of improving GCSE and A-level examination results ('A-level pass rate rises yet again' *Times Educational Supplement*, 16.8.96) – it cannot be the teachers and pupils who are working harder and performing better but rather evidence of a general 'dumbing down'. (*Sunday Telegraph*, 20.8.95 blamed the expansion of universities for 'spurring the devaluation of the A-levels, and in turn the devaluation of the GCSE'; 'The great declining achievement yawn', in *Times Educational Supplement*, 25.8.95.) League tables are fine for schools which score well in the A*–C category. What about those schools which are towards the bottom end of the tables but whose teachers are working wonders with pupils of limited ability whose optimum perform-ance may be D or E? To be named and shamed in the national and local press cannot be anything other than demotivating, and that is probably vastly understated. What effect does teachers' demotivation have on their teaching?

> If teachers believe that their work is not valued, then *their* motivation to motivate their pupils will be reduced. In other words, there is likely to be an interactive relationship between the motivation of teachers and that of their pupils. (Galloway *et al.*, 1998: 5)

As Galloway points out, it is hardly surprising that teachers adopt a 'what's the point attitude', just as their pupils do when they feel the investment of effort appears to have nil pay-off:

> The result is likely to be that teachers adopt a work avoidance response . . . , arising from a feeling of helplessness, or a self-worth motivated response which uses rejection of government policies to legitimise reduction in commitment to high education standards. (Galloway *et al.*, 1998: 143)

Summary

Of the multifarious factors which may contribute to a pupil's positive or negative evaluation of a subject, such as the learning environment, access to equipment, the textbook, the number in the class, etc., the teacher comes out on top for all cohorts in Leeds and Kiel. (This was also found in the OXPROD study: Filmer-Sankey, 1989, 1991. See also Clark & Trafford, 1995: 318, 321.) The teacher is a factor which permeates almost every issue investigated in this study relating to pupils' feelings about learning foreign languages/German and issues relating to the 'in-school' foreign language learning experience. The responses to the open questions where pupils have the opportunity to explain their views are particularly revealing. Again and again the teacher is named as the reason, for example, why they like/dislike German/French, why their learning experience has improved/deterio-rated, why they like/dislike school, how German/French could be improved, and so on. The teaching methodology, the textbook, the computers available count for little if the teacher–pupil relationship is lacking. The teacher carries an enormous burden of responsibility. It is hardly surprising that some teachers fold under the stress or wish to escape. (See 'One in three wants to quit' in *Times Educational Supplement*, 13.6.97. See also 'I'm divorcing my teacher husband, citing the school as his mistress' in *Times Educational Supplement*, 12.6.98.)

A particular aspect of the teacher's role revealed by the data which gives grounds for concern is the apparent absence of communication in Leeds with regard to pupil-progress. A disturbingly high percentage of pupils across all three cohorts claim not to know what their teachers' assessment of their progress is. (See Keys & Fernandes, 1993 who also found high percentages of pupils claiming little feedback from teachers.). So much time and effort have been spent in Leeds schools developing and implementing Records of Achievement for what appears, in the case of German, to be a very poor pay-off. The whole point of Records of Achievement is to attain transparency, for the pupils to know where they stand in terms of attainment so that new, realistic, achievable targets can be negotiated and agreed. On the basis of report from this sample of pupils from four Leeds schools (and in the absence of evidence from teachers and other documentation), the system appears not to be working. Why may this be so? Is it a question of time? Is it a question of the nature of the feedback given? This is not a simple issue and requires focused research.

This study is built on pupils' responses to the in-school experience with special reference to foreign languages and German in particular. They make clear the primacy of the role of the teacher. She is made responsible for good and ill. In spite of the absence of data from teachers, it was felt inappropriate to omit at least some insight into the context within which they are obliged to work and the challenges posed by their subject, the pupils' reaction to the subject and the government policy which shapes what goes on in their schools within and beyond their subject. The following chapter provides some strategies which may help the troubled teacher meet the challenges faced.

Chapter 10

What Can we Learn From the Germans?

Reports on comparative research (Green & Steedman, 1993; HMI, 1986, 1991; Mason et al., 1992; Steedman & Hawkins, 1993) and the media (Channel 4: Dispatches: 'All our Futures', 1993) often refer to the German approach to education (among other things) as a model of excellence. More Germans have competence in English than do English speakers in German (Hagen, 1992; Wright & Wright, 1994). Germans' competence in English is generally better than that of English-speakers in German (European Commission, 1989). This chapter looks for clues as to why this may be so, whether teachers of English in Germany encounter the same motivational challenges as teachers of German in the UK and, if so, how these are tackled. What can we learn from the Germans?

Introduction

The British appear to have something of a problem with the Germans. We want to be better than them but never quite manage. They have beaten England in every meaningful football match since 1966, usually by the narrowest of margins: one goal in five in 1970; penalties in 1990; penalties in Euro96. They now own that very British institution, Rolls-Royce. They lead the UK in league tables for attainment in mathematics and science (Keys *et al.*, 1995b). They are going to get their way with the Euro. The UK media add to the frustration by painting a glowing picture in which all things German seem to be held up as a model of excellence (Channel 4 Television, 1993; MacLeod, 1995). The only way we can try to regain the high ground is to make jokes about the war (e.g. *Allo! Allo!* BBC) and caricature their alleged attempts to monopolise the sunbeds in Spanish holiday locations.

In terms of foreign language learning, is the picture in Germany as rosy as we might think? If so, what can we learn from the Germans to enhance the learning experience of UK learners?

What Can be Learned from the Germans?

There exists a popular perception that motivation to learn foreign languages is a greater problem for the British than it is for other nationalities, not least the Scandinavians, Dutch and Germans. The work of Milton and Meara (1998) shows how other countries attach much greater importance to the teaching and learning of English than we do to French and German in Britain. This is reflected in Table 10.1 relating to the approximate number of hours of foreign language tuition received by 14–15 year olds in their study:

Heuer (1983: 104ff.) conducted research into motivation and the learning of English with Year 7 pupils (12 year olds) in the *Hauptschule* (roughly the equivalent of the secondary modern school in Britain). He found that of the 845 pupils involved, 81.9% recognised the value of English for travel and future career and had used it in some way, usually in connection with television, records, reading, interaction with tourists and travel; 33.3% had read an English newspaper or magazine.

A similar study was conducted with pupils in Years 5 (10 year olds) to 9 (14 year olds) by Fengler and Fischer (1983, 112ff.). In response to the question, 'Why learn English?', the 310 pupils responded as follows: 33.3% because it is a compulsory subject; 68.7% travel; 67.1% career; 72.4% of the boys and 59.7% of girls claimed to come from families with English-speaking competence.

It may not be all sweetness and light within the foreign language learning context in Germany, however. Mreschar (1991) reports that pupils there too have 'attitude problems'. He concludes that German pupils generally have a low opinion of their teachers especially with regard to their poor level of communicative competence and inability to bring relevance to the real world into their lessons. The system of assessment with its pressure to achieve also contributes to a less than positive attitude to school. Piepho (1983: 119ff.) worked with 1700 pupils of all abilities in Years 7 (12 year olds) to 9 (14 year olds) in order to ascertain their likes and dislikes and aspects of English learning which influenced motivation. While he found the majority of pupils keen to learn, problems were caused by unimaginative

Table 10.1 Approximate hours of foreign language tuition received by subjects

British students learning French	210
British students learning German	80
German students learning English	400
Greek students learning English	660

Table 10.2 Vocabulary scores from LLEX Lingua vocabulary tests

	Mean (%)	Mean (words)	S.D.
Greek students learning English (63)	70	1680	290
German students learning English (80)	50	1200	440
British students learning French (54)	30	660	310
British students learning German (8)	41	984	156

approaches to introducing vocabulary, the exploitation of texts and grammar drills. Boring, unattractive worksheets, uninteresting texts, meaningless oral exercises and disappointing test results were also identified by pupils as doing little to enhance the enjoyment of learning English.

It is reassuring perhaps for the frustrated teacher of foreign languages in the UK that pupils in Germany have complaints too. The difference in outcome, however, remains disconcerting. Some German pupils find aspects of language learning boring but still appear to reach a level of competence which seems so much higher than that attained by UK learners of French and German. In Milton and Meara's comparative study (1998), 187 14–15-year-old foreign language learners in Britain, Germany and Greece were tested using versions of Meara's (1995) LLEX Lingua vocabulary tests. The results are summarised in Table 10.2.

Milton and Meara's findings reflect not only the greater knowledge of vocabulary of Greek and German English-learners over their British French- and German-learning peers but also the greater length of time spent on foreign languages (see Table 10.1) and the greater demands made on the Greeks and Germans in English examinations in comparison to GCSE.

The research above suggests that the foreign language teaching situation in Germany, at least in terms of pupil reaction to provision, seems little different from that in the UK. The major difference appears to lie in the area of perceived relevance. German learners attach (or live and learn in a context in which they are made to feel obliged to attach) considerably greater importance to foreign language learning, it seems, than their British peers and as a result may be prepared to tolerate a teaching approach which they may find less than inspiring. This is targeted as an area of investigation in the survey and interviews in this study. What are the other similarities and differences between responses from Leeds pupils and their Kiel counterparts? Each of the important areas for which Leeds data have already been provided will be taken in turn (with the exception of the ethnocentric dimension for which the Leeds/Kiel comparison has been made in Chapter 7) to identify factors of significance from which lessons may be drawn. (See Chapter 4, p. 60ff for important differences between the Leeds and Kiel contexts.)

German Pupils' Likes and Dislikes

Is the reaction of Kiel pupils to their language learning experience different from that of their Leeds counterparts? (See Table 10.3.)

As is the case for Leeds, pair work and group work are much enjoyed in English lessons in Kiel and are identified as the most popular activities. Computer work is done as rarely in Kiel as it is in Leeds (13/92 83.2%; 15/94 82.0%; n = 139 in each case). ('The ratio of computers to children in

Table 10.3 Percentages of Kiel pupils responding to the question: 'How much do you enjoy the following activities in English lessons?

Activity	Age/yr	I do not like this at all 1	2	I don't mind this 3	4	I enjoy this Not done[a]	Sample	Mean[b]	S.D.[b]
Pair work	13/92	1.5	8.8	24.8	54.0	10.9	137	3.48	0.74
	15/94	0.7	3.6	24.6	60.1	10.9	138	3.62	0.61
Group work	13/92	0.7	7.2	18.0	48.9	25.2	139	3.54	0.71
	15/94	0.7	4.3	21.6	59.0	14.4	139	3.62	0.62
Literature	13/92	5.9	6.6	12.5	8.8	66.2	136	2.72	1.05
	15/94	6.6	7.4	18.4	11.8	55.9	136	2.80	1.01
Speaking	13/92	3.7	14.0	36.8	45.6	0.0	136	3.24	0.83
	15/94	5.0	11.5	37.4	46.0	0.0	139	3.25	0.85
Computer	13/92	2.2	2.9	1.5	10.2	83.2	137	3.17	1.15
	15/94	2.2	0.7	2.9	12.2	82.0	139	3.40	1.04
Reading	13/92	6.5	19.4	38.8	27.3	7.9	139	2.95	0.89
	15/94	5.8	18.0	38.1	32.4	5.8	139	3.03	0.89
Listening exercise	13/92	3.0	20.0	37.0	22.2	17.8	135	2.96	0.81
	15/94	3.7	11.9	45.2	21.5	17.8	135	3.03	0.77
Writing exercise	13/92	10.9	17.4	47.8	23.2	0.7	138	2.84	0.91
	15/94	8.7	20.3	47.1	23.9	0.0	138	2.86	0.88
Project/ coursework	13/92	0.7	4.3	15.9	12.3	66.7	138	3.30	0.75
	15/94	2.9	2.9	9.5	16.8	67.9	137	3.25	0.97

[a] 'Not done' – to indicate activities which pupils feel they do not engage in in class.
[b] Includes only those pupils who claim to participate in activities, i.e. excludes those under 'not done'.

secondary schools (10–18 years) is only 1:1200 – and many schools have no computers', Cohen, 1997.) Those who have had this experience share the enthusiasm of their Leeds peers. Apart from speaking (4th most popular activity), the four skills (one cannot refer to ATs in the German context) do not score terribly well, especially writing (least popular). Listening does not only feature towards the bottom of the enjoyment table (2nd least popular) but is claimed not to be done by 18% of learners of English at age 13 and 24.6% at age 15. Given the nature of this skill and its basic importance, these appear disturbingly high percentages. This may be an indication of a teaching methodology which is largely based on written texts, comprehension and discussion/question and answer in the target language. This may be thought to preclude the need for formal listening comprehension exercises. (See Mreschar, 1991 and Chambers, 1991 who criticise a 'sterile' and 'unimaginative' approach to the teaching of English in Germany.)

It is interesting to note that a small number of pupils take the opportunity in the open questions to raise objections to the target language approach which they find difficult and off-putting: 'Englisch finde ich schlecht – die Lehrerin redet nur Englisch' *I don't like English — the teacher only speaks English.* (15 year old).

Project/coursework in English lessons is experienced by few, enjoyed by some but not by others.

Other Influential Factors in English Lessons

Do Leeds and Kiel pupils share the same perceptions on the factors influencing how they view their in-class foreign language learning experience? (See Table 10.4.)

Leeds and Kiel pupils are in agreement as to the most important factors contributing to a positive view of their foreign language learning experience:

- the teacher;
- the textbook;
- the equipment;
- teacher-made materials.

That the teacher should top the list for both Kiel and Leeds pupils is not surprising. (See below.) The textbook assumes considerable importance in Kiel. Anecdotal evidence combined with the outcomes of the question on enjoyment suggest that work in Kiel in English lessons may be much more textbook-based than tends to be the case in German classes in Leeds. (See Mreschar, 1991 and Chambers, 1991.) It is interesting that Kiel pupils should

Table 10.4 Percentages of 13–15 Kiel cohort responding to the question: 'How important to you are the following in English lessons?'

Factors	Age/Yr	Unimportant 1	2	Reasonably important 3	4	Very important 5	Sample	Mean	S.D.
Teacher	13/92	5.0	3.6	18.0	25.2	48.2	139	4.08	1.12
	15/94	0.7	1.4	10.1	25.2	62.6	139	4.48	0.79
Textbook	13/92	4.4	3.7	32.4	36.0	23.5	136	3.71	1.01
	15/94	2.2	6.5	32.4	32.4	26.6	139	3.75	0.99
Equipment	13/92	5.3	9.0	32.3	34.6	18.8	133	3.53	1.06
	15/94	3.6	5.1	42.0	28.3	21.0	138	3.58	1.00
Teacher-made materials	13/92	5.9	9.6	36.8	27.2	20.6	136	3.47	1.10
	15/94	2.9	6.5	41.3	28.3	21.0	138	3.58	0.99
No of pupils	13/92	11.7	8.0	24.1	19.0	37.2	137	3.62	1.36
	15/94	4.3	5.1	15.9	33.3	41.3	138	4.02	1.08
Exchange	13/92	6.7	19.3	24.4	18.5	31.1	135	3.48	1.29
	15/94	15.2	12.3	27.5	18.1	26.8	138	3.29	1.38
Computers	13/92	36.7	23.3	16.7	11.7	11.7	120	2.38	1.39
	15/94	41.7	10.2	17.3	8.7	22.0	127	2.59	1.61
Penpals	13/92	22.4	25.4	23.9	16.4	11.9	134	2.70	1.31
	15/94	30.7	25.5	25.5	10.9	7.3	137	2.39	1.23
Classroom	13/92	50.7	24.3	13.2	6.6	5.1	136	1.91	1.17
	15/94	51.1	12.2	21.6	5.8	9.4	139	2.10	1.34

attach importance to equipment, given that they appear to use so little of it, as indicated in the previous section. They have little access to computers, for example, nor do they appear to use cassette-recorders or listening-posts. Teacher-made materials are possibly given importance as pupils may see them as an attempt to get away from the textbook and introduce more variety.

The *t*-test for independent samples was applied to identify any differences between the reponses of pupils in Leeds and Kiel at age 13 and two years later at age 15.

The only areas which provide a significant difference between Leeds and Kiel 13 year olds in 1992 are: the number of pupils in the class: $t = 4.12$, df = 249, $p < 0.001$ – Kiel pupils view the number of pupils in a class as important, increasingly so as they get older; the exchange: $t = 4.18$, df = 239, $p < 0.001$. In contrast to Leeds pupils, Kiel pupils tend to attach importance to the influence of exchanges. The exchange visit represents an opportunity to put to the test in an authentic context the competence gained so far at school.

Two years later the picture changes. At age 15 there are significant differences between the responses of Leeds and Kiel pupils in almost all areas:

Teacher:	$t = 2.03$, df $= 252$, $p < 0.05$
Textbook:	$t = 2.17$, df $= 252$, $p < 0.05$
Teacher-made materials:	$t = 2.35$, df $= 250$, $p < 0.05$
Equipment:	$t = 3.73$, df $= 250$, $p < 0.001$
Computers:	$t = 2.94$, df $= 231$, $p < 0.001$
Number of pupils in the class:	$t = 6.52$, df $= 251$, $p < 0.001$
Exchange:	$t = 6.43$, df $= 248$, $p < 0.001$

The only areas in which there is no significant difference are the classroom and penpals. Why there should be this difference in response between pupils at age 13 and 15 is difficult to explain. One possibility, admittedly difficult to prove, may be that Leeds pupils have the opportunity to drop foreign language learning after GCSE (and the majority take advantage of this) while their Kiel peers are obliged to continue. As a result they may take the above considerations rather more seriously. This view may be supported by the importance Kiel pupils attach to English learning generally.

The Usefulness of Foreign Language Learning

When Leeds pupils were asked to comment on the usefulness of the subjects on their timetable, mathematics, English and science came out on top. (See Chapter 6, p. 85ff.) In the words of one 13 year old pupil: 'We have more lessons in science than in anything else, so I suppose it must be the most useful'. Foreign languages were generally not perceived as useful. The Kiel pupils regarded mathematics, English and German as the three most useful subjects. Their interview responses reflect the importance they attach to foreign languages in general:

> 'Fremdsprachen sind total wichtig. Innerhalb des zusammenwachsenden Europas ist es wichtig, daß man sich mit Leuten anderer Nationen verständigen kann. Sobald man die Sprache kann, und sich mit den Leuten verständigen kann, hat man die Möglichkeit, ein Land ganz anders kennenzulernen.'
> *Foreign languages are extremely important. Within an integrating Europe it is important that you can make yourself understood to other nationalities. As*

Table 10.5 Percentages of Leeds and Kiel pupils responding to the request to complete the statement with the phrase which appeared applicable to them: If German/English were not taught in the school, I would probably . . .

	Age/Year	Leeds (%)	Kiel (%)
not bother learning	13/92	54.9 (n = 113)	30.9 (n = 139)
German/English at all	15/94	70.4 (n = 115)	27.0 (n = 137)
try to get lessons in	13/92	22.1 (n = 113)	33.8 (n = 139)
German/English somewhere else	15/94	13.0 (n = 115)	43.1 (n = 137)
pick up German/English in	13/92	10.6 (n = 113)	33.1 (n = 139)
everyday situations (books,	15/94	10.4 (n = 115)	24.1 (n = 137)
mags, newspapers, etc.)			

> soon as you can speak the language and make yourself understood, you have the opportunity to get to know the country in a completely different way. (Year 8 pupil)

– and English in particular:

> 'Mit Englisch kann man überall durch.' *You can manage with English everywhere* (Year 10 pupil).
> 'Englisch ist die Weltsprache.' *English is the world language* (Year 10 pupil).
> 'Jedes Kind kann Englisch, in jedem Land.' *Every kid can speak English, in every country* (Year 6 pupil).

In order to gain some insight to the importance attached by pupils to learning German/English, Leeds and Kiel pupils were asked to respond to what they would do, in the hypothetical situation where English were not taught at school (see Table 10.5).

There appears to be a clear distinction between the more pro-active reaction of Kiel pupils and the rather apathetic response of Leeds pupils. Up to 70.4% of Leeds pupils opting not to bother learning German at all seems to suggest that Leeds pupils rather struggle to appreciate any real relevance or importance it may have. The contrast with the reaction of Kiel pupils (in terms of English) is striking. More than two-thirds of German pupils claim that they would make an effort to learn English elsewhere or in different ways. This may indicate an awareness of English competence as an important life skill.

Table 10.6 Percentages of Kiel pupils responding to statements in relation to: If French were not taught in the school, I would probably . . .

Response	Age/Year	Percentage
not bother learning French	13/92	33.3 ($n = 42$)
at all	15/94	63.4 ($n = 42$)
	15/92	12.5 ($n = 8$)
	17/94	12.5 ($n = 8$)
try to get lessons in	13/92	33.3 ($n = 42$)
French somewhere else	15/94	19.5 ($n = 42$)
	15/92	62.5 ($n = 8$)
	17/94	75.0 ($n = 8$)
pick up French in	13/92	31.0 ($n = 42$)
everyday situations	15/94	14.6 ($n = 42$)
(books, mags,	15/92	25.0 ($n = 8$)
newspapers, etc.)	17/94	12.5 ($n = 8$)

Table 10.7 Percentages of pupils completing the sentence: 'I believe German/English should be . . .'

	Age/Yr	Leeds (%) ($n = 188$)	Kiel (%) ($n = 198$)
taught to all pupils	13/94	15.4 ($n = 188$)	62.6 ($n = 198$)
	13/92	13.3 ($n = 113$)	64.5 ($n = 138$)
	15/94	4.3 ($n = 115$)	68.3 ($n = 139$)
	15/92	0.0 ($n = 13$)	72.4 ($n = 58$)
	17/94	30.8 ($n = 13$)	71.9 ($n = 57$)
taught only to	13/94	79.8 ($n = 188$)	34.8 ($n = 198$)
those pupils who	13/92	85.8 ($n = 113$)	34.1 ($n = 138$)
wish to learn it	15/94	93.0 ($n = 115$)	30.9 ($n = 139$)
	15/92	100 ($n = 13$)	27.6 ($n = 58$)
	17/94	69.2 ($n = 13$)	26.3 ($n = 57$)
omitted from the	13/94	4.8 ($n = 188$)	2.5 ($n = 198$)
school curriculum	13/92	0.9 ($n = 113$)	1.4 ($n = 138$)
	15/94	2.6 ($n = 115$)	0.7 ($n = 139$)
	15/92	0.0 ($n = 13$)	0.0 ($n = 58$)
	17/94	0.0 ($n = 13$)	1.8 ($n = 57$)

The Kiel reaction to French is not quite so enthusiastic but still more positive than is the case for Leeds pupils' response to German (see Table 10.6).

The responses of the 10% sample interviewed corroborates the above distinction between Leeds and Kiel pupils. Between 44% and 53% of Leeds interviewees claim they would not take a German course elsewhere if it were not on offer at their school. In excess of 80% of Kiel pupils respond positively with regard to learning English.

Are languages so important that they should be taught to all pupils? (See Table 10.7). Again the Kiel pupils are much more *dirigiste* than their Leeds counterparts, keener on a *laissez-faire* approach.

What is it all for in any case? What do pupils intend to do with any language competence they may gain? (See Table 10.8.) Once again the generally more positive attitude of the Kiel pupils is apparent. There is little doubt that the Kiel pupils attach an importance to English competence which most of their Leeds peers fail to appreciate with regard to their learning of German. Given that a learner's perception of the importance of the subject of learning is a key factor in the quality of the learner's motivation, this is a depressing but all too predictable outcome for Leeds teachers.

How English Learning Could be Enhanced

The trends for Kiel 11–13 and 13–15 cohorts (English and French) broadly replicate the responses of Leeds learners of German (see Chapter 8, p. 131ff). (See Tables 10.9 and 10.10)

Where any changes are suggested, the emphasis in responses to open questions and interview questions appears to be on greater attention given to activities relating to oral work:

'Mehr reden; nicht so viel lesen; weniger Grammatik; nicht so viele sture Vokabel machen; mal was anders.' *More speaking; not so much reading; less grammar; less boring old vocabulary; something different for a change.* (Year 10)

'Möglichst viel sprechen. Ein Sprachgefühl entwickeln.' *As much speaking as possible. Develop a feeling of the language.* (Year 8)

'Mehr Sprachübung. Wenn man im Ausland ist, sollte man fragen können, wo das Postamt ist, zum Beispiel.' *More speaking practice. When you're in a foreign country, you should be able to ask where the post-office is, for example.* (Year 8)

There is certainly a demand for greater variety:

'Der Unterricht ist ziemlich langweilig.' *The lessons are fairly boring.* (Year 10)

One pupil outlines what this means in practice:

'Einen Satz durcharbeiten; die Hausaufgabe; am nächsten Tag Haus-

Table 10.8 Future intentions re German/English. Pupils were asked to tick the statement/s which applied to them.

Statement	Place/Age/Year	Percentage
I am working towards getting a good GCSE grade	Leeds/13/94	54.1 ($n = 194$)
	Leeds/13/92	80.0 ($n = 115$)
	Leeds 15/94	89.6 ($n = 115$)
I want to take A-level German	Leeds/13/94	16.5 ($n = 194$)
	Leeds/13/92	27.0 ($n = 115$)
	Leeds 15/94	8.7 ($n = 115$)
I want to take Abitur[a] English – main subject	Kiel/13/94	21.0 ($n = 204$)
	Kiel/13/92	27.3 ($n = 139$)
	Kiel/15/94	16.5 ($n = 139$)
I want to take Abitur[a] English – subsidiary subject	Kiel/13/94	11.3 ($n = 204$)
	Kiel/13/92	15.1 ($n = 139$)
	Kiel/15/94	23.0 ($n = 139$)
I want to study German at university I want to study English at university	Leeds/13/94	5.7 ($n = 194$)
	Leeds/13/92	10.4 ($n = 115$)
	Leeds 15/94	0.0 ($n = 115$)
	Kiel/13/94	0.0 ($n = 204$)
	Kiel/13/92	3.6 ($n = 139$)
	Kiel/15/94	2.2 ($n = 139$)
I want to speak German well enough to get a job there I want to speak English well enough to get a job there	Leeds/13/94	15.5 ($n = 194$)
	Leeds/13/92	20.0 ($n = 115$)
	Leeds 15/94	11.3 ($n = 115$)
	Kiel/13/94	34.3 ($n = 204$)
	Kiel/13/92	50.4 ($n = 139$)
	Kiel/15/94	46.8 ($n = 139$)
I want to give it up as soon as I can	Leeds/13/94	21.1 ($n = 194$)
	Leeds/13/92	4.3 ($n = 115$)
	Leeds 15/94	12.2 ($n = 115$)
	Kiel/13/94	0.5 ($n = 204$)
	Kiel/13/92	0.0 ($n = 139$)
	Kiel/15/94	1.4 ($n = 139$)
I haven't really thought about it	Leeds/13/94	41.2 ($n = 194$)
	Leeds/13/92	38.3 ($n = 115$)
	Leeds 15/94	27.8 ($n = 115$)
	Kiel/13/94	29.4 ($n = 204$)
	Kiel/13/92	25.2 ($n = 139$)
	Kiel/15/94	24.5 ($n = 139$)
I don't care about German because I am no good at it I don't care about English because I am no good at it	Leeds/13/94	11.3 ($n = 194$)
	Leeds/13/92	0.0 ($n = 115$)
	Leeds 15/94	5.2 ($n = 115$)
	Kiel/13/94	0.5 ($n = 204$)
	Kiel/13/92	0.7 ($n = 139$)
	Kiel/15/94	1.4 ($n = 139$)

[a] Abitur: A-level equivalent

Table 10.9 Percentages of 13 and 15 year old Kiel pupils in 1992 and the same pupils in 1994 responding to the question: 'If you had the opportunity to change the way *English* is taught in your school, what would you do?'

Suggestion	13/92 (15/94) (n = 139)	13/94 (n = 204)	15/92 (17/94) (n = 59)
No change	21.6 (18.0)	18.6	11.9 (5.1)
More interesting teaching methods	36.7 (6.5)		39.0 (49.2)
Change teacher	12.2 (6.5)	10.3	3.4 (6.8)
More interesting texts			(13.6)
Other	10.8 (31.6)		32.1 (3.3)
No response	18.7 (37.4)	44.1	13.6 (22.0)

Some pupils give responses appropriate to more than one category

Table 10.10 Percentages of 13 and 15 year old Kiel pupils in 1992 and the same pupils in 1994 responding to the question: 'If you had the opportunity to change the way French is taught in your school, what would you do?'

Suggestion	13/92 (15/94) (n = 42)	15/92 17/94 (n = 8)
No change	19.0 (11.9)	12.5 (12.5)
More interesting teaching methods	31.0 (11.9)	(12.5)
More exchanges		(12.5)
Change teacher	7.1	25.0
Other	14.3 (33.3)	(12.5)
No response	28.6 (42.9)	62.5 (50.0)

Some pupils give responses appropriate to more than one category

aufgabe vergleichen; wenn man es nicht macht, kriegt man Ärger, muß es nacharbeiten, doppelt machen; wieder neue Seite, durcharbeiten; zwischendurch erzählt er was aus seiner Jugend oder über England.'
Work your way through a sentence; homework; check the homework next day; if you haven't done it, you're given a hard time and have to do it later, twice; then a new page; work your way through it; in between he tells you something about when he was young or about England. (Year 10)

The demand for variety may be met by the implementation of a wider range of media:

'Ab und zu mal englische Nachrichten im Fernsehen zeigen, damit man die englische Sprache auch vom hören kennenlernt.' *Show us the English news on television from time to time so that we can also get to know what the English language sounds like.* (Year 6)

'Mehr englische Filme gucken.' *Watch more English films.* (Year 10)

It is interesting to note that 25% of 13-year-old Kiel pupils interviewed in 1992 suggest a reduction in the amount of scolding as a potential enhancement in English lessons.

'Der Lehrer soll nicht so viel herumbrüllen.' *The teacher shouldn't yell and scream so much.* (Year 6)

'Nicht so streng sein; nicht so viele Strafen.' *He shouldn't be so strict; shouldn't give out so many punishments.* (Year 8)

'Manche Lehrer flippen schnell aus.' *Many of the teachers quickly lose their cool!* (Year 10)

One 15 year old (1994) appeals for a calmer approach:

'Mehr Zeit, Geduld und Ruhe.' *More time, patience and quiet.* (Year 10)

A 17 year old (1994) appears critical of the teacher's English competence and suggests the requirement for all teachers of English to spend a year in an English-speaking country:

'Alle Englischlehrer müßten ein Jahr oder mehr im englischsprachigen Ausland verbringen, um "lebendiges Englisch" zu lernen.' *All English teachers should be required to spend at least a year in an English-speaking country, in order to learn English as it is really spoken.* (Year 12)

A feeling of *Schadenfreude* on the part of Leeds teachers may be misplaced, however. Some respondents are very happy with their teacher's provision:

'Den Unterricht macht er schon witzig genug.' *Lessons are already great fun.* (Year 6)

'Sie hat den Unterricht bis jetzt so gut gemacht, da gibt's nichts zu verbessern' *Up to now the lessons have been fine; there is nothing to improve upon.* (10)

'Ich bin mit dem Unterricht recht zufrieden.' *I am perfectly happy with the lessons.* (Year 8)

These findings concur broadly with those of Solmecke (1983, 130ff.) who surveyed over 2000 16–19 year olds on their reaction to the quality of their English-learning experience: 57.5% regarded it as bad, 25% as acceptable, only 17.4% as good and 14% chose not to comment. In terms of how the teaching could be improved the following suggestions were made:

– more oral work (6%)
– use of 'proper' English (7.3%)
– more intensive teaching (3%)
– more variety (7.7%)
– the appointment of properly qualified teachers (7.1%): 'Wir wollen richtige Englischlehrer und keine ausrangierten Erdkundelehrer' *We want proper English teachers and not discarded geography teachers.*

Other suggestions included: optional learning of English; an earlier start to English learning; change everything; more resources – less focus on textbook; travel to England; contact with speakers of English.

The Shared Perception of Effort and Progress

Much was made in Chapter 9 (see also Chapter 3) of the importance of the teacher and pupil sharing a perception of the amount of effort and progress being made. It was argued that this had an important role to play in the quality of the teacher–pupil relationship. It was a source of some disappointment that the majority of pupils appeared not to know what their teacher thought. Was the picture any different in Kiel? (See Table 10.11.)

Table 10.11 Percentage of Kiel pupils aged 13 in 1992 and 15 in 1994 who claim not to know what their teacher thinks regarding their effort and progress in English

	Don't know re: effort	*Don't know re: progress*
Kiel: 13/92	28.1	32.4
Kiel: 15/94	37.4	41.2

Table 10.12 Percentage of Kiel pupils aged 13 in 1992 and 15 in 1994 who claim not to know what their teacher thinks regarding their effort and progress in French

	Don't know re: effort	*Don't know re: progress*
Kiel: 13/92	38.1	40.5
Kiel: 15/94	47.6	50.0

The responses of Kiel pupils learning English are remarkably similar to those of their Leeds counterparts. The same problem of pupils' ignorance of what their English teachers think about their progress and effort exists in Kiel but to a lesser extent. Again this is disturbing in a learning context where so much store is put by continuous assessing. Learners of French also claim to be kept in the dark. (See Table 10.12.)

There appears to be a serious information gap in terms of feedback from teachers to pupils on their effort and progress. The German approach to assessment includes regular formal tests. On the basis of responses from pupils in this sample, it appears that these tests seem to be summative rather than formative in nature, given that pupils claim to be unaware of any messages provided by any feedback. The product rather than the quality of the learning appears to be at issue.

Parental Influence

Kiel pupils in 1992 and the same pupils in 1994 were surveyed in the same way as their Leeds peers, to test the hypothesis that their home context offers greater opportunities for the use of English and for support from parents than is the case for German in Leeds. (See Table 10.13.)

Although Kiel pupils feel that the amount of encouragement they receive increases between the ages of 11 and 13 ('Wenn ich ein gutes Zeugnis bekomme, dann bekomme ich eine Überraschung und meine Eltern helfen mir, damit ich die Überraschung bekomme.' *If I get a good report, I get a surprise and my parents help me so that I get the surprise*, 11 year old), the trend for other cohorts in both locations suggests a slight diminution over the two years. This is difficult to rationalise with any confidence. It may be the case that younger pupils are more attracted to higher scores, almost regardless of the question. Aged 13 and again at age 15, they may be more reflective and critical. Perhaps they have reached the stage where they are striving for independence and do not wish to admit to support and encouragement

Table 10.13 Percentages of Kiel pupils responding to the question: 'How much do your parents encourage you to learn foreign languages?'

	Not at all		*A little*		*Very much*			
	1	*2*	*3*	*4*	*5*	*Sample*	*Mean*	*S.D.*
Kiel 11/92	9.7	9.2	26.0	24.5	30.6	196	3.57	1.27
Kiel 13/94	8.4	3.4	24.0	28.9	35.3	204	3.78	1.23
Kiel 13/92	5.9	6.6	21.3	33.8	32.4	136	3.80	1.14
Kiel 15/94	8.0	10.1	26.8	25.4	29.7	138	3.59	1.24
Kiel 15/92	3.4	13.6	18.6	28.8	35.6	59	3.80	1.17
Kiel 17/94	13.8	6.9	31.0	20.7	27.6	58	3.41	1.34

from parents ('Meine Eltern ermutigen mich aber mit geringem Erfolg. Muß ich selber wissen.' *My parents encourage me but with little success. It's up to me!* 15 year old;). Perhaps age and increasing maturity are also factors. ('Ich bin ziemlich auf mich selbst angewiesen.' *I am fairly self-sufficient.*15 year old.) (See Oskamp, 1977 and Chapter 3, p. 45ff.) This trend does not apply to pupils aged 15 in 1992 who feel most encouraged ('Meine Eltern freuen sich, daß ich so gut bin.' *My parents are pleased that I'm so good!*).

The encouragement to learn foreign languages perceived by Kiel pupils may be explained by the importance attached to English by the German education system and society in general. Without English qualifications, job opportunities are limited. It may be the case that Kiel parents are in a better position to offer encouragement in the form of support, given that more of them have English competence than seems to be the case for parents with German competence in Leeds (see Chapter 6, p. 87ff). Unlike Kiel, Leeds did not have a 'languages for all' policy in all schools until the advent of the National Curriculum. If pupils measure encouragement in terms of how much their parents can help them with their homework, and responses of interviewees suggest that they do, then it is hardly surprising that the scores in Leeds are generally lower. Interview responses also provide evidence to suggest some pupils interpreting parents' threats and punishments as a form of encouragement to enhance performance: 'Sie geben Druck. Wenn ich für die Schule nicht lerne, dann darf ich nicht weg.' *They put pressure on. If I don't do my schoolwork, then I' m not allowed out.'* This was not evident in the responses of Leeds pupils.

The Teacher's Burden

Pupils in Kiel and Leeds appear to hold their teachers responsible for all that is good and bad in their foreign language learning experience. This burden may be arguably more onerous for the teacher of German in Leeds than it is for the teacher of English (and to a lesser extent French) in Kiel, given the discrepancy between some of the factors contributing to the pupils' motivation, not least that relating to perceived usefulness. The foreign language teaching context (especially regarding English) and the data provided here by pupils, suggest that Kiel teachers enjoy a number of advantages over their Leeds colleagues:

(1) English enjoys high status on the school curriculum; Kiel pupils start learning English earlier than those in Leeds and are obliged to learn it for longer; English is allocated more time on the school timetable. (See Chapter 4, p. 61ff.)
(2) Kiel pupils are conscious of the importance and usefulness of English and its status as the 'world language'; many more Kiel pupils than is

Table 10.14 Percentage of 11–13 and 13–15 cohorts responding to the request to give their reason/s for learning German/English: 'I am learning German/English because . . . '

Reason	Place/Age/Year	I disagree 1	2	Neutral 3	4	I agree 5	Sample	Mean	S.D.
I enjoy it	Leeds/13/94	25.5	15.1	24.5	20.3	14.6	192	2.83	1.39
	Leeds/13/92	5.3	4.4	18.4	28.1	43.9	114	4.01	1.13
	Leeds/15/94	15.9	8.8	29.2	28.3	17.7	113	3.23	1.30
	Kiel/13/94	30.3	20.2	24.7	9.6	15.2	198	2.59	1.40
	Kiel/13/92	31.9	22.2	23.0	11.9	11.1	135	2.48	1.34
	Kiel/15/94	27.3	17.3	33.1	11.5	10.8	139	2.61	1.29
It will allow	Leeds/13/94	10.5	8.9	32.6	24.7	23.2	190	3.41	1.23
me to meet	Leeds/13/92	1.7	7.8	22.6	34.8	33.0	115	3.90	1.01
and talk with	Leeds/15/94	6.1	4.4	23.7	42.1	23.7	114	3.73	1.07
more people	Kiel/13/94	42.7	18.6	21.6	10.1	7.0	199	2.20	1.28
	Kiel/13/92	47.1	16.9	15.4	14.7	5.9	136	2.15	1.32
	Kiel/15/94	56.5	18.1	15.2	6.5	3.6	138	1.83	1.13
I think it will	Leeds/13/94	20.0	20.0	29.5	14.7	15.8	190	2.86	1.33
help me to get	Leeds/13/92	5.3	8.8	40.4	20.2	25.2	114	3.51	1.12
a good job	Leeds/15/94	6.2	6.2	38.9	34.5	14.2	113	3.44	1.02
	Kiel/13/94	22.3	22.3	39.6	8.6	7.1	197	2.56	1.14
	Kiel/13/92	18.4	25.7	35.3	11.8	8.8	136	2.67	1.17
	Kiel/15/94	24.6	18.1	37.7	8.7	10.9	138	2.63	1.25
An educated	Leeds/13/94	13.1	7.9	28.8	19.9	30.4	191	3.47	1.36
person should	Leeds/13/92	13.0	9.6	26.1	23.5	27.8	115	3.44	1.34
be able to	Leeds/15/94	17.7	8.8	35.4	26.5	11.5	113	3.05	1.24
speak a	Kiel/13/94	20.0	15.4	33.3	20.5	10.8	195	2.87	1.26
foreign	Kiel/13/92	25.9	19.3	28.1	16.3	10.4	135	2.66	1.31
language	Kiel/15/94	26.8	26.1	28.3	10.9	8.0	138	2.47	1.22
I am interest-	Leeds/13/94	26.8	26.8	31.6	8.9	5.8	190	2.40	1.15
ed in German/	Leeds/13/92	13.9	21.7	35.7	14.8	13.9	115	2.93	1.22
English people	Leeds/15/94	20.4	17.7	36.3	22.1	3.5	113	2.71	1.13
and their way	Kiel/13/94	10.8	17.4	30.8	23.1	17.9	195	3.20	1.23
of life	Kiel/13/92	21.5	21.5	22.2	15.6	19.3	135	2.90	1.42
	Kiel/15/94	14.5	21.7	28.3	15.9	19.6	138	3.04	1.32
I have to take	Leeds/13/94	50.7	14.5	19.9	9.5	5.5	190	2.05	1.26
a foreign	Leeds/13/92	49.1	15.8	19.3	10.5	5.3	114	2.07	1.26
language	Leeds/15/94	62.6	8.7	10.4	9.6	8.7	115	1.93	1.38
	Kiel/13/94	29.3	17.7	23.2	12.6	17.2	198	2.71	1.44
	Kiel/13/92	29.6	17.8	23.0	10.4	19.3	135	2.72	1.47
	Kiel/15/94	26.8	10.9	24.6	15.2	22.5	138	2.96	1.50

the case for Leeds (re: German) (a) think that English should be taught to everyone (see Table 10.7) and (b) express the intention to use their English competence in the future (see Table 10.8).

(3) Leeds pupils regard enjoyment as the main reason for learning German. This is not the case to anything like the same extent with pupils in Kiel who generally feel the need to learn it regardless of the level of enjoyment.

It is interesting to note that when this question was asked of German pupils in the interview context, they found it very difficult to come up with a reason for their learning English without prompting. Is this an indicator that they take the learning of English for granted? Is it simply something which has to be done and is not up for dicussion?

(4) Kiel pupils' preferred travel destinations tend to be English-speaking countries (see Table 7.3). This is also the case for those who express an interest in working abroad. Only a small percentage of Leeds pupils nominate countries where German is spoken (see Table 7.8).

(5) Kiel pupils enjoy more frequent opportunities to practise their English competence in authentic situations (see Table 6.12). (Caveat: for Leeds pupils there appears to be no statistically significant relationship between having this opportunity and their perception of the usefulness of German.)

(6) Kiel pupils experience travel abroad at an earlier age than Leeds pupils. (See caveat for 5.)

(7) Where Kiel parents encourage pupils in specific subjects as opposed to providing encouragement generally, English is likely to be one of those subjects.

(8) A higher percentage of Kiel parents have competence in English than is the case for Leeds parents' competence in German and are therefore in a stronger position to offer practical support. (See Chapter 6, p. 87ff.)

Summary

So what can be learned from the Germans? Kiel secondary school pupils learning English (and in some cases French) seem to hold similar views to their Leeds peers. They have broadly the same likes and dislikes. They articulate the same complaints. The buck stops with the teacher, be the perception positive or negative.

The difference in perception is linked to the foreign language learning/teaching context. The Kiel pupils find themselves in a context where English competence is important. It is seen as a life skill. The place of English on the school timetable is not questioned; it is almost taken for granted. Because pupils see the importance of English, they may be prepared to put up with a learning experience which may be regarded as boring or not much fun. 'It has to be done, so let's get on with it,' appears to be the attitude. The Leeds context produces a very different mindset.

Chapter 11

'I Did It My Way!'

A broad conclusion which may be drawn from this and other studies (e.g. Gardner & Lambert, 1972) is that pupils learn for two reasons: (1) because they find the subject of learning useful; (2) because they find the subject of learning enjoyable.

The purpose of this chapter is to provide some tried and proven suggestions as to how teachers may be able to: (a) give pupils a more positive view of the utilitarian value of foreign languages; and (b) amend their standard approaches to foreign language teaching with minimal extra work, in order to enhance the learning experience for their pupils.

Introduction

You may recall Wayne, Chris, Hannah and Norman who were introduced in Chapter 1. These pupils displayed some of the identifying characteristics for pupils who may be categorised as 'disaffected', 'demotivated' or 'switched-off language learning'. What follows are some examples of attempts to switch Wayne, Chris, Hannah and Norman and similar pupils back on to languages, if only for a limited period, and take the 'de' out of their apparent or real demotivation. They have been tried out with real pupils, the same pupils to whom I have given the names above and who stimulated the study behind the writing of this book. It must be recognised, however, that these approaches worked in one particular context, for one particular teacher working with one particular group of pupils. Although reasonably confident that that which follows can be transferred from one teaching/learning context to another, I cannot guarantee it. The risk is worth taking. 'Feel the fear and do it anyway' (Jeffers, 1991).

Some of what follows is anecdotal. I make no apologies for this. Although conscious of the dangers of generalising from a sample of one, I feel nevertheless that much can be learned from an analysis of the experience and the approach adopted. Details are provided which may at first seem superfluous. Although they add colour to the anecdotes, this is not their purpose. They form part of the tapestry contributing to the positive outcome. This, I trust, will be drawn out in the analysis.

Bread and Butter Activities

Before exploring activities which may not belong to 'the norm', those which require special preparation or are associated with the exploitation of an 'exceptional' opportunity, it is important to acknowledge the significance of those activities which may belong to the everyday agenda of the modern languages classroom.

Personal identification

This topic has the potential to pose problems in that pupils may complain that describing themselves is boring, and what is the point of it anyway? It may pose particular problems for teachers of second foreign languages in that pupils have done it all before in their first foreign language. A simple solution may be provided by giving each pupil an alternative identity. Each may become a pop or sports star, a famous actor or politician from the present or past. The problem for the pupil, however, is that she is kept in the dark as to the persona she has taken on. The new identity is written on a sticker which is affixed to the pupil's back. In order to establish her new name, the pupil then has to go around the class asking others questions which may be answered only with a 'Oui/Ja/Si' or 'Non/Nein/No': e.g. 'Bin ich ein Mann?' *Am I a man?* 'Lebe ich noch?' *Am I still alive?* 'Bin ich jung?' *Am I young?* 'Bin ich oft in den Nachrichten?' *Am I often in the news?* Eventually the pupil may establish the newly acquired identity. Perhaps not. This does not matter too much as the effort invested is more important than a successful outcome. Pupils do not react as having failed but as having enjoyed the process.

This activity often succeeds because it has a point. There is an information-gap which pupils have to fill. They are challenged. They are not asking a question to which they already know the answer (in the fashion of the teacher asking 'Was ist das?'/'Qu'est-ce que c'est?' ' while presenting the flashcard of a rabbit; she knows it is a rabbit; all the pupils know it is a rabbit; what is the point in asking the question?). Pupils are also given the opportunity to get out of their chairs, to break the formal straitjacket, to move around the classroom, to interact with their classmates, to make some noise (purposeful and of acceptable volume).

The activity is not without risk, however. The teacher who remains unconvinced that her classroom management is up to the challenge of up to 30 pupils all moving around the room and talking at the same time, is better advised to postpone this activity until such times as the full co-operation of the pupils is assured. How can the teacher be sure that the pupils are all interacting in the target language? How can she be sure that one pupil is not simply telling the other the name on the sticker? This calls for a high level of trust and monitoring. How misled it is to regard pupil-centred activities as the opportunity for the teacher to have a breather. There is no respite.

Experience has taught me that under the appropriate conditions the risks are worth taking. The activity allows so many pupils to practise the same vocabulary and structures again and again without becoming bored or realising that they are engaged in what amounts to little more than a drilling exercise.

Himmel und Hölle

This game has been around for a very long time. The chances are that you played it as a child. The chances are that your pupils have already played it, albeit outside the foreign language learning context. This should be seen as an advantage rather than a reason to avoid it. The example provided below is again on the theme of *Personal Identification* but has the flexibility to cover all manner of topic areas including *Shopping, Holidays, Hobbies inter alia*.

Pupils are provided with a square piece of paper as illustrated in Figure 11.1. They are given oral instructions on how to fold the piece of paper in the target language. (This is the ideal. Whether the instructions on how to play the game are given in the target language or mother-tongue depends on the level of ability of the class. Consideration of investment and pay-off is important. If it is going to take too long to complete this first phase of the task in the target language and/or the pupils are going to become frustrated because of the degree of difficulty and consequently lose any enthusiasm for the activity, then resorting to the mother-tongue is justified.) Pupils work in pairs. Partner A indicates a number. Partner B has to count up to this number while moving the model in and out. Partner A selects a name. Partner B then has to move the model in an out while spelling out the selected name. Having done this, parter A unfolds the model at the appropriate place and interprets the illustration to describe the attributes of the person identified.

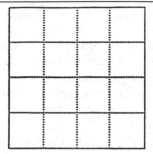

Give each pupil a square piece of paper (20 cm × 20 cm). If the illustrations are already drawn in the squares (see Figure 11.2), this makes life easier. It is also possible, however, to give the pupils a blank square of paper on which they can draw their own illustrations. This works much better once pupils are familiar with the model.

Give the pupils the following instructions in the target language:

- Put the square of paper onto your desk with the drawings face down (*Legt bitte das Blatt auf den Tisch mit den Bildern unten.*)
- Fold the paper along the lines drawn, like this (*Faltet bitte das Blatt so, und dann so . . .*) (The pupils manage to follow the instructions as much as a result of what they observe as of what they hear.)

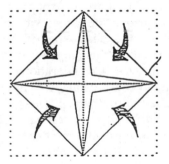

- Turn the paper over (*Dreht das Blatt um*)
- Take one corner and fold it to the middle, like this (*Nehmt bitte die erste Ecke und faltet sie zur Mitte, so . . .*)
- Take the second/third/fourth corner and fold it to the middle like this (*. . . und dann die zweite/dritte/vierte Ecke, so . . .*)

Figure 11.1 Himmel und Hölle – instructions
(The illustrations are taken from *TIP* 3/90 Tiefdruck Schwann-Bagel)

- Now you have created a smaller square (*Jetz habt ihr ein kelineres Quadrat*)
- Turn the paper over (*Dreht das Blatt um*)

- Repeat the above, i.e.
  take one corner and fold it to the middle, like this (*Nehmt bitte die erste Ecke und faltet sie zur Mitte, so ...*
  Take the second/third/fourth corner and fold it to the middle like this (*... und dann die zweite/dritte/vierte Ecke, so ...*)
- Now you have created a very small square *Jetz habt ihr ein ganz kleines Quadrat*)
- Press down in the middle of the square (*Drückt die Mitte ein*)
- If you have followed the instructions, the numbers are on the outside and the illustrations on the inside. (*Wenn ihr alles richtig gemacht habt, sind die Ziffern außen und die Bilder innen.*)

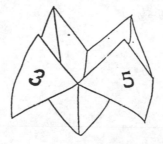

Figure 11.1 (*cont.*)

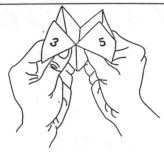

- Put the thumb and first finger of your right hand under two of the corners, like this (*Mit dem Daumen und dem ersten Finger der rechten Hand unter diese zwei Klappen, so . . .*)
- Put the thumb and first finger of your left hand under the other two corners like this (*Mit dem Daumen und dem ersten Finger der linken Hand unter diese zwei Klappen, so . . .*)

Figure 11.1 (*cont.*)

Figure 11.2 Himmel und Hölle – an example

This activity has much to commend it:

- pupils are given a real reason to listen; if they do not listen and watch they cannot make the model;
- pupils are given the opportunity to learn kinesthetically (an important issue in terms of differentiation: some pupils learn best visually; some learn best aurally; others learn best kinesthetically – by touching, feeling, making and moving.);
- they practise counting;
- they practise the alphabet (for which they seem to need lots of consolidation work);
- There is a point to the activity – they do not know the attributes of the people named on the model; they are required to find out and relay this to their partners in the target language.
- They practise the same language and structures again and again without feeling the pain of the drill in which they are engaged; they do not see it as a drill; for them it is a game.

Role-play

Role-play is a feature of so many modern languages classes. It has to be. Given that Scotty cannot beam us across to France/Germany/Spain, *Star Trek* style, we have to pretend from time to time. The point of so many of the pre-communicative presentation-and practice-tasks is to get ever closer to the stage where we try to create the plausible, (not quite) communicative context of the pupil buying stamps at the French/German/Spanish post-office, albeit at the teacher's desk in the classroom. At the beginning of Year 7 pupils appear to enjoy role-play so much. With time, however, and with replication of the same approach and same outcomes, pupils' enthusiasm diminishes to the point of extinction. What can be done to keep the fires of enthusiasm burning? How can the standard approach to the progression from presentation to 'production' (in the classroom context a pot of gold at the end of the rainbow) be 'spiced up' to make the role-play experience more enjoyable or at least tolerable?

I asked my pupils. They came up with the idea of making the pretence even more extreme. Rather than pretending they were in Germany, they wanted to change their identity and make the context even more contrived. They were making an appeal for their imagination and creativity to be exploited. We looked at some of the standard GCSE role-play situations and the pupils provided their ideas on alternative contexts (see Table 11.1).

Some of the suggested contexts on the right of Table 11.1 can apply to more than one of the role-play situations on the left. Pupils wanted to take on the persona of their favourite pop-star or transpose the context to that

Table 11.1 Role-play situations

Topic	New context
Directions	In space
At the doctor's	A soap opera
Holidays	On a desert island
In the hotel	As a famous person
Shopping	Limited budget
At the post office	Change of mood
Hobbies	In prison
Daily routine	As a German/French speaking animal
My family	

of their favourite soap-opera. Authenticity, plausibility and context-related appropriateness of the target language were non-issues. The most important feature for me was the enthusiasm shown by the pupils and their application to a task of which they felt they had ownership. The pay-off was very positive but of limited duration. It is a sad truth that most of the 'novel' ideas which seem to work in the classroom have a limited shelf-life. Once the sell-by date is reached, what was once enjoyable and fulfilling becomes old-hat and boring. The teacher is then challenged to find the next novel idea or to relaunch an old idea but in different packaging.

(It is not by accident that the language of the marketplace features in the above paragraph. Schools and their teachers have become purveyors of a product. The consumers (the pupils and their parents) are demanding and expect to be entertained and seduced by a wide range of goods in smart wrappers which they can enjoy. If they do not like what is on offer, some vote with their feet by opting for different products (subjects) or even by transferring to different outlets (schools); others, who find themselves in more restricting circumstances, are obliged to stay with their local outlet but they register their objections in their negative behaviour and attitude.)

The robbery

The enjoyment of role-play can be enhanced by giving the pupils the opportunity to dress up. Many teachers of foreign languages keep a bag of jumble in their classrooms so that pupils can change their persona and really get into the role. When dressing up is added to a video recording of the performance, motivation is often enhanced. Pupils sometimes show a heightened determination to get the language absolutely correct. Pupils, who otherwise have shown a mild indifference to details of grammar and pronunciation, have been heard to say: 'Oh, I got that wrong. Can I do it again?' Not only does the opportunity to be immortalised on the silver screen have a positive influence on their motivation, but the dressing up sometimes seems to provide pupils with the mask behind which some need to hide in order to be able to set aside their inhibitions and cover up any embarrassment felt when speaking in this strange code.

On one occasion per class, the dressing up may be taken a stage further. The teacher arranges for a colleague or an older pupil to dress up in a bizarre fashion; for example, hat, sunglasses, false beard, striped shirt, kilt and wellington boots. Ten minutes into the lesson, this partner bursts into the room brandishing a toy gun. He (in my experience it has mostly been a man or boy) points the gun at the class and demands silence. He then directs his attention towards the teacher and demands: 'Hände hoch oder ich schieße!' *Put up your hands or I'll shoot!* The teacher makes her shock and terror overt and puts her hands in the air. The robber (because that is what he is) then conducts a search, finds the teacher's purse and makes his exit. Once the pupils have settled down (some are open-mouthed in their amazement at such an interruption; others giggle because they recognise the identity of the robber) and the teacher has regained her composure (I did this on one occasion when my 'partner in crime' genuinely did frighten me half to death so violent was his entry, so threatening his demeanour and so violent his body search), it is their task to put together a target language description of the robber and reconstruct the robbery for the police who are sure to be on their way to the scene of the crime. (Now you can understand why this only works on one occasion with each class.)

Does the investment of time, energy, preparation and persuasion skills produce a commensurate pay-off? I think so. Even though this is very much a 'one off', the reaction of the pupils and sometimes the quality of their work suggest that this can be one of the highlights of their foreign language learning year. It may be the first thing which springs to mind when they recall their foreign language learning at school in later life.

What has been provided so far is a highly edited version of the plethora of day-to-day activities which form part of the language learning process. Each teacher will have her favourites. The most effective are normally the simplest and often require little preparation. They should not be devalued because of this.

What follows are examples reflecting a 'project approach'. They require more preparation and rather than forming part of one lesson, cover a series of lessons.

The Project Approach I

It was obvious from a very early stage in their German learning experience that this Year 9 group to which Wayne, Chris, Hannah and Norman belonged had an aversion to textbooks, indeed any reading material beyond *Just 17*, *Viz* and in two or three cases, publications of the more adult variety. Some effort had to be made to provide them with tasks which were practical, purposeful and with concrete, short-term outcomes and rewards. This appeared at first more easily said than done but with some thought and a little good fortune, this theory eventually became the underpinning to what turned out to be successful practice.

I met Mrs Young at the school Barn Dance. She was a parent with a daughter at the school and, most importantly, a native speaker of German. Having broken the ice and touched on my difficulty with Year 9 over the pie and pea supper (is it not sad that I had nothing else to talk about other than Year 9?) I contacted Mrs Young more formally at the beginning of the following week and described in greater detail the challenge posed by Year 9 disenchantment. We met over coffee and collaborated in the planning of a devious, little ruse.

The topic of the unit of work to be undertaken was 'personal idenfica-tion'. None of the pupils in the class had ever met a real, live German before. I therefore suggested to them that rather than carrying on with our usual work we could invite a native speaker whom I knew to a little party and chat. I did not mention that what the party and chat represented was, in truth, practice in the four skills including a European and cross-curricular dimension. The good news was that we would not have to use the boring, old textbook (which is in fact far from boring and very new!). The 'bad' news was that we would have to do it all in German! I cannot claim that their cups were overflowing with enthusiasm but the general grunts and mutterings seemed to indicate a semblance of a positive response, more so for the 'little party' element than for the 'chat'. The change represented a deviation from the norm, in terms of their in-class experience. They seemed to accept it not necessarily as something potentially better but rather something that could hardly be worse. (Does Initial Teacher Training prepare one for the blows to be rained on one's self-esteem by members of the 'cool', 'anti-education culture' (Whitehead, 1996?)

The pupils and I discussed – in English – what would have to be written in the letter of invitation. With some help from me and a great deal of dictionary work, groups of pupils cobbled together a rough draft in German on the wordprocessor. We then collaborated in knocking off the rough edges and printed off the final version which was sent off with some anticipation to Frau Young.

While we waited for Frau Young's response – 'I bet she doesn't come!' 'I don't care. We won't understand what she says anyway!' – we spent the interim working on the questions we would like to ask her. These included all the questions included in any unit on personal identification:

> Wie alt sind Sie? *How old are you?* (A little rude perhaps but all in the name of German learning!)
> Wo wohnen Sie? *Where do you live?*
> Wohnen Sie in einer Wohnung oder in einem Haus? *Do you live in a flat or a house?*
> Sind Sie verheiratet? *Are you married?*
> Haben Sie Kinder? *Do you have any children?*
> Was sind Ihre Hobbys? *What are your hobbies?*
> and so on.

We struggled a little bit with the *Sie* polite form of address, but knowing Frau Young as I did, I did not have to worry that she would be offended if the pupils demonstrated inappropriate familiarity with the *du* form. We also worked on possible answers which Frau Young was likely to provide. It is all very well being able to ask the questions, but what was the point if we could not understand the answers? Do you remember the first time you asked for directions in the target language in the target language country?

In time for the first lesson of the following week Frau Young's response to our letter of invitation arrived. The pupils fought and argued for the right to open the envelope and read the contents. How much motivation can a teacher cope with? I asked a challenging revision question (Wie sagt man auf deutsch: 'with best wishes'? *What is the German for* . . . – this was how we had finished our letter to Frau Young), and the first pupil to answer correctly (after about 10 attempts we got pretty close) opened the letter – only to find it was all written in funny, German writing! We got our heads together, however, to ascertain that Frau Young had agreed to join us. We had a week to prepare.

The pupils were quite nervous on the day of Frau Young's visit. They had worked very hard and seemed anxious not to get things wrong. Each pupil had a specific responsibility as there were so many details to be covered: welcoming Frau Young; chairing the question and answer session (jetzt bist du dran! *now it's your turn!*); catering; taking photographs. Frau Young arrived armed with photo albums. She not only answered the pupils' (sometimes embarrassing) questions but also illustrated her answers with reference to the photographs. The pupils gathered around her and listened and looked with interest. It resembled storytelling time at primary school. (Why do we not do this in the secondary school foreign language class? Why do we leave behind so much good practice at the time of transfer from primary to secondary?) Frau Young used simple German and spoke at an appropriate pace. When it was obvious that comprehension was being threatened by the need for unfamiliar, rather complex target language usage, she slipped into English. With consummate skill she did not allow this to become the thin edge of the wedge. Even if she had, I would not have been concerned, in view of how interested the pupils were and of what her input was doing for the pupils' motivation.

After about 40 minutes we transferred to the food technology department where the pupils had been busy during the lunch break preparing various cakes and fruit flans, following a recipe from *Cooking the German Way* (Hobart & Sofier, 1986). The *Kaffee und Kuchen* slipped down a treat! Ignore the cultural dimension at your peril! The question and answer session continued – in English – as the pupils demonstrated their curiosity in the light of what Frau Young had told them about the war, the Wall and her life in the old East Germany. The bell for the end of school marked the end of the visit. Frau Young was thanked with a short, prepared speech in German and we exchanged 'auf Wiedersehen, Tschüs and bis zum nächsten Mal!' *Goodbye, cheerio and until the next time!* To my relief, the first phase of the visit had been a success.

Frau Young's VW Golf disappearing into the distance did not mark the end of the project, however. Just as we had worked on the invitation, so we had to get down to writing a letter of thanks. Once this had been wordprocessed and sent off we set to work on our photo-montage. Chris had acted as photographer and had done a fine job. He had never had such a good time in German before. At last he had found there was something positive he could contribute to the German lesson. The photographs were selected, mounted onto coloured card, annotated in German and displayed on the wall. Once we felt that perfection had been reached, we invited the Headteacher and the Head of Year 9 to our next lesson. They were very impressed by the pictorial record of our undertaking and were suitably effusive in their praise. (Sadly they could not comment on the quality of the German. Please see earlier reference to the absence of suitable role-models in Chapter 1, p. 4; see also Chapter 12, p. 201 on the status of foreign languages in schools.) You could almost see the pupils' hearts swell with pride. For most of them it was the first time that a member of the school hierarchy had spoken to them in anything other than vituperative terms.

What were the indicators that the project had been a success?

- Pupils had remained motivated throughout a unit which covered material which they had already dealt with in French and which is sometimes viewed as childish and tedious in terms of the manner in which it is taught.

- They learned and retained the material.
- They said they wanted more of the same: 'When can Frau Young come back?' 'Do you know any other Germans?' 'I thought Germans were all fat and dead boring but they're not, are they?'
- They had collaborated successfully, taken responsibility seriously and were proud of the products of their efforts.
- They appeared more interested and enthusiastic on their return to 'traditional' German lessons: they asked more questions about how to say certain English expressions in German; they wanted to know more about German life and culture; they wanted to meet more native speakers.

Why did the approach seem to work? Frau Young's visit was underpinned by the hunch that pupils learn because they perceive what is to be learned as useful and/or enjoyable. They were given short-term goals and specific responsibilities in accordance with what they thought they were good at; their opinions were valued; everything they did had a purpose; their efforts were recognised and praised.

The Project Approach II

A similar approach was adopted as a result of a visit to a coffee shop located at the back of a delicatessen not far from the school. As I relaxed in the peace and quiet of the empty room with its wooden floor and furniture and the authentic coal fire burning in the range, I noticed the posters on the wall, advertising the Nürnberger Spielzeugmuseum (*the Nürnberg toy museum*), the Nürnberger Weihnachtsmarkt (*the Nürnberg Christmas market*) as well as various German cheeses, wines and other specialities not too common on the shelves of local supermarkets. This led to a conversation with the waitress who told me that the elderly lady who owned the delicatessen and coffee shop was a German native. I immediately thought of Year 10, bottom set. 'Food and drink' was on the agenda. This was a topic area they had visited before with their previous teacher. They were sure to make this clear to me, in no uncertain terms. They were certain to regard it as 'boring'. I could see another opportunity to get away from the textbook and to revisit a topic in a novel and arguably more plausible manner.

I arranged another visit to the coffee shop to meet the owner. Frau Römer was delightful. As I had done with Mrs Young, I explained the situation I faced with my relatively small Year 10 class (20 pupils) and outlined my proposal and what I hoped to achieve. Frau Römer was very enthusiastic and only too pleased to help. We negotiated a day and time and a special price for a 'Kaffee und Kuchen' visit for the pupils. The language of interaction on the visit was to be German. All that remained was to sell the idea to the pupils. This proved less difficult than I had feared. They welcomed every opportunity to get out of school. The steps which followed were similar to those adopted for the visit of Mrs Young:

- we collaborated on the writing of a letter, seeking permission to visit the shop *en masse*;
- the pupils seemed to enjoy receiving and reading Frau Römer's response;
- they worked harder than usual on preparing for the visit: learning appropriate vocabulary relating to food and drink; asking for the menu; ordering; asking for the bill; paying, etc.

On the day of the visit we were welcomed warmly by Frau Römer in clear, simple, slightly accented German. The pupils were slightly shy at first. I was rather surprised at how quiet they were. I scarcely remembered them so reticent in class! It was clear that they were taking in the unique ambience, so different to the McDonald's atmosphere to which they were more accustomed. I observed them looking into the flames of the fire, the posters on the wall (there were now even more in German), the menu (which Frau Römer had written out in German). They were reading for real reasons. It was now time to order. Frau Römer and an assistant (another German native speaker and trainee teacher: 'Beziehungen sind das halbe Leben!' *It's not what you know; it's who you know!*) made their way around the tables gently and patiently, teasing out of the pupils what they would like to eat and drink. None of the exchanges took place in English. The pupils seemed to have been seduced by the context in which they found themselves and the native speakers with whom they were now interacting. The pupils spoke to each other in English. I did not think it appropriate for me to intrude in this. We were not in class. I did not want to break the spell. I felt that the potential motivational pay-off was too great to meddle at this stage.

When the cakes and drinks were delivered, the pupils responded appropriately and seemed thoroughly to enjoy the German specialities before them. These were cakes the like of which they had rarely, if ever, seen before: *Bienenstich; Schwarzwälder Kirschtorte* (the real thing); *Apfel-streuselkuchen; Berliner; Zwetschenkuchen* – all 'mit Sahne' (*with cream*) of course.

Once the *Kuchen* had been eaten and the *Kaffee* (*und Cola*) had been drunk, the pupils asked for the bill. Frau Römer and her assistant obliged and, as they collected the money, engaged in little cameo conversations in German with the pupils: had they enjoyed the cake? which sort did they like best? do they prefer coffee or tea or some other drink? The material for a GCSE role-play – and more – had been covered. It all appeared to me to be so unforced, so uncontrived (in spite of the fact that it all had been set up).

It was Catrina's job to immortalise the event in photographs. She had been taking pictures throughout the one hour visit and wanted a group photo to mark the occasion. Frau Römer and her assistant joined us to make the pictorial record complete.

We expressed our thanks to our hostess, said our goodbyes and made our way back to school discussing the experience in some detail. What followed replicated the approach to Frau Young's visit:

– letter of thanks to Frau Römer;
– annotated photomontage on the walls of the classroom;
– visit from the head of year.

Again the experience was exclusively positive. The motivational pay-off was considerable, albeit for a limited period of time.

Possible Project Approach III

What follows are some thoughts on another potential 'project', stimulated by a 'chance encounter'. No steps have been taken to realise the potential as yet. The seed has been planted, however. It has been put to one side to await the appropriate conditions for it to grow to fruition.

I was obliged to visit the central library to do some research for a non-foreign languages specific 'European Work Placement' project. There I was able to access a database which provided the names, addresses and telephone numbers of all the companies within a 10 mile radius of the city with subsidiaries and branches in France and Germany. I was surprised to find a total of 65.

It occurred to me that this must have enormous potential for making my teaching more practical, meaningful and vocational. Could I take the pupils to one or more of these companies to see how German/French is used in an authentic context on a day-to-day basis? If we could not visit a company, could a representative of a company come to us? Is there any aspect of a company's work to which pupils could contribute in a mutually helpful manner? Surely there must be some way in which the company and the languages department of the school could collaborate to help pupils see the importance and practical usefulness of foreign language competence. There must also be cross-curricular potential begging to be exploited: geography – routes taken between the UK and the European mainland: mathematics – mileage between cities; fuel consumption; currency exchange rates. There must be the possibility of pupils working on foreign language materials to help publicise the company's products or to assist German/French lorry drivers and company representatives when they come to the UK. The potential is enormous.

But 'Every Silver Lining Has a Cloud!'

The Mrs Young and Frau Römer projects described above were 'one-offs'. Although other similar projects have been tackled since the initial success, it is acknowledged that it is not practicable for the scheme of work to consist of this type of exercise exclusively. The teacher simply does not have enough hours in the day or sufficient energy to sustain that. There is a considerable risk that the positive attitudes to German and the Germans which were engendered by Frau Young's visit and the afternoon spent in Frau Römer's coffee shop might dissipate if something were not done, if not to maintain pupils' enthusiasm – a tall and arguably unrealistic order – then to refreshen it at intervals. It may be the case that the adoption of a local company may have more lasting potential. This remains to be seen.

Why were the projects described a success?

- The 'normal' approach to teaching and learning German had been adjusted to obviate the need for a textbook (in the foreground at least).
- The pupils recognised that their learning had a real purpose.
- We practised all four attainment targets: listening to a native speaker for a real purpose; speaking to an authentic, German listener for a real purpose; reading authentic material for a real purpose; writing to an authentic readership for a real purpose.
- The inclusion of the cultural dimension: this applied not only to Frau Young's input but also the *Kaffee und Kuchen* prepared from a German recipe book.
- The cross-curricular dimension: the wordprocessing; the photography; the presentation of the wall display; the preparing of the *Kaffee und Kuchen*; the social skills in the negotiation, collaboration and team work.
- The positive feedback from authority figures.
- It may seem sacrilegious – but the use of English played an important role in the pupils retaining 'ownership' of the contents of the letters, the questions they wanted to ask and the structure and content of the visit. This could not have been done had German been used almost exclusively as the language of classroom interaction. This does not mean, however, that the target language was neglected, far from it. I would even suggest that more quality German was used because the pupils were aware of why they needed it, approved of the enterprise and therefore were committed to it. So often the focus is on the quantity used in the classroom (most coming from the teacher). In this case the emphasis was on pupil-centred quality.

In the introduction to this chapter the reader was forewarned that detail was to be included which may appear superfluous. This may include the references to the Barn Dance or to the visit to the coffee shop. These were 'chance encounters' which led to something different being done inside and outside the classroom to enhance the pupils' German learning experience and their perception of German, Germany and the Germans. The message behind the inclusion of these details is that opportunities often arise per chance and the teacher has to be awake to them and their potential. He who hesitates is lost. Foreign languages are all around us. With some justification we bemoan the fact that we teach French/German/Spanish in an English speaking environment. There are nonetheless opportunities surrounding our schools to show our pupils that foreign languages are relevant and useful and spoken by our neighbours. Is there a German delicatessen or a tapas bar or French restaurant near your school? Do you have any native speakers who are parents in your school? I am sure my working context is far from unique. You may get a negative response. Maybe I have been exceptionally lucky. You will never know if you don't ask. Fortune favours the brave.

The project approach may enhance pupils' enjoyment of the language. The involvement of local industry may enhance enjoyment *and* help pupils see the importance and influence of foreign language competence. Are there other ways of promoting the utilitarian value of foreign languages?

Local Hero

I happened to be listening to a radio programme in which the centre forward (let's call him Alan – when approached about his inclusion in this book, he expressed a preference to remain anonymous) for the local first division football team at that time, was being interviewed. He happened to mention that he had been studying for a degree in French and German prior to signing for his first professional contract. My ears immediately pricked up! Here was the opportunity to provide some disaffected German-learning teenagers with a role-model with an interest in foreign languages.

It was a long shot, I know, but I wrote to 'the 30 goals a season man' inviting him to join one of our lessons to provide the pupils with an insight into his foreign language learning experience, why he had opted for languages and to what extent they had been useful to him in his career. To my amazement he responded in the affirmative. Now I was really worried. Quite apart from the natural apprehension about setting up such a high profile visit, I also had to consider the fact that 50% of the pupils were supporters of Alan's team's deadly local rivals. If the situation were not handled properly, I could find myself with a riot on my hands!

For the day of the visit I had booked the large lecture theatre so that it could accommodate all of the Year 9 pupils and those in Year 10 who were available. Alan arrived and was introduced to the audience. The reaction of the pupils, both sets of fans, was strange. I don't think they had honestly believed that the real Alan was coming. It would probably be a look-alike or a different Alan from the third eleven. No! It was really him – in the flesh. After the introduction we had 40 minutes of questions and answers relating to Alan's experience of languages at school, why he had taken A-level languages and then started a degree. He told of how useful his foreign language competence had been in his football career, especially when playing in Europe, not least in his confrontations with referees and over-zealous German defenders. He advised pupils to take their languages seriously as we were becoming increasingly integrated into Europe and could well be at a disadvantage on the jobs front without them. He told them of how much fun he had had in learning French and German, in meeting target language speakers and indeed other nationalities from the Eastern bloc for example, with whom he shared German as the common language.

Alan did a wonderful marketing job for languages. Interestingly, he said nothing that I had not said to the pupils a hundred times before. This time they listened, however, and appeared to take it all in. The difference appeared to be that Alan was a real person and a success in life, as opposed to a little Irish teacher with a moustache! I did not feel offended by this realisation. So long as the message had got through, my sensitivities could take the strain.

BMW versus Nissan Micra

Chris had left the school two years previously. Having taken A-level German he went straight into an attractive job at Deutsche Bank. I bumped into him on a shopping expedition one weekend and he updated me on his progress. He told me of the courses he had been on in Germany and how he used his German on a daily basis. I asked him if he would be likely to have an afternoon free to share his experiences with the current Year 9. He said he would make the necessary arrangements with his employer.

On the agreed day, at the appointed time, Chris arrived at the school in a gleaming, bright red BMW. He had the insensitivity to park it next to my clapped out, dirty white Nissan Micra. As he and I walked to the front of the lecture theatre, the pupils were taken by this handsome, young man in the Armani suit, silk tie and without a hair out of place. They seemed impressed by the fact that Chris' car, appearance, body language and confident demeanour seemed to say, 'I have made it!' and that was after only two years in the 'real world' and in spite of having opted for German at school!

Again Chris told the pupils nothing that they did not know already. His German competence had helped get him a job which he enjoyed enormously, rewarded him handsomely, allowed him to travel the world and gave him access to a wide range of (largely German-speaking) people. He had no regrets about opting for German and shared with the pupils some of the anecdotes from his school experience, much to my embarrassment. Again he had done a good sales job on my behalf. Again he was worth listening to because he was from a context beyond school, was devastatingly good-looking and had a nice car, as opposed to me, who – well my self-concept had been sufficiently shattered!

Summary

What I have endeavoured to describe above are examples of attempts made to stimulate and refresh the interest of pupils who might be described as 'demotivated' or 'disaffected'. Such an approach may be appropriate to all pupils, not just the 'switched-off'. We all flag a little from time to time, for one reason or another, regardless of our commitment or level of ability, and need something to regenerate our enthusiasm. It is important to note, however, that I make no claims for the 'transferability' of the above. The exercises worked for me and my pupils in our teaching and learning context. It may be very different for you in your school.

Why did the approach seem to work? The visits made by Frau Young and to Frau Römer's coffee shop focused on the useful, enjoyable and purposeful; short-term goals; specific responsibilities governed by individuals' particular talents; sharing and valuing of opinions; praise and self-esteem. The visits of Alan and Chris had a different aim. In these cases the focus was not on a specific unit of work but on the whole point of learning a language. The pupils needed role-models who could show them that their investment in learning German (and other languages) had the potential of a real pay-off in the long term.

You may claim not to have a Frau Young, an Alan or a Chris but I bet you have. I suggest that we do not exploit our environment enough in our foreign language teaching. German, Germany and the Germans are all around us. How many companies within 20 miles of your school have links with Germany? Do you have a local delicatessen, restaurant or clothes shop, for example, which is run by a native speaker? Frau Römer is only too happy to work with our pupils on little projects. We do not need to pretend we are in a German café. We have one just up the road.

It is only practicable to adopt the above approach on an infrequent basis. It is important, however, in motivational terms, to abandon the textbook from time to time and exploit the context within which the pupils live.

Alternative resources are on the doorstep. The educational and local press periodically feature projects which take the pupils away from what might be regarded as 'traditional' teaching in an attempt to enhance their motivation to learn. 'Premier league tackles 3Rs' (*Times Educational Supplement*, 5.12.97) for example describes how under-achievers attend after-school classes at their local football clubs in Newcastle, Leeds and Sheffield. At the time of writing the World Cup in France dominates the media. A plethora of ideas of how this 'one in every four years' opportunity can be exploited in the classroom, and the modern languages classroom in particular, jump out of the pages of the press: 'Cup fever feeds wider world of knowledge' (*Times Educational Supplement*, 19.6.98) summarises how a number of schools approached the tournament in a cross-curricular way to enhance not only pupils' linguistic and cultural awareness but also their knowledge of mathematics and geography *inter alia*. The effect on the pupils is encapsulated in the following comment from one of the teachers involved:

> The World Cup has provided the energy for all of this. The children are highly motivated and totally focused. (*Times Educational Supplement*, 19.6.98)

How often can we say this about our pupils? It is unrealistic to harness this motivation and focus all of the time. To venture into the reality of the pupils' environment on those occasions when the opportunity arises can have enormous pay-off which more than compensates for the undoubted investment of time, effort and imagination.

Chapter 12

So What Are We Going To Do About It?

So where do we go from here? What have we learned from this attempt to access the motivational perspectives of pupils learning foreign languages? What remains to be done that scope of the study could not accommodate? What messages need to be sent to our 'highers' if not 'betters'?

Implications of this Study for a Theoretical Model of Motivation

Ajzen's theory of planned behaviour (1988 and this study Chapter 2) provided three main strands at its basis, 'perceived behavioural control', 'attitude towards the behaviour' and 'subjective norm', which offered categories of influence on a given behavioural intention. This was adequate for the review of the literature for this study but, as it turns out, fails to meet the needs of the description and analysis of the data. Ajzen's model needs to be adapted to meet the differing dependent factor upon which his three categories of independent factors have influence. Ajzen's dependent factor is 'the intention to carry out the behaviour'. In the case of this book, however, the dependent factor is the pupils' perspectives on the behaviour, that is their attitudes towards the behaviour which in the present case is the actual learning of German. It transpires that the independent factors contributing to these are: (1) perceived associations and utility; (2) transnational attitudes; (3) reactions to experience of classroom learning; (4) attitudes and influence of others. It is apparent that the four independent factors are interlinked in their influencing of the dependent factor. What comes out of the analysis, however, is the dominating, central role played by perceived associations and utility which take on the role of dependent *and* independent factor. The pupils' perception of a subject's usefulness is dependent on its status in society and on the school curriculum; the more enhanced this status, the more likely pupils are to feel encouraged by parents at home; this leads in turn to a more positive attitude to the in-school experience; if pupils perceive a subject's utility as positive then the enjoyment of the in-school experience is helpful but not an overriding factor; in the case of modern languages, experience of other countries and other nationalities may contribute to the perception of usefulness but the latter is not dependent upon the former.

The model of motivation develops into the form shown in Figure 12.1. This model focuses on the perspectives of the 'consumers', in this case learners of German. Their views taken independently of those of other influential participants in the learning process, for example teachers and parents, inevitably provide a one-sidedness but at the same time an insight into the feelings of those at the receiving end. In the same way that a hotel manager may feel that feedback from guests may be unfair in that it takes little account of the constraints under which she and her staff may be working, she is advised nonetheless to take note of the criticisms and do what is possible to bolster any weaknesses. This model therefore has the potential to provide valuable information for policy makers, teachers, parents and others interested in the learning experience of secondary school pupils.

The application of the project methodology behind the model has a developmental dimension in that it accesses pupils' perspectives on each of two occasions, two years apart, giving 'consumers' the opportunity to articulate how their views may have changed in the course of that period. This provides information on the extent of their enthusiasm at the beginning of the survey, how that enthusiasm is affected by the learning process after two years and reasons for any change.

Central amongst the independent factors in the model are pupils' perceived associations and utility of a given learning goal. (See Chapter 10, p. 160ff.) Other independent factors, within the learning context (in the case of this study, the classroom and the school) and extrinsic to the learning context (for example the influence of parents), are fed by and feed into perceived utility. This factor takes on the dual role of dependence and independence. If a subject is perceived as useful, parents are more likely to provide support and encouragement; the more encouragement and support provided by parents, the more likely learners are to perceive the subject as useful. Similarly, if the subject has high status within the school, pupils are more likely to perceive its usefulness and adopt a more positive attitude to the learning process. If pupils fail to see its usefulness, then insofar as they may be motivated to any extent, this is likely to depend on their enjoyment of the subject. This puts a great onus on the teacher. No subject can be entertaining all of the time.

Given the centrality of perceived utility in the shaping of pupils' views of learning a given subject, this model has serious implications for teachers

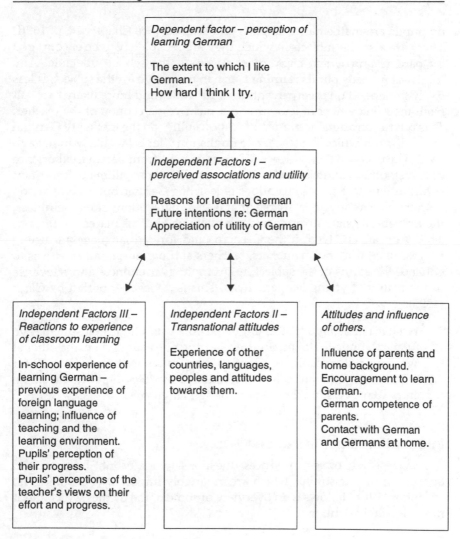

Figure 12.1 Model relating to motivational perspectives of pupils learning German

of modern foreign languages, especially those in the UK. The data in this book suggest that pupils bring with them an enthusiasm for a wide range of subjects, including German, to their secondary school experience. As the years pass, however, this enthusiasm for German diminishes as does pupils' perception of its usefulness. The most useful subjects as perceived by pupils are mathematics, English and science. (See Chapter 10, p. 160ff) These are also the subjects in which they are most likely to be encouraged by parents and which enjoy most space on the school timetable. Any motivation Leeds pupils learning German may have for the subject, is less likely to depend on their perception of its utility and more likely to result from their enjoyment of lessons and a positive perception of the teacher. This puts a considerable burden of responsibility on the teacher of German in Leeds with which the teacher of English in Kiel is less likely to have to cope. The classroom experience, encouragement from parents, experience of travel, other countries and other nationalities may all make important contributions to pupils' perceptions of learning German but in comparison with the apparently key variable, that is their perceptions of its usefulness, the influential relationship seems relatively weak. This places the responsibility on all involved in the German (and foreign languages) learning process, including policy makers, teachers and parents, to make efforts to enhance the status of the subject, to promote its usefulness and relevance in the reality of young learners' lives. This is a view supported by Clark (1995):

> What is needed is a radical linguistic policy and huge investment: two foreign languages for all children starting one at age seven, the other at age nine, with a choice of vocational or academic streams from 12 for pupils with different career inclinations. By 2005 there should be no entry to university without two foreign languages.

Information Gaps Still to be Filled

Any research project produces questions which cannot be answered because of the constraints which are invariably imposed. This book is no exception. What follows is an overview of some of the themes which merit more detailed attention.

Pupils opting out of German

This book adopted as its focus of attention the perceptions of pupils learning German. This immediately excluded a constituency of some size and significance, that is, those pupils who opt out of German. Had time and space permitted, it would have been of considerable import, not least to those interested in increasing numbers taking German, to access the reasons why pupils choose not to continue with this particular foreign language to GCSE level and why pupils choose to continue with an alternative foreign language or opt out of foreign languages altogether at A-level.

Perceived status of subject in school

The comparative dimension of this book stimulated the consideration of the potential influence of the status of a given subject on the school curriculum on pupils' perceptions of its usefulness and relevance. Given that Kiel pupils start learning English earlier, spend more time in English lessons each week and continue learning it for longer than their Leeds peers do on German, it may be the case that this contributes, along with a plethora of other factors, to their perception of the language as a subject of importance. It was not the aim of this study to examine this area in detail but it seems worthy of further investigation, not least in the light of the comment of the Leeds pupil who thought science was the most useful subject because it was allocated most time (see Chapter 10, p. 160ff: 'We have more lessons in science than in anything else, so I suppose it must be the most useful'). It is not suggested that such an investigation into pupils' views should be restricted to foreign languages. It has a much wider application than this.

Parental encouragement

There is a suggestion, raised by the data in this study, of a possible link between on the one hand the status of a subject on the school curriculum and in the perception of the society in which we live, and on the other hand the level of encouragement which parents give to their children to do well in that subject. Again, this study focuses on the views of pupils. It would be interesting to access the views of parents on the question of what it is that stimulates them to encourage their child to work hard at one subject rather than another.

The same applies to the form which this encouragement takes. Leeds pupils suggest that most parents encourage them by asking them about their homework, urging them to do it, checking it and helping them with it. Some Kiel pupils suggest that their parents apply a system of reward and reproof which they interpret as encouragement. What do parents think? How do they perceive the encouragement which they feel they offer their child? Do they feel adequately equipped to provide the help which is needed or do they need support? If this is so, how can this be accommodated?

Records of achievement

The importance of the influence of the teacher in successful learning is well documented and is corroborated by the findings in this study. The data raise one particular aspect of the teacher's role in establishing a sound relationship with her pupils and contributing to motivating them to reach their potential, which gives grounds for concern. This relates to the area of communication between teacher and pupil with regard to assessment of progress. An all too high proportion of pupils both in Leeds and Kiel claim not to know the views of their teacher regarding their effort and progress. It must be remembered that only the views of the pupils have been accessed. It would surely be of value to seek the opinions of the teachers on this subject. As far as Leeds is concerned, Records of Achievement (RoA) are already in place and a great deal of time and effort is spent in consultation, negotiation and goal-setting by teachers and pupils. These data appear to be suggesting that, on the basis of this sample and with regard to German, the system is not working. Anecdotal evidence suggests that RoA are becoming ever more peripheral to the point of irrelevant with the advent of League Tables and the associated significance of A*–C scores at GCSE. These force some schools to concentrate their efforts on setting targets (as opposed to negotiating targets) for those pupils around the C/D borderline to the virtual exclusion (at least in terms of target setting) of the high fliers (who can look after themselves) and the poor performers (a lost cause?).

The forgotten third skill

This heading is the title of a book written by Marcelle Kellerman (1981) and deals with the topic of reading and why it is the activity most neglected in the modern languages classroom. This question is as relevant in 1998 as it was in 1981. Since the publication of Kellerman's book much progress has been made to provide material which is appropriate to the interests, abilities and other needs of the range of pupils in any given class. In spite of this, however, the reading of extended texts, certainly for the 11–16 age group, does not form part of many German/French lesson plans. It would be of interest to ascertain the views of teachers as to why reading remains '*The forgotten third skill*'.

When pupils do read in class the text is more likely to be an advertisement, short newspaper article or letter rather than an extended text in the form of a poem, playlet or short story. Any text which might be described as an example of literature, on the basis of these data, does not become part of the German programme until well into the A-level course. This is another area of concern on two fronts:

(1) Pupils are being denied access to a wealth of reading material with the potential to stimulate their imaginations and give them insights into cultural background, 'grammar in action', consolidation of vocabulary which they already know and access to new vocabulary in context. Literature does not have to mean the work of the 'greats'. There is a wealth of material written, for example, by German authors for German

children of school age, which UK learners could potentially read with enjoyment.

(2) Having opted to take A-level German, some pupils (given that literature is optional on the syllabus of some examination boards) are expected to be able to read, appreciate and discuss examples of German literature, having been brought up on a diet of advertisements and newspaper cuttings. This is akin to building a castle in the sand.

Much might be gained from an action research project on reading and reading materials, especially for pupils in the 11–16 age group. The results could have considerable significance and serve to enhance pupils' reading and general learning experience, and not just in foreign languages.

Exchanges and visits abroad

The value of school exchanges, visits abroad generally and to the target language country in particular, is an area of some controversy. The APU (DES/DENI/WO,1985: 390), for example, maintains that pupils with experience in the target language country are more likely to feel positive towards learning the language of that country than those pupils who have not had this experience. The data in this book, however, suggest, albeit tentatively, that travel abroad, exchanges and experience of native speakers at home and abroad, be it in the target language country or in other holiday destinations, has little bearing on pupils' assessment of German and its usefulness and may indeed have a negative affect on their evaluation of German people. A research exercise which cleared up this ambiguity would serve teachers well who invest so much in an effort to ensure that pupils have a positive experience of travel and sojourns abroad.

It was also suggested in the discussion of the data that the full potential of exchange visits was not being exploited, especially in the preparation and follow-up phases where there is so much scope for letter-writing with a real purpose, exchange of video and audio recordings, cross-curricular project work and so on. This could give German and foreign language learning generally the practical application and meaningful activities to enhance its image in the perceptions of pupils. An investigation into current practice and the determination of what may function as 'good practice' could have wide-ranging benefits. (See Berry 1998: 'School exchange trips aren't always the success they should be. But giving both parties a focus – such as working on a play together – can be the way to achieve a truly rewarding experience'.)

The second foreign language in UK and Germany

The scope of this project did not allow detailed insights into pupils' views of French in Kiel. This subject is of interest because of the status of French as the second foreign language in Kiel schools, a position it shares generally with languages other than French in UK schools. It would be of interest and some value to examine whether second foreign languages in different countries encountered the same problems, for example, of perceived status, time allocation, the demand to reach the same standard as in the first foreign language but in fewer years, and as a result were less highly regarded by pupils. UK schools may have much to learn from their neighbours on the European mainland who generally have broader experience of second and indeed third foreign language teaching.

The influence of the soap opera

When Kiel pupils were invited to explain why they were attracted to visit and work in Australia, there was a strong suggestion that the advent of the soap opera on German television had something to do with this. They seemed attracted by the presentation of a version of a lifestyle which seemed to involve almost exclusively beautiful people who spent most of their time engaged in watersports and dealing with the complications of relationships with the opposite sex.

The influence of the soap opera has been a topic of debate since the early days of Coronation Street. Recent research funded by The Women's Nationwide Cancer Control Campaign (Haigh, 1995) concludes that children regard television soaps as important sources of information, more important than teachers, parents or friends. The influence of the soap opera on the motivation of viewers to learn the target language, however, is an area yet to be investigated. The German soap opera, *Schwarzwaldklinik*, was given a run on British television but enjoyed little success. It had little or no influence on German learners because few watched it, not least because of its late transmission time. To generalise from this one example would be erroneous. To look into the influence of a range of soap operas transmitted in countries other than the country of origin, on viewers' interest in that country and its language, could provide data with a bearing on the variety of effective media available to teachers.

Recommendations

What then are the recommendations which can be made as a result of the findings relating to this study? Some may appear idealistic. Some are fraught with difficulty. If we are serious about education and the place of foreign language learning in education, then surely a little idealism is not misplaced; surely the difficulties are worth confronting.

(1) If the motivation which Kiel pupils have for learning English is to be matched by Leeds pupils learning German, then major policy decisions have to be made to enhance the prestige of German (and other foreign languages) in schools:

- the programme of diversification of first foreign languages needs to be reborn to change the traditional position of French as the first foreign language; diversification is a term now rarely used in the context of foreign language learning and teaching; it appears to have been crushed beneath the landslide of other reforms, league tables and OFSTED inspections;
- a foreign language should be compulsory until pupils leave school; arguably, it should be a university entrance requirement (see Clark, 1995);
- rather than a second foreign language being squeezed out of a packed National Curriculum, it should be given its proper place on the school timetable as is the case in most other European countries; Claude Allègre, French Education Minister, announced in July 1998 (*Times Educational Supplement*, 10.7.98) the requirement for *Lycéens* to have competence in at least two foreign languages by the time they leave school. By contrast, David Blunkett, British Secretary of State for Education and Employment, announced in the same month of the same year (*Times Educational Supplement*, 10.7.98) that some pupils should be allowed to drop a modern foreign language in Key Stage 4. Is it so unrealistic for us to have the same aspirations as the French in this regard?

If reforms such as those suggested above were to be implemented, then future generations of pupils would be more likely to see for themselves the importance of foreign languages, obtain greater encouragement from parents who would not only share this perception of the importance of foreign language competence but also be able to offer practical support to their children because of their own competence.

(2) There is a desperate need for the EC resolution of 24 May 1988 and the subsequent DES policy statement (February 1991), requiring the inclusion of a European Dimension in the National Curriculum, to be implemented with enthusiasm and energy, at least at KS1 and KS2. There are examples of good practice throughout the country but they tend to be the exception rather than the rule and to focus on French.

Pupils must be given insight into a wider range of languages, people and cultures if problems of ignorance and ill-founded prejudice are to be obviated.

(3) The teacher has a key role to play in motivation. She is more important than the methodology, working environment or equipment. Her support, enthusiasm, positive approach in providing a learning experience which has practical application, vocational value and is enjoyable and fulfilling are key motivational components. It is important that teachers access their pupils' views on their learning experience in order to provide for their varying needs. If these needs are to be met teachers must be provided with the necessary in-service training (for example in ICT and autonomous / flexible approaches to learning), the necessary resources (for example computer hard- and software and adequate teaching space, preferably in the form of smaller classes), time (to plan and prepare lessons properly), support (classroom assistants and, in the increasingly technological world of modern language teaching and learning, technicians; why should technicians be limited to the support of science and technology teachers?) and a syllabus which takes them away from purely transactional language into greater linguistic variety.

(4) Lee and Dickson (1991) identify two areas of particular concern to UK teachers of modern languages, that is size of the teaching group and the length and frequency of lessons:

> A view strongly expressed by the majority of teachers in the survey was the need for lower ability pupils to be in small teaching groups; a maximum of 10 was suggested by one teacher. Several teachers explained that languages should be seen as a practical subject, requiring small class sizes. (Lee & Dickinson, 1991)

The introduction of Local Management of Schools (LMS) and the general tightening of budgets is more likely to lead to larger classes rather than smaller:

> In addition to small classes, the teachers stressed the need for languages to be taught in short periods (one suggested no more than 30-minute sessions), with frequent lessons during the week: the 'little and often' approach. (Lee & Dickinson, 1991)

A timetable which seems in most schools to be driven by science and technology departments is unlikely to provide much scope for single lessons. An allocation of one or two teaching periods per week of 70 minutes duration for foreign languages appears to be the norm. This falls some way short of meeting the needs of learners, especially the disaffected (Chambers, 1992) for whom a 'little but often' approach is almost certainly more appropriate.

(5) Pupils value regular feedback on their performance which should take the form of meaningful interaction between learner and teacher. Motivation may break down when pupils are unsure that their perception of their progress and the perception of the teacher are not the same. When perceptions are shared, discussed and agreed upon, there is much less risk of self-fulfilling prophecy of the negative kind.

(6) The positive motivational influence of visits to the target language country is not being exploited fully. Much more attention needs to be given to the integral role which the preparation and follow-up phases of such visits should play in giving purpose to classroom activities. This applies to all age groups.

(7) Greater insights should be given to cultural background, perhaps in the form of 'a day in the life of . . . ' in the target language communities. This may be of interest to language learners and others at every stage and may serve to prevent stereotyping and the consolidation of prejudice based on ignorance. If pupils cannot go to the country, then the country should come to them in the form of visits from foreign nationals who live and work locally, visits to local businesses who communicate and trade with our EU partners, the organisation of German/French days inside and outside school. If motivation is to be high, then the foreign language, as a subject of practical and vocational application and intrinsic interest, as opposed to an item on the school timetable, must be kept high on the agenda.

Summary

Much has been learned from the pupils in this study. Their views deserve to be listened to and taken seriously. They confirm that there are two main reasons why they learn: (1) because the subject of the learning is useful; (2) because it is enjoyable.

Much of the onus for making learning enjoyable rests on the shoulders of the teacher. Her shoulders have to be broad because learning cannot always be enjoyable. There are aspects of learning which demand endeavour, tenacity and hard graft. This can be tolerated if the subject of the learning is perceived as useful. This is not always the case for modern foreign languages. This is not the teacher's fault. She needs the support of the school, of the government and of society. Currently this support, if it exists at all, is very limited. How does she cope in the absence of support of any real substance? How does she retain her commitment, professionalism, energy and good humour, especially in the absence of the real credit she deserves? Who knows? For how long can she go on?

Year 7 (11year olds) Leeds Questionnaire

NAME . . . . . . SCHOOL . . . . . . CLASS . . . . .

1. How much have you been looking forward to going to secondary school. Indicate by circling a number somewhere along the scale.
   (1 or 2 = not looking forward to it; 3 = you don't mind either way; 4 or 5 = you are looking forward to it)

Not looking forward to it at all		Neutral		Really looking forward to it
1	2	3	4	5

2. Please explain why: . . . .

3. Below you will find a list of 12 subjects. Think about each of them and consider how much you have been looking forward to taking each subject at secondary school. Indicate by circling a number somewhere along the scale.

	Not looking forward to it at all		Neutral		Really looking forward to it
Maths	1	2	3	4	5
English	1	2	3	4	5
French	1	2	3	4	5
Geography	1	2	3	4	5
History	1	2	3	4	5
Science	1	2	3	4	5
PE	1	2	3	4	5
German	1	2	3	4	5
Technology	1	2	3	4	5
Music	1	2	3	4	5
RE	1	2	3	4	5
Art	1	2	3	4	5

4. Which subject were you looking forward to most of all? . . ..

5. Why? . . . .

6. Which subject were you dreading most of all? . . . . . .

7. Why? . . . .

8. How do you feel about the prospect of learning a foreign language?
    Tick the answer which best describes how you feel:

    Excited
    Quite looking forward to it
    Don't really care
    Am not really looking forward to it
    Hate the thought of it

9. Explain why . . . .

10. Did you learn any foreign languages before coming to secondary
    school? . . .

11. Which language/s? . . . . . .

12. For how long? . . . . .

13. Did you enjoy it? Circle a number on the scale to indicate how you
    feel:

I did not enjoy it		It was OK		I enjoyed it very much
1	2	3	4	5

14. Why? / Why not?
    . . . .

15. Have you ever been to a foreign country? . . . .

16. Which one/s? . . . .

17. Choose one of the foreign countries you have visited and say what
    the people were like there by completing the following sentence:

    The people in . . . . were . . . .

18. Which other country would you like to visit? . . . .

19. Why? . . . .

20. If the language of that country was not English, would you try to learn
    it before you went? . . . .

21. Why? / Why not? . . . .

22. Would you consider trying to get a job in a foreign country when you leave school? . . . .

23. Which foreign country/countries? . . . .

24. Why this country/these countries? . . . .

25. Here are some words that pupils your age have used to describe people from other countries:
    pushy unpleasant stupid ambitious loud friendly boring polite pleasant unfriendly impolite beautiful interesting clever ugly

    Please complete the following sentences by writing down one or more of these words. You can use your own words if you want to:
    I think German people are . . . .
    I think French people are . . . . . .
    I think British people are . . . .

26. How much do your parents encourage you to learn foreign languages? Circle a number on the scale 1–5 to indicate this:

Not at all		A little		Very much
1	2	3	4	5

27. Have you ever had the opportunity to hear German used outside school? . . .

28. If so, please give an example: . . . .

29. Do you know any Germans? . . .

30. About how many? . . .

31. How much German does your mother know?
    Circle a number on the scale to indicate what you think:

None		Some		Lots
1	2	3	4	5

32. How much German does your father know?
    Circle a number on the scale to indicate what you think:

None		Some		Lots
1	2	3	4	5

33. **Think about each of the subjects below. How useful is each of them? Indicate on the scale how you feel.**

	Useless		Quite useful		Very useful
Maths	1	2	3	4	5
English	1	2	3	4	5
French	1	2	3	4	5
Geography	1	2	3	4	5
History	1	2	3	4	5
Science	1	2	3	4	5
PE	1	2	3	4	5
German	1	2	3	4	5
Technology	1	2	3	4	5
Music	1	2	3	4	5
RE	1	2	3	4	5
Art	1	2	3	4	5

34. **Which subject do you think is the most useful?** . . . .

35. **Why?** . . . .

36. **Which subject do you think is the least useful?** . . . . .

37. **Why?** . . . .

38. **Have you been in a situation where it would have been useful to be able to speak German?** . . . .

39. **Complete the following sentence by filling in the blank at the beginning with the name of your favourite subject:**

    . . . . . is my favourite subject because . . .
    (Now tick the boxes which best match how you feel)

	Untrue	Partly true	True
. . . it will be useful in getting me a job	❏	❏	❏
. . . it is fun in class	❏	❏	❏
. . . the teacher is good	❏	❏	❏
. . . I get the right amount of homework	❏	❏	❏
. . . my test marks are good	❏	❏	❏
. . . the work is satisfying	❏	❏	❏
. . . the work is varied	❏	❏	❏
. . . the work is interesting	❏	❏	❏

Other reasons you may wish to add:

. . . .

Appendix 2

Year 9 (13 year olds) Leeds Questionnaire

NAME...... SCHOOL..... CLASS ...

1. Has secondary school been as good / bad as you expected it would be? Indicate on the scale how you feel:

Worse than expected		What I had expected		Better than expected
1	2	3	4	5

2. **Explain why:** ....
    . . . .

3. **Have individual subjects been as good / as bad as you expected they would be? Indicate on the scale how you feel:**

	Worse than expected		What I had expected		Better than expected
Maths	1	2	3	4	5
English	1	2	3	4	5
French	1	2	3	4	5
Geography	1	2	3	4	5
History	1	2	3	4	5
Science	1	2	3	4	5
PE	1	2	3	4	5
German	1	2	3	4	5
Technology	1	2	3	4	5
Music	1	2	3	4	5
RE	1	2	3	4	5
Art	1	2	3	4	5

4. **Give reasons for your feelings about French if you do French:**

    . . . .

    . . . .

5. **Give reasons for your feelings about German if you do German:**

    . . . .

    . . . .

6. **Please put a circle somewhere along the scale below to indicate how much you like German compared to all your other subjects:**

German is my *least* preferred subject				German is my *most* preferred subject
1	2	3	4	5

7. **Please circle a number in statements (a) to (f) to indicate your reason/s for learning German: (1 or 2 = you disagree; 3 = you neither agree nor disagree; 4 or 5 = you agree)**

    I AM LEARNING GERMAN BECAUSE

	I Disagree		Neutral		I Agree
(a) I think it will help me to get a good job	1	2	3	4	5
(b) I am interested in German people and their way of life	1	2	3	4	5
(c) It will allow me to meet and talk with more people	1	2	3	4	5
(d) An educated person should be able to speak a foreign language	1	2	3	4	5
(e) I enjoy it	1	2	3	4	5

    (f) Any other reason:

    . . . .

8. **Think about each of the subjects below. How useful is each of them? Indicate on the scale how you feel.**

	Useless		Quite useful		Very useful
Maths	1	2	3	4	5
English	1	2	3	4	5
French	1	2	3	4	5
Geography	1	2	3	4	5
History	1	2	3	4	5
Science	1	2	3	4	5
PE	1	2	3	4	5

	Useless		Quite useful		Very useful
German	1	2	3	4	5
Technology	1	2	3	4	5
Music	1	2	3	4	5
RE	1	2	3	4	5
Art	1	2	3	4	5

9. Which subject do you regard as the *most* useful? . . . . . .

10. Why? . . . .

11. Which subject do you regard as the *least* useful? . . . . . .

12. Why? . . . .

13. How often have you come across a situation where it would have been useful to be able to speak German?
    . . . .

14. What do you enjoy *most* about coming to school?
    . . . .

15. What do you enjoy *least* about coming to school?
    . . . .

16. If you were asked to judge whether a subject was good or not, how much importance would you attach to the following considerations? Circle the number which best matches how you feel (1 = unimportant; 5 = very important)

	Unimportant		Reasonably important		Very important
How useful it is in getting you a job	1	2	3	4	5
How much fun it is in class	1	2	3	4	5
How good the teacher is	1	2	3	4	5
How much homework you get	1	2	3	4	5
How good your test marks are	1	2	3	4	5
How satisfying the work is	1	2	3	4	5
How varied it is	1	2	3	4	5
How interesting it is	1	2	3	4	5
How much you can mess around with your pals	1	2	3	4	5

Other aspects not included in the above list

. . . .

17. **Please tick the statement which best applies to you:**
    I try very hard in German lessons
    I try quite hard in German lessons
    I don't really try at all in German lessons

18. **What does your teacher think?**
    S/he thinks I try very hard in German lessons
    S/he thinks I try quite hard in German lessons
    S/he thinks I don't really try at all in German lessons
    I don't know what s/he thinks

19. **Please tick the statement which best applies to you:**
    I am making excellent progress in German
    I am doing well in German
    I am making satisfactory progress in German
    I am making poor progress in German

20. **What does your teacher think?**
    S/he thinks I am making excellent progress in German
    S/he thinks I am doing well in German
    S/he thinks I am making satisfactory progress in German
    S/he thinks I am making poor progress in German
    I don't know what s/he thinks

21. **Tick all the statements** that apply to you:
    I am working towards a good GCSE grade
    I want to take A-level German
    I want to study German at university
    I want to speak German well enough to get a job there
    I want to give it up the first chance I can get
    I haven't really thought about it
    I don't care about German because I am no good at it
    Other . . . .

22. **How much do you enjoy the following activities in German lessons?**
    Circle a number or the letter N to indicate on the scale how you feel:

	I do not like this at all		I don't mind this		I enjoy this	We don't do this
Group work	1	2	3	4	5	N
Pair work	1	2	3	4	5	N
Listening exercises	1	2	3	4	5	N
Writing exercises	1	2	3	4	5	N
Reading quietly	1	2	3	4	5	N

	I do not like this at all		I don't mind this		I enjoy this	We don't do this
Speaking	1	2	3	4	5	N
Work with computer	1	2	3	4	5	N
Literature	1	2	3	4	5	N
Project work/coursework	1	2	3	4	5	N

23. **How important to you are the following in helping you feel positive about German?**

	Unimportant		Reasonably important		Very important
The teacher	1	2	3	4	5
The textbook	1	2	3	4	5
Teacher-made materials (worksheets, OHP transparencies, flashcards, etc.)	1	2	3	4	5
Good quality equipment	1	2	3	4	5
Availability of computers	1	2	3	4	5
A nicely furnished classroom	1	2	3	4	5
Number of pupils in class	1	2	3	4	5
Penpals	1	2	3	4	5
Exchange with German school	1	2	3	4	5
Television	1	2	3	4	5
Influence from home	1	2	3	4	5

Other . . . .

24. **Have you ever been to a foreign country?** . . . .

25. **Which one/s?** . . . .

26. **Choose one of the foreign countries you have visited. Complete the following sentence by saying what the people were like there:**
    The people in . . . . . were . . . .

27. **What did you like most about the country/countries you visited?**
    . . . .

28. **What did you like least about the country/countries you visited?**
    . . . .

29. **Which other country would you like to visit?** . . . . . .

30. **Why?** . . . .

31. **If the language of that country was not English, would you try to learn it before you went?**
    . . . .

32. **Why? / Why not?** . . . .

33. **Would you consider trying to get a job in a foreign country when you leave school?** . . .

34. **Which foreign country/countries?** . . . .

35. **Why this country / these countries?** . . . .
    . . . .

36. **Here are some words that pupils your age have used to describe people from other countries:**

    pushy unpleasant stupid ambitious loud friendly stupid polite pleasant unfriendly impolite beautiful interesting clever ugly

    Please complete the following sentences by writing down one or more of these words. You can use your own words if you want to:

    I think German people are . . . .
    I think French people are . . . .
    I think British people are . . . .

37. **Please place a tick next to the statement which appears most applicable to you. If German were not taught in the school, I would probably**

    (a) not bother learning German at all
    (b) try to get lessons in German somewhere else
    (c) pick up German in everyday situations (i.e. read German books and newspapers, try to speak it when possible, watch German films)
    (d) none of these (explain) . . . .

38. **After GCSE, I will probably**

    (a) try to use my German as much as possible
    (b) try to use my German a little

(c) not use German at all

(d) do none of these (explain) . . . .

39. **If I had the opportunity to change the amount of German which is taught in our school, I would**

(a) increase the number of lessons

(b) keep the number of lessons as it is

(c) decrease the number of lessons

40. **I believe German should be**

(a) taught to all pupils

(b) taught only to those pupils who wish to learn it

(c) omitted from the school curriculum

41. **If you had the opportunity to change the way German is taught in your school, what would you do?**

. . . .

. . . .

42. **How much German does your mother know? Circle a number on the scale to indicate what you think:**

None		Some		Lots
1	2	3	4	5

43. **How much German does your father know? Circle a number on the scale to indicate what you think:**

None		Some		Lots
1	2	3	4	5

44. **How much do your parents encourage you to learn German? Circle a number on the scale 1–5 to indicate how you feel:**

Not at all		A little		Very much
1	2	3	4	5

45. **Have you ever had the opportunity to hear German used with friends of the family?** . . .

46. **Please give an example:**

. . . .

47. **Do you know any people who speak German as their mother-tongue?**

. . .

48. **About how many?** . . .

49. **Has your opinion of German and German lessons changed in the last two years?***

     . . . .

50. **If so, how and why?***

     . . . .
     . . . .

Many thanks for your co-operation.
G. N. Chambers.

*Questions asked in 1994 only.

Appendix 3

Year 11 (15 year olds) Leeds Questionnaire

NAME . . . . . . SCHOOL . . . . . . CLASS . . .

1. **Please circle a number in statements a to f to indicate your reason/s for learning German: (1 or 2 = you disagree; 3 = you neither agree nor disagree; 4 or 5 = you agree)**

I AM LEARNING GERMAN BECAUSE

	I disagree		neutral		I agree
(a) I think it will help me to get a good job	1	2	3	4	5
(b) I am interested in German people and their way of life	1	2	3	4	5
(c) It will allow me to meet and talk with more people	1	2	3	4	5
(d) An educated person should be able to speak a foreign language	1	2	3	4	5
(e) I enjoy it	1	2	3	4	5
(f) I have to take a foreign language at GCSE level	1	2	3	4	5

(g) Any other reason: . . . .

2. **Think about each of the subjects below. How useful is each of them? Indicate on the scale how you feel.**

	Useless	Quite useful		Very useful	
Maths	1	2	3	4	5
English	1	2	3	4	5
French	1	2	3	4	5
Geography	1	2	3	4	5
History	1	2	3	4	5
Science	1	2	3	4	5

	Useless	Quite useful		Very useful	
PE	1	2	3	4	5
German	1	2	3	4	5
Technology	1	2	3	4	5
Music	1	2	3	4	5
RE	1	2	3	4	5
Art	1	2	3	4	5

3. Which subject do you regard as the <u>most</u> useful? . . . . . .

4. Why? . . . .

5. Which subject do you regard as the <u>least</u> useful? . . . .

6. Why? . . . .

7. How often have you come across a situation where it would have been useful to be able to speak German? . . . .

8. What do you enjoy <u>most</u> about coming to school?
    . . . .

9. What do you enjoy <u>least</u> about coming to school?
    . . . .

10. If you were asked to judge whether a subject was good or not, how much importance would you attach to the following considerations? Circle the number which best matches how you feel (1 = unimportant; 5 = very important)

	Unimportant		Reasonably important		Very important
How useful it is in getting you a job	1	2	3	4	5
How much fun it is in class	1	2	3	4	5
How good the teacher is	1	2	3	4	5
How much homework you get	1	2	3	4	5
How good your test marks are	1	2	3	4	5
How satisfying the work is	1	2	3	4	5
How varied it is	1	2	3	4	5
How interesting it is	1	2	3	4	5
How much you can mess around with your pals	1	2	3	4	5

Other aspects not included in the above list
. . . .

11. **Please tick the statement which best applies to you:**

    I try very hard in German lessons
    I try quite hard in German lessons
    I don't really try at all in German lessons

12. **What does your teacher think?**

    S/he thinks I try very hard in German lessons
    S/he thinks I try quite hard in German lessons
    S/he thinks I don't really try at all in German lessons
    I don't know what s/he thinks

13. **Please tick the statement which best applies to you:**

    I am making excellent progress in German
    I am doing well in German
    I am making satisfactory progress in German
    I am making poor progress in German

14. **What does your teacher think?**

    S/he thinks I am making excellent progress in German
    S/he thinks I am doing well in German
    S/he thinks I am making satisfactory progress in German
    S/he thinks I am making poor progress in German
    I don't know what s/he thinks

15. **Tick all the statements** that apply to you:

    I am working towards a good GCSE grade
    I want to take A-level German
    I want to study German at university
    I want to speak German well enough to get a job there
    I want to give it up the first chance I can get
    I haven't really thought about it
    I don't care about German because I am no good at it
    Other . . . .

16. **How much do you enjoy the following activities in German lessons?**
    Circle a number or the letter N to indicate on the scale how you feel:

	I do not like this at all	I don't mind this		I enjoy this	We don't do this
Group work	1	2	3	4	5	N
Pair work	1	2	3	4	5	N
Listening exercises	1	2	3	4	5	N
Writing exercises	1	2	3	4	5	N
Reading quietly	1	2	3	4	5	N

	I do not like this at all		I don't mind this		I enjoy this	We don't do this
Speaking	1	2	3	4	5	N
Work with computer	1	2	3	4	5	N
Literature	1	2	3	4	5	N
Project work/ coursework	1	2	3	4	5	N

17. **How important to you are the following in helping you feel positive about German?**

	Unimportant		Reasonably important		Very important
The teacher	1	2	3	4	5
The textbook	1	2	3	4	5
Teacher-made materials (worksheets, OHP transparencies, flashcards, etc.)	1	2	3	4	5
Good quality equipment	1	2	3	4	5
Availability of computers	1	2	3	4	5
A nicely furnished classroom	1	2	3	4	5
Number of pupils in class	1	2	3	4	5
Penpals	1	2	3	4	5
Exchange with German school	1	2	3	4	5
Television	1	2	3	4	5
Influence from home	1	2	3	4	5
Other					

18. **Have you ever been to a foreign country?** . . . .

19. **Which one/s?** . . . .

20. **Choose one of the foreign countries you have visited. Complete the following sentence by saying what the people were like there:**
    The people in . . . . . were . . . .

21. **What did you like most about the country/countries you visited?**
    . . . .

22. **What did you like least about the country/countries you visited?**
    . . . .

23. **Which other country would you like to visit?** . . . . . .

24. **Why?** . . . .

25. If the language of that country was not English, would you try to learn it before you went?

. . . .

26. Why? / Why not? . . . .

27. Would you consider trying to get a job in a foreign country when you leave school? . . .

28. Which foreign country / countries? . . . .

29. Why this country / these countries? . . . .

. . . .

30. Here are some words that pupils your age have used to describe people from other countries:

pushy unpleasant stupid ambitious loud friendly stupid polite pleasant unfriendly impolite beautiful interesting clever ugly

Please complete the following sentences by writing down one or more of these words. You can use your own words if you want to:

I think German people are . . . .
I think French people are . . . .
I think British people are . . . .

Please place a tick next to the statement which appears most applicable to you.

31. If German were not taught in the school, I would probably

   (a) not bother learning German at all
   (b) try to get lessons in German somewhere else
   (c) pick up German in everyday situations (i.e. read German books and newspapers, try to speak it when possible, watch German films)
   (d) none of these (explain) . . . .

32. After GCSE, I will probably

   (a) try to use my German as much as possible
   (b) try to use my German a little
   (c) not use German at all
   (d) do none of these (explain) . . . .

33. **If I had the opportunity to change the amount of German which is taught in our school, I would**

    (a) increase the number of lessons
    (b) keep the number of lessons as it is
    (c) decrease the number of lessons

34. **I believe German should be**

    (a) taught to all pupils
    (b) taught only to those pupils who wish to learn it
    (c) omitted from the school curriculum

35. **If you had the opportunity to change the way German is taught in your school, what would you do?**

    . . . .
    . . . .

36. **How much German does your mother know? Circle a number on the scale to indicate what you think:**

None		Some		Lots
1	2	3	4	5

37. **How much German does your father know? Circle a number on the scale to indicate what you think:**

None		Some		Lots
1	2	3	4	5

38. **How much do your parents encourage you to learn German? Circle a number on the scale 1–5 to indicate how you feel:**

Not at all		A little		Very much
1	2	3	4	5

39. **Have you ever had the opportunity to hear German used with friends of the family? . . .**

40. **Please give an example:**

    . . . .

41. **Do you know any people who speak German as their mother-tongue?**
    . . .

42. **About how many? . . .**

43. **Has your opinion of German and German lessons changed in the last two years?***

    . . . .

44. If so, how and why?*

. . . .

. . . .

Many thanks for your co-operation.
G. N. Chambers.

*Questions asked in 1994 only

Appendix 4

Year 13 (17 year olds) Leeds Questionnaire

NAME . . . . . . SCHOOL . . . . . . CLASS . . .

1. **Please circle a number in statements (a) to (f) to indicate your reason/s for learning German: (1 or 2 = you disagree; 3 = you neither agree nor disagree; 4 or 5 = you agree)**

    I AM LEARNING GERMAN BECAUSE

	disagree		neutral		agree
(a) I think it will help me to get a good job	1	2	3	4	5
(b) I am interested in German people and their way of life	1	2	3	4	5
(c) It will allow me to meet and talk with more people	1	2	3	4	5
(d) An educated person should be able to speak a foreign language	1	2	3	4	5
(e) I did not get good enough grades to allow me to do a different A-level subject	1	2	3	4	5
(f) I enjoy it	1	2	3	4	5
(g) Any other reason:					

2. **Think about each of the subjects below. How useful is each of them? Indicate on the scale how you feel.**

	Useless		Quite useful		Very useful
Maths	1	2	3	4	5
English	1	2	3	4	5
French	1	2	3	4	5
Geography	1	2	3	4	5
History	1	2	3	4	5

	Useless	Quite useful			Very useful
Science	1	2	3	4	5
PE	1	2	3	4	5
German	1	2	3	4	5
Technology	1	2	3	4	5
Music	1	2	3	4	5
RE	1	2	3	4	5
Art	1	2	3	4	5

3. Which subject do you regard as the <u>most</u> useful? . . . .

4. Why? . . . .

5. Which subject do you regard as the <u>least</u> useful? . . . .

6. Why? . . . .

7. How often have you come across a situation where it would have been useful to be able to speak German? . . . .

8. What do you enjoy <u>most</u> about coming to school?
   . . . .

9. What do you enjoy <u>least</u> about coming to school?
   . . . .

10. If you were asked to judge whether a subject was good or not, how much importance would you attach to the following considerations? Circle the number which best matches how you feel (1 = unimportant; 5 = very important)

	Unimportant	Reasonably important			Very important
How useful it is in getting you a job	1	2	3	4	5
How much fun it is in class	1	2	3	4	5
How good the teacher is	1	2	3	4	5
How much homework you get	1	2	3	4	5
How good your test marks are	1	2	3	4	5
How satisfying the work is	1	2	3	4	5
How varied it is	1	2	3	4	5
How interesting it is	1	2	3	4	5
How much you can mess around with your pals	1	2	3	4	5

Other aspects not included in the above list
. . . .

11. Please tick the statement which best applies to you:

I try very hard in German lessons
I try quite hard in German lessons
I don't really try at all in German lessons

12. What does your teacher think?

S/he thinks I try very hard in German lessons
S/he thinks I try quite hard in German lessons
S/he thinks I don't really try at all in German lessons
I don't know what s/he thinks

13. Please tick the statement which best applies to you:

I am making excellent progress in German
I am doing well in German
I am making satisfactory progress in German
I am making poor progress in German

14. What does your teacher think?

S/he thinks I am making excellent progress in German
S/he thinks I am doing well in German
S/he thinks I am making satisfactory progress in German
S/he thinks I am making poor progress in German
I don't know what s/he thinks

15. Tick all the statements that apply to you:

I am working towards a good A-level grade
I want to study German at university
I want to speak German well enough to get a job there
I want to give it up the first chance I can get
I haven't really thought about it
I don't care about German because I am no good at it
Other . . . .

16. How much do you enjoy the following activities in German lessons? Circle a number or the letter N to indicate on the scale how you feel:

	I do not like this at all		I don't mind this		I enjoy this	We don't do this
Group work	1	2	3	4	5	N
Pair work	1	2	3	4	5	N
Listening exercises	1	2	3	4	5	N
Writing exercises	1	2	3	4	5	N
Reading quietly	1	2	3	4	5	N
Speaking	1	2	3	4	5	N

	I do not like this at all		I don't mind this		I enjoy this	We don't do this
Work with computer	1	2	3	4	5	N
Literature	1	2	3	4	5	N
Project work/ coursework	1	2	3	4	5	N

17. **How important to you are the following in helping you feel positive about German?**

	Unimportant		Reasonably important		Very important
The teacher	1	2	3	4	5
The textbook	1	2	3	4	5
Teacher-made materials (worksheets, OHP transparencies, flashcards, etc.)	1	2	3	4	5
Good quality equipment	1	2	3	4	5
Availability of computers	1	2	3	4	5
A nicely furnished classroom	1	2	3	4	5
Number of pupils in class	1	2	3	4	5
Penpals	1	2	3	4	5
Exchange with German school	1	2	3	4	5
Television	1	2	3	4	5
Influence from home	1	2	3	4	5
Other					

18. **Have you ever been to a foreign country?** . . . .

19. **Which one/s?** . . . .

20. **Choose one of the foreign countries you have visited. Complete the following sentence by saying what the people were like there:**

    The people in . . . . . were . . . .

21. **What did you like most about the country/countries you visited?**
    . . . .

22. **What did you like least about the country/countries you visited?**
    . . . .

23. **Which other country would you like to visit?** . . . .

24. **Why?** . . . .

25. If the language of that country was not English, would you try to learn it before you went?

. . . .

26. Why? / Why not? . . . .

27. Would you consider trying to get a job in a foreign country when you leave school? . . .

28. Which foreign country / countries? . . . .

29. Why this country / these countries? . . . .

. . . .

30. Here are some words that pupils your age have used to describe people from other countries:

pushy unpleasant stupid ambitious loud friendly stupid polite pleasant unfriendly impolite beautiful interesting clever ugly

Please complete the following sentences by writing down one or more of these words. <u>You can use your own words if you want to</u>:

I think German people are . . . .
I think French people are . . . .
I think British people are . . . .

Please place a tick next to the statement which appears most applicable to you.

31. **If German were not taught in the school, I would probably**

    (a) not bother learning German at all
    (b) try to get lessons in German somewhere else
    (c) pick up German in everyday situations (i.e. read German books and newspapers, try to speak it when possible, watch German films)
    (d) none of these (explain) . . . .

32. **After A-level, I will probably**

    (a) try to use my German as much as possible
    (b) try to use my German a little
    (c) not use German at all
    (d) do none of these (explain) . . . .

33. **If I had the opportunity to change the amount of German which is taught in our school, I would**
    (a) increase the number of lessons
    (b) keep the number of lessons as it is
    (c) decrease the number of lessons

34. **I believe German should be**

    (a) taught to all pupils
    (b) taught only to those pupils who wish to learn it
    (c) omitted from the school curriculum

35. **If you had the opportunity to change the way German is taught in your school, what would you do?**
    . . . .
    . . . .

36. **How much German does your mother know? Circle a number on the scale to indicate what you think:**

None		Some		Lots
1	2	3	4	5

37. **How much German does your father know? Circle a number on the scale to indicate what you think:**

None		Some		Lots
1	2	3	4	5

38. **How much do your parents encourage you to learn German? Circle a number on the scale 1–5 to indicate how you feel:**

Not at all		A little		Very much
1	2	3	4	5

39. **Have you ever had the opportunity to hear German used with friends of the family?** . . .

40. **Please give an example:**
    . . . .

41. **Do you know any people who speak German as their mother-tongue?** . . .

42. **About how many?** . . .

43. **Has your opinion of German and German lessons changed in the last two years?***
    . . . .

44. If so, how and why?*

. . . .

. . . .

Many thanks for your co-operation.
G. N. Chambers.

*Questions asked in 1994 only

Bibliography

Ajzen, I. (1988) *Attitudes, Personality and Behavior*. Milton Keynes: Open University Press.

Ajzen, I. and Timko, C. (1986) Correspondence between health attitudes and behavior. *Journal of Basic and Applied Social Psychology* 7, 259–76.

Alexander, R., Rose, J. and Woodhead, C. (1992) *Curriculum Organisation and Practice in Primary Schools*. DES.

Alexander, T., Bastiani, J. and Beresford, E. (1995) *Home-School Policies: A Practical Guide*. Nottingham: JET Publications.

Alison, J. (1993) *Not Bothered? Motivating Reluctant Learners in Key Stage 4*. London: CILT.

Aplin, R. (1991) Why do pupils opt out of foreign language courses? A pilot study. *Educational Studies* 17(1), 3–13.

Atkinson, J., McClelland, D., Clark, R.A. and Lowell, E.L. (1953) *The Achievement Motive*. New York: Appleton.

Atkinson, T. (1992) Le hamster a mangé mon pneu: Creative writing and IT. *Language Learning Journal* 6, 68–70.

Ball, C. (1995) Presidential address to the North of England Education Conference.

Bandura, A. (1989) Human agency in social cognitive theory. *American Psychologist* 44, 1175–84.

Bandura, A., Adams, N. and Beyer, J. (1977) Cognitive processes mediating behavioral change. *Journal of Personality and Social Psychology* 35, 125–39.

Barber, M. (1994a) Born to be better. *Times Educational Supplement*, 18 March.

Barber, M. (1994b) How classwork can compete with the telly. *The Independent*, 21 July.

Barton, A. (1997) Boys' under-achievement in GCSE modern languages: Reviewing the reasons. *Language Learning Journal* 16, 11–16.

Bello, J. (1989) *Spanish as First Foreign Language in Schools*. Oxford: OXPROD, University of Oxford Department of Educational Studies.

Berry, K. (1998) Dramatic finish. *Times Educational Supplement*, 10 July.

Bialystok, E. (1978) A theoretical model of second language learning. *Language Learning* 28, 69–83.

Bialystok, E. (1990) *Communication Strategies*. Oxford: Basil Blackwell.

Bjørg, S. (1988) Attitudes and 'cultural distance' in second language acquisition. *Applied Linguistics* 9, 357ff.

Blackburne, L. (1993) England is trailing at GCSE level. *Times Educational Supplement*, 26 March.

Blatchford, P. (1992) Children's attitudes to work at 11 years. *Educational Studies* 18(1), 107–17.

Blum, P. (1998) *Surviving and Succeeding in Difficult Classrooms*. London: Routledge.

Brookman, J. (1994) Homeland's rockers find their tongues. *Times Educational Supplement*, 4 February.

Brophy, J. and Good, T. (1974) *Teacher–Student Relationships*. New York: Holt, Rinehart & Winston.

Brophy, J. and Good, T. (1976) *Die Lehrer- Schüler- Interaktion*. Munich: Oldenbourg.

Brown, H. (1981) Affective factors in second language learning. In J. Alatis, P. Alatis and H. Altman (eds) *The Second Language Classroom: Directions for the 1980s*. New York: Oxford University Press.

Brown, R. (1993) Developing IT in modern languages. *Language Learning Journal* 8, 51–3.

Bruner, J. (1966) *Towards a Theory of Instruction*. Cambridge, MA: Harvard University Press.

Buckby, M., Bull, P., Fletcher, R., Green, P., Page, B. and Roger, D. (1981) *Graded Objectives and Tests for Modern Languages*. London: Schools Council.

Burstall, C. (1968) *French from Eight: A National Experiment*. Slough: NFER.

Burstall, C. (1975) French in the Primary School: The British Experiment. *Canadian Modern Languages Review* 31, 388–402.

Burstall, E. (1995) Watershed no bar to square-eyed. *Times Educational Supplement*, 10 November.

Burstall, C., Cohen, S., Hargreaves, M. and Jamieson, M. (1974) *Primary French in the Balance*. Windsor: NFER.

Callaghan, M. (1998) An investigation into the causes of boys' underachievement in French. *Language Learning Journal* 17, 2–7.

Campaign for Learning (1998) *Attitudes to Learning '98. MORI State of the Nation Survey: Summary Report*. London: Campaign for Learning.

Campbell, J. and Neil, S. (1994) *Curriculum Reform at Key Stage 1*. London: Longman.

Carroll, J. (1974) Learning theory for the classroom teacher. In G. Jarvis *The Challenge of Communication*. ACTFL Review of foreign language education No. 6. Skokie, IL: National Textbook Company.

Carroll, J. (1981) Conscious and automatic processes in language learning. *Canadian Modern Language Review* 37, 462–74.

de Cecco, J. and Crawford, W. (1974) *The Psychology of Learning and Instruction*. Englewood Cliffs, N J: Prentice-Hall.

Chambers, G. (1991) A win in anyone's language. *The Guardian*, 30 July.

Chambers, G. (1992) Modern languages and the timetable. *Language Learning Journal* 5, 55–9.

Chambers, G. (1993) Taking the 'de' out of demotivation. *Language Learning Journal* 7, 13–16.

Chambers, G. (1994) A snapshot in motivation at 10+, 13+ and 16+. *Language Learning Journal* 9, 14–18.

Chambers, G. (1995) Binational problem solving. *German Teaching* 11, 14–17.

Chambers, G. (1996) Listening. Why? How? *Language Learning Journal* 14, 19–22.

Chambers, G. and Higham, J. (1993) Information technology: The school dimension. *Information Technology in Initial Teacher Education: The Modern Languages Perspective*. York: National Council for Educational Technology, University of York.

Chambers, G. and Sheppard, A. (1993) *Diversification of First Foreign Language in Leeds Schools*. University of Leeds: School of Education.

Chambers, G. and Sugden, D. (1994) Special education in Schleswig-Holstein – the modern languages dimension. *German Teaching* 9, 22–5.

Channel 4 Television (1993) *Dispatches: All our Futures.* London: Channel 4 Television Publications.

Clark, A. and Trafford, J. (1995) Boys into modern languages: An investigation of the discrepancy in attitudes and performance between boys and girls in modern languages. *Gender and Education* 7(3), 315–25.

Clark, A. and Trafford, J. (1996) Return to gender: Boys' and girls' attitudes and achievements. *Language Learning Journal* 14, 40–9.

Clark, R. (1995) A tongue-tied time warp. *Times Higher Educational Supplement*, 13 October.

Clément, R. (1980) Ethnicity, contact and communicative competence in a second language. In H. Giles, W. Robinson and P.M. Smith (eds) *Language: Social Psychological Perspectives.* Oxford: Pergamon.

Cohen, L. and Manion, L. (1991) *Research Methods in Education.* London and New York: Routledge.

Cohen, M (1997) Germans play game of catchup on the Net. *The Guardian Education*, 6 May.

Convery, A. and Coyle, D. (1993) *Differentiation – Taking the Initiative.* London: CILT.

Convery, A. *et al.* (1997) *Pupils' Perceptions of Europe.* London: Cassell.

Council of Europe (1996) *Common European Framework for Reference for Language Learning and Teaching.* Strasbourg.

Crooks, G. and Schmidt, R. (1991) 'Motivation': Reopening the research agenda. *Language Learning* 41 (4), 469–512.

Dean, C (1994) A Utopia for the disenchanted. *Times Educational Supplement*, 22 July.

DES/WO (1983) *Foreign Languages in the School Curriculum. A Consultative Paper.* London: HMSO.

DES/WO (1985) *Boys and Modern Languages.* London: HMSO.

DES/DENI/WO (1985) *Foreign Language Performance in Schools: A Report on the 1984 Survey of French.* London: HMSO, APU.

DES/DENI/WO (1986) *Foreign Language Performance in Schools: A Report on the 1983 Survey of French, German and Spanish.* London: HMSO, APU.

DES/DENI/WO (1987) *Foreign Language Performance in Schools: A Report on the 1983 Survey of French, German and Spanish.* London: HMSO, APU.

DES (1989) *A Survey of the Teaching and Learning of Modern Foreign Languages in a Sample of Inner City and Urban Schools.* London: HMSO.

DES (1991) *Differentiation in Action.* London: HMSO.

DES/WO (1991) *Modern Languages in the National Curriculum.* London: HMSO.

DFE/WO (1991) *The European Dimension in Education.* London: HMSO.

DFEE/WO (1995) *Modern Languages in the National Curriculum.* London: HMSO.

DFEE/WO (1998) *Statutory Approval of Qualification under Section 400 of the Education Act 1996: Circular 3/98.* London: HMSO.

Doe, R. (1982) Lessons for linguists – is an enquiry necessary? *Times Educational Supplement*, 5 February.

Drew, F. and Ottewill, R. (1998) Implications of the increasing provision of OALF for course design and delivery. *Language Learning Journal* 17, 75–80.

Ellis, R. (1985) *Understanding Second Language Acquisition.* Oxford: Oxford University Press.

Elston, T. (1991) Are your students good listeners? *Francophonie* 4, 13–14.

European Commission (1989) *Young Europeans in 1987.* Brussels: European Commission.

Evans, M. (1993) Flexible learning and modern languages teaching. *Language Learning Journal* 8, 17–21.

Fawkes, S. (1993) Reading for pleasure and the National Curriculum. *Francophonie* 8, 41–3.

Feenstra, H. (1969) Parent and teacher attitudes: Their role in second language acquisition. *Canadian Modern Languages Review* 26, 3–13.

Feenstra, H. and Gardner, R. (1968) Aptitude, attitude and motivation in second language acquisition. *Research Bulletin 101*. London, Canada: University of Western Ontario.

Fengler, A. and Fischer, A. (1983) Wie sehen Schüler den Englischunterricht? Eine Nachuntersuchung zur Motivation im Englischunterricht. In G. Solmecke (ed.) *Motivation und Motivieren im Fremdsprachenunterricht.* Paderborn: Schöningh.

Filmer-Sankey, C. (1989) *A Study of First-Year Pupils' Attitudes Towards French, German and Spanish.* OXPROD, University of Oxford, Department of Educational Studies.

Filmer-Sankey, C. (1991) *A Study of Second-Year Pupils' Attitudes Towards French, German and Spanish.* Oxford: OXPROD, University of Oxford Department of Educational Studies.

Findlay, J. (1932) The psychology of modern language learning. *British Journal of Educational Psychology* 2, 319–31.

Finn, J. (1972) Expectations and the educational environment. *Review of Educational Research* 42, 387–410.

Freud, S. (1964) *An outline of psycho-analysis.* London: Hogarth Press/Institute of Psychoanalysis.

Frost, R. (1995) Cheap calls compensate for a late start. *Times Educational Supplement Computers Update,* 24 March.

Fürntratt, E. (1976) *Motivation des schulischen Lernens.* Weinheim: Beltz.

Gagnon, M. (1974) Quelques facteurs déterminant l'attitude vis-à-vis l'anglais, langue seconde. In R. Darnell (ed.) *Linguistic Diversity in Canadian Society 4.* Edmonton: Linguistic Research Inc.

Galloway, D., Rogers, C., Armstrong, D. and Leo, E. (1998) *Motivating the Difficult to Teach.* Harlow: Longman.

Gardner, R. (1966) Motivational variables in second language learning. *International Journal of American Linguistics* 32, 24–44.

Gardner, R. (1968) Attitudes and motivation: Their role in second language acquisition. *TESOL Quarterly* 2, 141–50.

Gardner, R. (1985) *Social Psychology and Second Language Learning.* London: Arnold.

Gardner, R. and Lambert, W. (1972) *Attitudes and Motivation in Secondary Language Learning.* Rowley, MA: Newbury House.

Gardner, R. and Santos, E. (1970) Motivational variables in second language acquisition: A Phillipine investigation. *Research Bulletin 29.* London, Canada: Department of Psychology, University of Western Ontario.

Gardner, R. and Smythe, P. (1975) Motivation and second language acquisition. *Canadian Modern Languages Review* 31, 218–30.

Giles, H. and Byrne, J.L. (1982) An intergroup approach to second language acquisition. *Journal of Multilingual and Multicultural Development* 1, 17–40.

Girard, D. (1977) Motivation: The responsibility of the teacher. *English Language Teaching Journal* 31(2), 97–102.

Goethe-Institut (1998) *Spotlight on Europe, Manchester.* Goethe-Institut.

Gold, K. (1995) Choosing from Dearing's pick 'n' mix. *Times Educational Supplement*, 20 January, Section 2, p. 5.

Green, P.S. and Hecht, K. (1989) Investigating learners' language. In C.J. Brumfit and R. Mitchell *Research in the Language Classroom*. ELT Docs 133: MEP (British Council).

Green, A. and Steedman, H. (1993) *Educational Provision, Educational Attainment and the Needs of Industry: A Review of Research for Germany, France, Japan, the USA and Britain*. London: National Institute of Economic and Social Research.

Grenfell, M. and Harris, V. (1993) How do pupils learn? *Language Learning Journal* 8, 22–5.

Gunn, O. (1998) Excellence for all children. Meeting special educational needs. *Teaching Today* 19, 8–9.

Hagedorn, J. (1993) Truants select lessons to miss from school. *The Independent*, 26 June.

Hagen, S. (1992) *The Foreign Language Needs of British Business: A CTC Response*. London: City Technologies Trust Ltd.

Haigh, G. (1995) Clean-living tips gleaned from soaps. *Times Educational Supplement*, 10 November.

Hargreaves, D. (1972) *Interpersonal Relationships and Education*. London: Routledge & Kegan Paul.

Hargreaves, D. (1982) *The Challenge for the Comprehensive School*. London: Routledge & Kegan Paul.

Hastings, N. (1992) Questions of Motivation. *Support for Learning* 7(3), 135–7.

Hawkins, E. (ed.) (1997) *30 Years of Language Teaching*. London: CILT.

Heuer, H. (1983) Zur Motivation im Englischunterricht. In G. Solmecke (ed.) *Motivation und Motivieren im Fremdsprachenunterricht*. Paderborn: Schöningh.

HMI (1985) *Survey of Boys and Modern Languages*. London: HMSO.

HMI (1986) *Education in the Federal Republic of Germany: Aspects of Curriculum Development and Assessment*. London: HMSO.

HMI (1989) *A Survey of the Teaching and Learning of Modern Foreign Languages in a sample of Inner City and Urban Schools*. London: DES.

HMI (1991) *Aspects of Vocational Education and Training in the Federal Republic of Germany*. London: HMSO.

Hobart, A. and Sofier, R. (1986) *Cooking the German Way*. Leicester: Admiral.

Hockett, C. (1958) *A Course in Modern Linguistics*. New York: Macmillan.

Holec, H. *et al.* (1996) *Strategies in Language Learning and Use*. Strasbourg: Council of Europe.

Hooley, G. and Newcomb, J. (1988) Ailing British exports: Symptoms, causes and cures. In M. Thomas and N. Waite (eds) *The Marketing Digest* (pp. 397–410). London: Heinemann.

Hull, C. (1943) *A Behaviour System and Principles of Behaviour*. New York: Yale University Press.

Hurd, S. (1998) 'Too carefully led or too carelessly left alone'? *Language Learning Journal* 17, 70–4.

Jahnke, J. (1977) *Motivation in der Schulpraxis*. Freiburg: Herderbücherei.

James, W. (1890) *The Principles of Psychology*. London: Macmillan.

Jeffers, S. (1991) *Feel the Fear and do it Anyway*. London: Arrow Books.

Jones, W. (1966) *Bilingualism in Welsh Education*. Cardiff: University of Wales Press.

Jung, J. (1978) *Understanding Human Motivation*. New York/London: Macmillan.

Kellerman, M. (1981) *The Forgotten Third Skill*. Oxford: Pergamon.

Kelly, L.G. (1976) *25 Centuries of Language Teaching.* London: Newbury House.

Keys, W. and Fernandes, C. (1993) *What Do Students Think about School?* Slough: NFER.

Keys, W., Harris, S. and Fernandes, C. (1995a) *Attitudes to School of Top Primary and First-year Secondary Pupils.* Slough: NFER.

Keys, W., Harris, S. and Fernandes, C. (1995b) *Third International Mathematics and Science Study: First National Report, Part I.* Slough: NFER.

Klapper, J. (1992a) Reading in a foreign language: Theoretical issues. *Language Learning Journal* 5, 27–30.

Klapper, J. (1992b) Preliminary considerations for the teaching of FL reading. *Language Learning Journal* 6, 53–6.

Klapper, J. (1993) Practicable skills and practical constraints in FL reading. *Language Learning Journal* 7, 50–4.

Krashen, S. (1978) The monitor model for second language acquisition. In R. Gingras (ed.) *Second-language Acquisition and Foreign Language Teaching.* Arlington, VA: Center for Applied Linguistics.

Krashen, S. (1981) *Second Language Acquisition and Second Language Learning.* Oxford: Pergamon.

Krashen, S. (1982) *Principles and Practice in Second Language Acquisition.* Oxford: Pergamon.

Kyriacou, C. (1992) *Effective Teaching in Schools.* Hemel Hempstead: Simon & Schuster Education.

Lambert, W. (1961) *A Study of the Roles of Attitude and Motivation in Second Language Learning.* NDEA Project Report SAE – 8817. Montreal, Canada: NDEA.

Lambert, W. (1963a) Psychological approaches to the study of language Part I: On learning, thinking and human abilities. *Modern Language Journal* 14, 51–62.

Lambert, W. (1963b) Psychological approaches to the study of language Part II: On second language learning and bilingualism. *Modern Language Journal* 14, 114–21.

Lambert, W. (1967) A social psychology of bilingualism. *Journal of Social Issues* 23, 91–109.

Lambert, W. (1974) Culture and language as factors in learning and education. In F.E. Aboud and R.D. Meade (eds) *Cultural Factors in Learning and Education.* Bellingham, Washington: Fifth Western Washington Symposium on Learning.

Lambert, W. and Klineberg, O. (1967) *Children's Views of Foreign People.* New York: Appleton-Century-Croft.

Lee, B. (1994) Extending opportunities: Modern foreign languages for pupils with special educational needs. In A. Swarbrick (ed.) *Teaching Modern Languages* (pp. 88–100). London: Routledge.

Lee, B. and Dickson, P. (1991) *Foreign Languages for Lower Attaining Pupils.* Slough: NFER.

Lennon, P. (1993) The advanced learner: Affective, social and motivational factors. *Language Learning Journal* 8, 39–43.

Lewin, K. (1952) Field theory and experiment in social psychology. *Field Theory and Social Science.* London: Tavistock Publications.

Little, A.W. (1985) The child's understanding of the causes of academic success and failure: A case study of British school-children. *British Journal of Educational Psychology* 55, 11–23.

Littlejohn, A. (1983) Increasing learner involvement in course management. *TESOL Quarterly* 17, 595–608.

Littlewood, W. (1984) *Foreign and Second Language Learning*. Cambridge: Cambridge University Press.

Locke, E., Frederick, E., Bobko, P. and Lee, C. (1984) Effect of self-efficacy, goals and task-strategies on task performance. *Journal of Applied Psychology* 69, 241–51.

Long, M. and Porter, P. (1985) Group work, interlanguage talk, and second language acquisition. *TESOL Quarterly* 19, 207–28.

Lukmani, Y. (1972) Motivation to learn and language proficiency. *Language Learning* 22, 261–73.

MacLeod, D. (1995) Hands across the sea. *The Guardian Education*, 30 May.

Maley, A. and Duff, A. (1994) Drama techniques in language teaching. In A. Swarbrick *Teaching Modern Languages* (pp. 151–9). London: Routledge.

Martin, G., and Hampson, E. (1991) Using the concept keyboard in modern languages. *Language Learning Journal* 3, 59–60.

Maslow, A. (1954) *Motivation and Personality*. New York: Harper & Row.

Mason, G., Prais, S. and Van Ark, B. (1992) *Productivity, Education and Training: Britain and Other Countries Compared*. London: National Institute of Economic and Social Research.

Mathews, T. (1996) A case for increasing negative affect in foreign language classes. *Language Learning Journal* 13, 38–41.

McDevitt, B. (1997) Learner autonomy and the need for learner training. *Language Learning Journal* 16, 34–9.

McDonough, S. (1981) *Psychology in Foreign Language Teaching*. London: Allen & Unwin.

McKenna, N. and McKenna, P. (1999) Perception and reality: Bridging the Internet gap. *Language Learning Journal* 20.

Meara, P. (1995) *LLEX Lingua Vocabulary Tests*. Swansea: CALS.

Measor, L. and Woods, P. (1984) *Changing Schools*. Milton Keynes: Open University Press.

Milner, D. (1981) Racial prejudice. In J. Turner and H. Giles (eds) *Intergroup Behaviour*. Oxford: Basil Blackwell.

Milton, J. and Meara, P. (1998) Are the British really bad at learning foreign languages? *Language Learning Journal* 18, 68–76.

Mitchell, I. and Swarbrick, A. (1994) *Developing skills for independent reading*. Pathfinder, 22. London: CILT.

Mowrer, O. (1950) *Learning Theory and Personality Dynamics*. New York: Ronald.

Mreschar, R. (1991) Was Schüler von der Schule halten. *Kultur Chronik* 4, *Langenscheidts Sprach-Illustrierte* Heft 3.

Nash, R. (1976) *Teacher Expectations and Pupil Learning* London: Routledge & Kegan Paul.

National Commission on Education (1995) *Success against the Odds: Effective Schools in Disadvantaged Areas*. London: Routledge.

National Curriculum Council (1992) *Modern Foreign Languages Non-Statutory Guidance*. York: NCC.

Office for Standards in Education (OFSTED) (1993) *Access and Achievement in Urban Education*. London: HMSO.

Office for Standards in Education (OFSTED) (1993) *Modern Foreign Languages. Key Stage 3. First year, 1992–93*. London: HMSO.

Office for Standards in Education (OFSTED) (1995) *Modern Foreign Languages. A Review of Inspection Findings 1993/94*. London: HMSO.

O'Connor, M. (1993) The Balcarras Experiment. *Times Educational Supplement*, 14 May.

O'Connor, M. (1994) The voice of the pupil is heard. *Times Educational Supplement*, 14 January.

O'Keeffe, D. and Stoll, P. (1993) *Truancy in English Secondary Schools*. London: DES HMSO.

O'Leary, J. (1998) British students build new language barrier. *The Times*, 3 January.

Olivier, R. (1990) Learner Autonomy. In B. Page (ed.) *What do you Mean . . . It's Wrong?* London: CILT.

Oller, J. and Perkins, K. (1978a) Intelligence and proficiency as sources of variance in self-reported affective variables. *Language Learning* 28, 85–97.

Oller, J. and Perkins, K. (1978b) A further comment on language proficiency as a source of variance in certain affective measures. *Language Learning* 28, 417–23.

Oskamp, S. (1977) *Attitudes and Opinions*. Englewood Cliffs, NJ: Prentice Hall.

O'Sullivan, A. (1983) Aspects of motivation in foreign language learning. Unpublished dissertation for award of MA. University of London, Institute of Education.

O'Sullivan, A. (1990) The foreign language coursebook: A study of its role in learner motivation. Unpublished dissertation for award of PhD. University of London, Institute of Education

O'Sullivan, E. (1990) *Friend and Foe: The Image of Germany and the Germans in British Children's Fiction from 1870 to the Present*. Tübingen: G. Narr Verlag.

Page, B. (1990) *What do you Mean . . . It's Wrong?* London: CILT.

Page, B. and Hewett, D. (1987) *Languages Step by Step: Graded Objectives in the UK*. London: CILT.

Perry, P. (1992) Time for great expectations. *Times Educational Supplement*, 14 February.

Petty, G. (1993) *Teaching Today*. Cheltenham: Stanley Thornes.

Phillips, D. (1989) *Which Language? Diversification and the National Curriculum*. London: Hodder & Stoughton.

Phillips, D. and Clark, G. (1988) *Attitudes Towards Diversification*. Oxford: OXPROD, Oxford University Department of Educational Studies.

Phillips, D. and Geatches, H. (1989) *Diversification and 'Transfers-In'*. Oxford: OXPROD, Oxford University Department of Educational Studies.

Phillips, D. and Filmer-Sankey, C. (1993) *Diversification in Modern Languages Teaching: Choice and the National Curriculum*. London: Routledge.

Phillips, D. and Stencel, V. (1983) *The Second Foreign Language: Past Developments, Current Trends and Future Prospects*. London: Hodder & Stoughton.

Pidgeon, D. (1970) *Expectation and Pupil Performance*. Slough: NFER.

Piepho, H. (1981) Some psychological bases for learning strategies and exercises in the communicative teaching of English. In C. Candlin (ed.) *The Communicative Teaching of English*. London: Longman.

Piepho, H. (1983) Englischunterricht aus der Schülerperspektive. Ermittlungen zu Erwartungshaltungen und Urteilsstrukturen als Voraussetzung schülerischer Curriculumentwicklung. In G. Solmecke (ed.) *Motivation und Motivieren im Fremdsprachenunterricht*. Paderborn: Schöningh.

Place, J.D. (1997) 'Boys will be boys' – boys and under-achievement in MFL. *Language Learning Journal* 16, 3–10.

Pollard, A., Broadfoot, P., Croll, P., Osborn, M. and Abbott. D. (1994) *Changing English Primary Schools?* London: Cassell.

Powell R (1986) *Boys, Girls and Languages in School*. London: CILT.

Powell, R. and Batters, J. (1985) Pupils' perceptions of foreign language learning at 12+: Some gender differences. *Educational Studies* 11(1), 11–23.

Powell, R. and Littlewood, P. (1983) Why choose French? Boys' and girls' attitudes at the option stage. *British Journal of Language Teaching* 21(1), 37.

Prag, D. (1994) Do languages really matter? In G. Parker (ed.) *Languages for the International Scientist* 15–21. London: CILT.

Pritchard, R. (1987) Boys' and girls' attitudes towards French and German. *Educational Research* 29(1), 65–72.

Pritchard, R. (1991) *Motivating the Majority*. University of Ulster: CILT.

Pyke, N. (1992) Merit points provide no incentive. *Times Educational Supplement* 21 February.

Pyke, N. (1998) Time out plan for unhappy teenagers. *Times Educational Supplement* 30 January.

Reisener, H. (1992) *Motivierungstechniken im Fremdsprachenunterricht*. Ismaning: Max Hueber Verlag.

Remmert, D., (1997) Introducing autonomous learning in a low ability set. *Language Learning Journal* 15, 14–20.

Rivers, W. (1964) *The Psychologist and the Foreign Language Teacher*. Chicago: Chicago Press.

Ruddock, J. (1996) Testimony of the expert witnesses. *Times Educational Supplement* 28 June.

Schiefele, H. (1963) *Motivation im Unterricht*. Munich: Franz Ehrenwirth Verlag KG.

Schiefele, H. (1974) *Lernmotivation und Motivlernen*. Munich: Franz Ehrenwirth Verlag KG.

Schreuders, T. and Bethell, A. (1993) *Do schools fail children?* London: BBC.

Schröder, K. (1981) Methods of exploring language needs in industry. In R. Freudenstein, J. Beneke and H. Poenische (eds) *Language Incorporated* (pp. 43–56). Oxford: Pergamon.

Schumann, J. (1978a) The acculturation model for second language acquisition. In R. Gingras *Second Language Acquisition and Foreign Language Teaching*. Arlington VA: Center for Applied Linguistics.

Schumann, J. (1978b) Social and psychological factors in second language acquisition. In J.C. Richards (ed) *Understanding Second and Foreign Language Learning*. Rowley, MA: Newbury House.

Schusser, G. (1972) *Lehrererwartungen*. Munich: Franz Ehrenwirth Verlag KG.

Shirey, L. and Reynolds, R. (1988) Effect of interest on attention and learning. *Journal of Educational Psychology* 80, 159–66.

Sittig, F. (1992) Vom Niedergang der deutschen Hauptschule: "Lehrer stören da nur". *Welt am Sonntag*, 20 November.

Skinner, B. (1957) *Verbal Behaviour*. New York: Appleton-Century-Croft.

Solmecke, G. (ed.) (1983) *Motivation und Motivieren im Fremdsprachenunterricht*. Paderborn: Schöningh.

Stables A. and Wikeley, F. (1997) Changes in preference for and perceptions of relative importance of subjects during a period of educational reform. *Educational Studies* 23(3), 393–403.

Stables, A. and Wikeley, F. (1999) From bad to worse? Pupils' attitudes to modern foreign languages at ages 14 and 15. *Language Learning Journal* 20.

Steedman, H. and Hawkins, J. (1993) _Mathematics in Vocational Youth Training for the Building Trades in Britain, France and Germany._ London: National Institute of Economic and Social Research.

St John-Brooks, C. (1993) Pupils pushed into early disaffection. _Times Educational Supplement_, 29 January.

St John-Brooks, C. (1993) Secondary pupils operating in a void. _Times Educational Supplement_, 29 January.

Stern, H. (1983) _Fundamental Concepts of Language Teaching._ Oxford: Oxford University Press.

Stradling, R., Saunders, L. and Weston, P. (1991) _Differentiation in Action: A Whole School Approach for Raising Attainment._ London: NFER and DES.

Swarbrick, A. (ed.) (1994) _Teaching Modern Languages._ London: Routledge.

Thornton, B. and Cajkler, W. (1996) A study of Year 10 student attitudes to German language and life. _Language Learning Journal_ 14, 35–9.

Tomlinson P.D. (1981) _Understanding Teaching._ London: McGraw-Hill.

Turner, K. (1997) Reading: Meeting the demands of the National Curriculum. _Language Learning Journal_ 17, 8–13.

Weiner, B. (1972) _Theories of Motivation._ Chicago: Rand McNally College Publishing Company.

Weiner, B. (1980) _Human Motivation._ New York: Holt, Rinehart & Winston.

Weiner, B. (1986) _An Attributional Theory of Motivation and Emotion._ New York: Springer-Verlag.

West, A., Hailes, J. and Sammons, P. (1997) Children's attitudes to the National Curriculum at Key Stage 1. _British Educational Research Journal_ 23 (5), 615–22.

White, C. and Wacha, H. (1992) Information technology and modern languages. _Language Learning Journal_ 5, 40–3.

Whitehead, M. (1996) Hard to keep the customers satisfied. _Times Educational Supplement_, 5 April.

Whyte, J. (1981) Sex typing in schools. In A. Kelly (ed.) _The Missing Half – Girls and Science Education._ Manchester: Manchester University Press.

Wilce, H. (1997) Have you done your homework? _The Independent_, 13 March.

Wilkins, D. (1972) _Linguistics in Language Teaching._ London: Arnold.

Wilkins, D. (1974) _Second Language Learning and Teaching._ London: Edward Arnold.

Wright, M., (1996) The cultural aims of modern language teaching: Why are they not being met? _Language Learning Journal_ 13, 36–7.

Wright, C. and Wright, S. (1994) Do languages really matter? The relationship between international business success and a commitment to foreign language use. _Journal of Industrial Affairs_ 3(1), 3–14.

Wringe, C. (1994) Ineffective lessons: Reasons and remedies: jottings from the tutor's note-pad. _Language Learning Journal_ 10, 11–15.

Wringe, C. (ed.) (1996) _Formation Autonome. A European Self-Study Professional Development Project for Language Teachers._ Zürich and Rugby: FIPLV and ALL.

Index